Infrastructure and Regional Development

European research in regional science 1

Infrastructure and Regional Development

Editor   R W Vickerman

Series editor   P W J Batey

European research in regional science

ISBN 0 85086 150 0
ISSN 0960-6130

British Library Cataloguing in Publication Data
A CIP catalogue record British Library.

published by Pion Limited, 207 Brondesbury Park, London NW2 5JN

p

Printed in Great Britain by Page Bros (Norwich) Limited

Foreword

European Research in Regional Science is a new series initiated by the British Section of the Regional Science Association. The series will provide a showcase for the best of European regional science research and reflects a burgeoning interest in regional matters prompted by the expanded European Community, recent political reforms, and the prospects of economic integration. As series editor, I shall be advised by an editorial board made up of leading European regional scientists. Although the focus will be on Europe, contributions will come from researchers around the world. Each volume will be based on a specific theme and will comprise a collection of carefully selected, high-quality papers drawn from one or more of the regional science conferences and workshops held in Europe, including the annual European Congress.

The first volume, on *Infrastructure and Regional Development*, provides a good illustration of the general approach that will be followed in developing the series. It includes coverage of debates on the theoretical treatment of infrastructure, of questions of method in assessments of impacts, and of issues connected with the financing of infrastrcture. Survey papers are intended to define the state of the art in this field and to identify an agenda for future research. Widespread use is made of case studies to provide specific examples of major infrastructure projects and their relationship to regional development. The majority of the papers are taken from sessions at two Regional Science Association conferences held in 1990: the European Congress in Istanbul and the British Section meeting in Liverpool.

Volumes in the series will be published annually and the publishers are aiming for a ten-month turnaround of papers. Proposals for new volumes are welcome at any time and should be submitted either to myself or to one of the members of the Editorial Advisory Board.

P W J Batey
Series Editor
Department of Civic Design
University of Liverpool

July 1991

Contributors

M Antonioli   *Istituto di Economia Politica,*
Università Commerciale Luigi Bocconi, 20136 Milano,
Italy

D Biehl   *Institut für Öffentliche Wirtschaft, Geld und Währung,*
Johann Wolfgang Goethe Universität,
D-600 Frankfurt am Main 11, Germany

U Blum   *Volkswirtschaftlehre insbes. Wirtschaftspolitik,*
D-8600 Bamberg, Germany

F Bruinsma   *Faculty of Economics, Free University,*
1081 HV Amsterdam, The Netherlands

S Casini Benvenuti   *IRPET, 50137 Firenze, Italy*

B Gérardin   *Director of Research (France)*
European Investment Bank, c/o INRETS,
94114 Arcueil Cédex, France

K Greenan   *Faculty of Business and Management,*
University of Ulster, Newtownsabbey BT38 0QB,
Northern Ireland

S Illeris   *Department of Geography, Ruskilde University,*
DK-4000 Roskilde, Denmark

L Jakobsen   *Department of Geography, Ruskilde University,*
DK-4000 Roskilde, Denmark

L Lesley   *Department of Transport, Liverpool Polytechnic,*
Liverpool L3 5UZ, England

M McHugh   *Faculty of Business and Management,*
University of Ulster, Newtownsabbey BT38 0QB,
Northern Ireland

K Mallalieu   *School of Economic and Social Studies,*
University of East Anglia, Norwich NR4 7TJ, England

G Maltinti   *IRPET, 50137 Firenze, Italy*

P Nijkamp   *Faculty of Economics, Free University,*
1081 HV Amsterdam, The Netherlands

Contributors

A Pio
Istituto di Economia Politica,
Università Commerciale Luigi Bocconi, 20136 Milano,
Italy

L Resmini
Istituto di Economia Politica,
Università Commerciale Luigi Bocconi, 20136 Milano,
Italy

P Rietveld
Faculty of Economics, Free University,
1081 HV Amsterdam, The Netherlands

C Secchi
Istituto di Economia Politica,
Università Commerciale Luigi Bocconi, 20136 Milano,
Italy

P Townroe
School of Urban and Regional Studies,
Sheffield Polytechnic, Sheffield S1 1WB, England

R Vickerman
Channel Tunnel Research Unit, University of Kent,
Canterbury, Kent CT2 7NF, England

Contents

Infrastructure and Regional Development: Introduction

R W Vickerman
University of Kent at Canterbury

The role of infrastructure in the regional development process has, for a long time, been rather uncertain. It is obvious that dynamic growing regions have a well-developed infrastructure whereas lagging regions are typically deficient. However, long periods of regional development policies based on the creation of infrastructure in lagging regions have failed to make much impression on regional divergence. In Europe, in addition to national policies, the European Regional Development Fund, as the main agent of the European Community's regional policy, has over the fifteen years of its existence devoted over 80% of its funding to infrastructure projects. Regional disparities narrowed in the period to 1970, but then widened substantially in the 1970s before stabilising again in the 1980s. The average gross domestic product (GDP) per capita of the ten strongest regions was 3.1 times that of the ten weakest in 1980; this figure rose slightly to 3.35 by 1988 and the coefficient of variation increased from 0.26 to 0.275.

This might suggest that infrastructure is irrelevant to the real determinants of regional growth and development. Putting public money into infrastructure, especially subsidised infrastructure, can be seen as a waste of resources. Alternatively, it is possible to argue that the problem arises from an insufficient transfer of resources. Despite the investment in infrastructure as a deliberate tool of policy in lagging regions, the leading regions have seen an even greater investment in infrastructure to maintain their position. Furthermore much investment in lagging regions simply helped leading regions to enlarge the size of their markets. Because of such ambiguities in the way in which the benefits from new infrastructure are distributed between different regions, and problems in measurement of these, government appraisal techniques often specifically omit regional development benefits. Such a situation applies in the United Kingdom for measuring the benefits of transport investment, for example.

Now we are in a situation where infrastructure is again at the head of the agenda. At a European level it is increasingly recognised that there is a need for a genuinely European infrastructure, not just in the obvious areas of physical transport infrastructure, such as roads and railways, but including air traffic control systems, other public utility infrastructures, and what may be termed the 'soft infrastructure' of basic research and development and training networks. Infrastructure, in all its guises, is seen as an essential means of building the internal market of the European Community (EC). There is a more pragmatic reason for the level of interest, however. In many of the core industrial areas of the Community, infrastructure is wearing out. Much of the hidden infrastructure of underground services in cities dates from the late 19th century and is life expired. The overground infrastructure of these cities, typically dating from the period of postwar construction, is approaching the age when it too will need renewal. Furthermore, the changes in Eastern Europe have revealed a decayed and inadequate infrastructure urgently requiring investment as an absolute prerequisite to any economic progress, especially because of the need to open these economies to trade in a completely different direction. The cost of this renewal is enormous. For this reason the public sector, the traditional provider of infrastructure, cannot hope to do more than identify priorities and offer seedcorn finance. The private sector, the ultimate beneficiary of much new infrastructure, must take a share of this finance, including a share of the risk. But for the private sector to do this, it requires both improved means of assessing the impact and informed strategic guidance from the public sector. The consequences, both for regions where this new investment does take place, and for those where it does not, are serious.

It is against this background that this volume of papers has been assembled. Its aim is not to produce a definitive treatise on the role of infrastructure in regional development, but it does bring together an important collection of issues which contribute to the debates on the theoretical treatment of infrastructure, assessment of the impact of infrastructure, and financing infrastructure provision, together with some specific case studies. The intention is to define the state of the art in current research on the topic and set an agenda for future research initiatives, which must increasingly take place in an international context. The papers include a number presented at two conferences of the Regional Science Association in 1990, the European Meeting in Istanbul and the British Section Meeting in Liverpool. These form the core papers reflecting the state of research on the topic in Europe, to which have been added a number of additional papers on specific case studies of major transport infrastructure projects.

There is a dominance of transport infrastructure projects reflected in these papers because this is where the renewal of interest has started. Big projects such as the Channel Tunnel, Storebaelt, and Strait of Messina are important missing links in any European network. If we cannot analyse adequately how specific large infrastructures affect the pattern of regional development it will be much more difficult to identify the effects of new east–west corridors in Germany or a European high-speed rail network. It is important also not to consider individual transport projects in isolation, a new rail-based development in one part of Europe has synergies with other developments in other parts of Europe which will have important consequences for the use of rail throughout the Community. The interface between modes is also important, especially between air and rail, so that the assessment of regional airport provision becomes a major issue. It is easy to be overwhelmed by big projects to the exclusion of the role which a network of infrastructures plays within cities and regions. Increasingly there is concern at the role of Europe's major metropolitan areas, not just in terms of competition between London, Paris, Frankfurt, Milan, etc, but in terms of whether any of these can fulfil their role as world cities efficiently enough. Infrastructure does not sit alone, however. It is substitutable for other inputs into the productive process, how efficiently that substitution works depends on the effectiveness of the soft infrastructure. Its actual impact depends on the responsiveness of individual sectors to new opportunities.

The papers in this book fall into four broad groups. In the first of these, in chapters 2 and 3, we consider the general role of infrastructure in regional development. In a paper based on a large multinational study for the EC, Dieter Biehl assesses first the theoretical treatment of infrastructure and then uses this as a basis for an empirical model. The essential argument of this chapter is that infrastructure is best treated as a public good which can raise the productivity of investment in private goods in a region. However, this can only occur in certain circumstances, where the absence of this public good is providing a constraint on development and there is no bottleneck in the provision of private goods. This demonstrates clearly that infrastructure investment may not always be necessary and is rarely sufficient for regional development to take place. The empirical evidence is for NUTS Level II regions (Eurostat, 1990) of the European Community and is, of necessity, rather aggregate, but nevertheless gives an invaluable impression of the nature of the problem. There are two stages: first the weighting of the importance of the various dimensions to infrastructure into a composite index and second the estimation of a set of regional quasiproduction functions. This enables the classification of regions into four main types according to the underutilisation or overutilisation of infrastructure and other resources, with a further distinction as to whether this level of utilisation is constant, decreasing, or increasing through time. The vast majority of regions display either overutilisation or underutilisation of both types of resource. Only three out of 118 regions appeared to have roughly normal capacity utilisation. The largest subgroup (forty-one regions) showed a decreasing degree of underutilisation or overutilisation, that is, a trend towards normal capacity utilisation, and these include a number of the poorest regions of the Community at one extreme, and a number of the richest at the other. Some key regions do appear in the minority of regions where one type of resource or the other acts as a constraint—most notably South East England where infrastructure exerts a major constraint. However, the most general conclusion is that rich regions face overutilisation, and poor regions underutilisation, of all types of resource. Infrastructure can therefore only be one part of a programme for balanced regional development.

In chapter 3 Roger Vickerman provides a general introduction to the specific question of the impact of transport infrastructure and reviews the way in which European Community policy towards such infrastructure has evolved. This has two aspects: the identification of the role of transport in the process of economic integration and the specific role of identifying and eliminating bottlenecks of Community-wide significance. The clear conclusion emerging from this is that the evaluation of infrastructure often has to take place at a higher level than it currently does which has important implications for financing that investment. Nevertheless, the European Commission has had severe difficulties in gaining acceptance of a financed programme for infrastructure of Community significance. It has taken over four years, and a reduction in the size of the programme to around one third of that originally proposed, to agree on an essential programme for 1992 and the completion of the Single Market.

The second and largest group of papers deals with various aspects of the specific assessment of transport infrastructures and their regional consequences. In an introductory chapter, chapter 4, Bernard Gérardin outlines the spatial theory lying behind any assessment and how this can be used to provide empirical verification. The use of this methodology in the context of the impact on Northern France of the Channel Tunnel and TGV (Train à Grande Vitesse) Nord projects is discussed. Gérardin suggests various ways in which a redefinition of traditional thinking is required. Particular features of this are a better understanding of the organisation of logistic chains, linking sources of production of raw materials and intermediate goods, production plants, and distribution centres, and the way new establishments locate and old establishments relocate or expand. Only with an understanding of these microlevel decisions can the spatial impact of infrastructure be understood at a macrolevel.

This theme is continued in chapter 5 where Roger Vickerman looks at the ways in which infrastructure in one region will have spillovers into other regions. This chapter suggests ways in which a hierarchy of regional types in Europe could be used to assess such infrastructure investment based on research on the impact of the Channel Tunnel. A typology of regions is based on their economic importance, functional interdependence, and eligibility for regional assistance. The emphasis here is on the way regions interrelate with one another. It is suggested that a contrast needs to be drawn between on the one hand the core metropolitan regions of Northwest Europe and the newer, fast-growing city regions outside this traditional core, and on the other hand the less developed, more dependent regions in the geographical core, which can be viewed as an empty heartland, as well as the traditional problem peripheral regions. Infrastructure links in the perhipheral regions to the core, but much new infrastructure is also being used to create corridors through the central regions, simply linking together the major city regions. The traditional city regions face the problem of inadequate infrastructure and are beginning to stagnate. This suggests the need to seek a balance between centrifugal and centripetal forces.

The following four chapters take three of Europe's major new infrastructures and examine various specific impacts associated with them. In chapter 6 Sven Illeris and Leif Jakobsen examine the effects of the fixed link across the Great Belt in Denmark. A specific study examined the consequences on firms in the high-technology sectors as these would be both the most mobile and the most able to take advantage of improved accessibility for passenger traffic. The conclusion from this is that the regional consequences are likely to be less pronounced than first thought in planning the link, but there is some evidence that any redistributive consequences may be less important than a general benefit resulting from improvements in accessibility and a greater coherence of the country as a whole.

By contrast to the Great Belt project, which is going ahead and links the central regions of the Danish economy to the European mainland, chapter 7 is an examination of the Strait of Messina crossing. Carlo Secchi, Magda Antonioli, Alessandro Pio, and Laura Resmini discuss results of a research project into the regional consequences for some of the poorer regions of the EC from this proposal, which is currently awaiting a firm decision to be taken in 1992. This study emphasises some of the practical difficulties, outlined in earlier chapters, of predicting the consequences of a specific infrastructure.

Chapters 8 and 9 are both concerned with specific regional consequences of the Channel Tunnel, but in more distant regions of Northwest England and Northern Ireland. In chapter 8 Lewis Lesley considers the way in which the development of connecting infrastructure could lead to the redevelopment of port facilities in Liverpool which could serve a range of European regions and lead to the diversion of traffic from more central ports such as Rotterdam. This 'Landbridge' concept could have both direct and indirect effects on the local economy of the Merseyside area. The rail developments proposed as part of this are seen as being an important element in ensuring the development of more peripheral regions. They also illustrate clearly the importance of viewing all infrastructure in the context of an overall network which links various modes of transport together, rather than as separable piecemeal investments. Lesley paints an optimistic picture of what changes might happen, but his analysis also makes it clear the way that both a number of separate agencies, public and private, have to take a series of interrelated decisions, and others have to respond to these in a specific way. Lack of coordination of conflicting regional interests is likely to hinder this.

For any transport investment to have an impact on regional development it is critical that it is perceived as beneficial by the users of transport.

This applies both to existing firms within a region and to those seeking potential new locations. In chapter 9, Kate Greenan and Marie McHugh examine the impact of the Channel Tunnel on one sector, the food processing industry, in one region, Northern Ireland. This type of in-depth study is valuable in illustrating clearly many of the general issues raised in earlier chapters. The food industry is an important one in this region and needs both to be able to increase its own accessibility and competitiveness in major new European markets and to resist new competition in its existing main markets such as southern England. A lack of knowledge of changes in accessibility and of the potential consequences is identified. Firms seem to be aware that quality and reliability of delivery are important characteristics, but also seem happy to rely on these tiding them over any major change. The results are not encouraging to those looking for immediate and dramatic responses to new infrastructure and bear out, for a traditional industry, the results of Illeris and Jakobsen for a new industry in the Danish context. Nevertheless there are some signs of an increasing awareness of the need to respond, albeit cautiously.

Chapters 10 and 11 present a rather different approach. They both use traffic forecasting models, in effect as a surrogate for more general economic consequences. This highlights the way that infrastructure has to be seen as a supply constraint on the development of demand, and hence economic activity, but also as a potential generator of new demand and activity. The two case studies look at a general infrastructure affecting several regions and a specific infrastructure affecting one more directly.

In chapter 10, Ulrich Blum looks at the case for new East–West links within a unified Germany on the basis of a detailed forecasting model of traffic patterns to the year 2010. The process of economic integration is found to place enormous demands on the transport infrastructure which will require new investment. Only with this new investment will the potential for economic growth in the East be realisable. This chapter demonstrates many of the problems encountered in developing a macro-model to forecast traffic flows over a long period and relating these to infrastructure capacity. Just as with the regional development model of chapter 2, the traffic model in chapter 10 demonstrates that infrastructure is only one of many influences on total flows. The enormous growth in traffic flows deriving from unification over the next two decades, with rail traffic between the two former German states rising by a factor of seven, also poses some specific regional problems. Formerly peripheral regions now find themselves at the centre, with an inadequate infrastructure. New infrastructure poses for them the same problems as the heartland regions identified in chapter 5, that they face the problem of becoming just part of a corridor between Hamburg or Cologne or Frankfurt or Munich and Berlin. Specific routing of new infrastructure and provision of access to it is therefore vital to these regions.

In chapter 11 Stefan Benvenuti Casini and Giovanni Maltinti look at the case of an assessment of the need for, and optimum location of, a new airport for the city of Firenze. As well as the significance of airports as instruments of regional growth in their own right, airports raise critical issues about the interface between different modes of transport. Part of the argument about siting the airport is in terms of access modes, part of the argument about the need for it at all is whether air travel will continue to grow at the same rate as in the past, given changes in other modes of transport. The authors not only look at specific questions of the interrelationship between supply and demand, they also consider the important issue of externalities arising from the new infrastructure. A rather simpler forecasting model can be used than in the more ambitious German study.

The final two chapters raise two new issues, but ones which are present, at least implicitly, in a number of the earlier chapters.

Chapter 12 takes up the theme of the softer infrastructure of entrepreneurial advice and competence in a region. This is clearly important in its own right as a measure of a region's capacity for growth, but it is also important as a complement to the development of hard infrastructure to the extent that it enables firms in a region to capitalise on the changing potential from that new hard infrastructure. This is a critical aspect of the pressures for centralisation or decentralisation raised in chapter 5. Peter Townroe and Karl Mallalieu present the results of a study of new small businesses in two rural counties of Britain. The extent to which businesses had used, and benefitted from, a range of advice and training facilities available as either semipublic goods or private goods, was surveyed. The principal conclusion is that, although most firms clearly value the need for having such facilities available, they have not always used them widely, and those that have, have had mixed experiences. Rather as with hard infrastructure, such as transport facilities, the simple existence of soft infrastructure does not guarantee success for a region. It requires initiative and application to harness the potential they create before economic benefits are felt by the regional economy.

Chapter 13 presents a summary of work on the determinants of metropolitan development. Competition between cities, especially between the big cities of Europe, has become recognised as increasingly important. To some extent, this survey both of theoretical models and of three recent empirical studies of European cities, highlights shortcomings in both. Piet Rietveld, Frank Bruinsma, and Peter Nijkamp illustrate the way that infrastructure has not so far assumed a central role in models seeking to explain variations in metropolitan development—these have concentrated on more traditional economic explanations of productivity in terms of private goods. However, they demonstrate the importance of introducing an infrastructure element.

The development of cities is important, not just in its own right, but also because a city's economic development affects that of the region dependent on it and for one of the major cities, such as London or Paris, this will include not just its own region but also a whole nation or indeed more than a nation. As the results of chapter 2 suggest that there may be infrastructure constraints on development in the London region and that the Paris region has major overutilisation of both infrastructure and other resources, albeit that this is reducing, and similar overutilisation, but of lesser degree, can be found in the regions of Hamburg, Frankfurt, Munich, Milan and Brussels, this suggests an important potential future constraint on European development. The question is then whether such constraints are sensible in policy terms as a means of spinning benefits off into more peripheral areas or whether the health of the major urban centres is critical to the economic health of the Community as a whole. This seems to be one of the most critical areas of future research, for which the chapter clearly appeals.

This volume illustrates both the richness and diversity of European regional science research on this important issue. However, it also illustrates that there is much that still needs to be done to be able to provide adequate guidance to policymakers and investors about the priorities for new infrastructure development.

Reference
Eurostat, 1990 *Regions: Nomenclature of Territorial Units for Statistics* (Office for Official Publications of the EC, Luxembourg)

The Role of Infrastructure in Regional Development

D Biehl
Johann Wolfgang Goethe-Universität, Frankfurt am Main

1 Introduction

In this chapter I argue that infrastructure or social overhead capital is one of the main determinants of regional development measured in terms of income, productivity, and employment. The chapter is based on the regional development potential or potentiality factor approach developed by Biehl et al (1975) for the Federal Republic of Germany and later extended and applied to the regions of the European Community (Biehl, 1986). The basic proposition of this approach is that there is a special group of resources characterised by high degrees of 'publicness' that determines potential income, productivity, and employment. This group of resources comprises infrastructure and, in addition, geographical location, agglomeration, and sectoral structure. Infrastructure is defined as that part of the overall capital stock of national or regional economies that, because of their 'publicness', are normally not provided by free markets at all or only inefficiently. Thus, its provision is mainly left to political decisionmaking processes. On the one hand, this makes infrastructure an important public policy instrument, on the other it means that infrastructure disparities cannot be explained as 'market failures'.

The chapter starts with a brief summary of the theoretical concept which is more fully developed in Biehl (1986) as to the role of infrastructure as a determinant of regional development. In the next section, an empirical approach to quantifying regional infrastructure capacities is presented. The fourth section integrates infrastructure in a more comprehensive version of the regional development potential approach and shows how regional GDP per capita can be explained with a quasi-production function. In addition, it is demonstrated that these resources, which display characteristics rather like those of public goods (hereafter therefore referred to as public resources), can display significant differences in utilisation. This allows us to identify underutilisation and overutilisation both of infrastructure and of total regional development potential. A few conclusions are also drawn for regional policymaking in the European Community.

2 Infrastructure as a determinant of regional development potential—a theoretical approach

Economic facts are always the result of a multitude of factors working within a framework characterised by multiple conditions. Economic analysis cannot, therefore, isolate one single cause and explain a complex

reality in a unilateral way. To try to assess the contribution of infrastructure to regional development also implies the danger that the multiple
network of causes and effects is arbitrarily reduced to a few relationships
considered to be the most important. On the other hand, one of the goals
of economic theorising is to identify the most relevant causal relationships,
with the aid of which a satisfactory explanation of economic facts is
possible—it would be inefficient to try to take account of the total universe
of interrelationships, many of which will only marginally influence the facts
observed. However, when an economic theory goes too far in reducing the
complexity of reality or whether it comes really close to identifying the
most important causal relationships cannot be determined by a priori
considerations, but only after empirical testing of the implied hypothesis.

A necessary requirement for a theory that claims to be able to assess
the contribution of infrastructure to regional development is that it is not
restricted to infrastructure, but considers also other possible determinants
of regional development. Such a theory must, therefore, be a theory of
regional development rather than one restricted to infrastructure alone.
This is the case with the regional development potential approach to be
presented here.

According to classical economics, *land* (or better *natural resources*),
capital, and *labour* are the three basic resource categories that, appropri-
ately combined, allow the production of output and income. For a long
time, however, natural resources have been neglected, and capital and
labour have been defined quite narrowly as if they are 'private' goods only.
Since the development of the theory of 'public' goods, we have to distinguish between these two types of goods both for final goods and for
resources. According to Musgrave and Musgrave (1984, page 48), 'publicness' implies nonrivalness and nonexcludability, two properties of goods
that cause market failure. As a consequence, resources with a sufficiently
high degree of publicness will not be provided efficiently by private
markets, or even not provided at all. The latter possibility is usually
accepted for government services, such as legislation, defence, and other
public activities. Depending on the type of service and the intensity of
publicness, these goods will either be provided by government itself or by
private firms under government regulation.

Among the three resource categories, it is above all natural resources
and capital that can have high degrees of publicness. If the term 'infrastructure' is used in order to designate that part of the overall capital stock
of an economy that possesses high publicness, infrastructure becomes a
determining or limiting factor to growth as it will not be provided by
private transactions during economic growth. Admittedly, private capital
or labour can sometimes be a substitute for intrastructure—however, what
is important for economic development is the *cost* at which missing
infrastructure can be substituted. One basic assumption of the regional
development potential approach is that the cost of substitution increases

with increasing publicness of a resource. The well-known theory of comparative advantage can then be interpreted as meaning that the cost of substituting a nonexisting or already fully exploited resource is so high that it determines specialisation in production.

There is a large literature on infrastructure if one does not insist on the use of the term 'infrastructure', but on its substance. Already in times of mercantilism, many writers implicitly applied a similar reasoning as to publicness when they claimed that public activities by the 'prince' determined development and welfare. Even classical economists, who strongly rejected the excessive reliance on public activities and praised the benefits of individual action, like Adam Smith, did not fail to mention that roads, harbours, and waterways are important prerequisites of growth.

More recently the newly coined term of 'social overhead capital' has played an important role in the theories of authors like Hirschman (1958), Tinbergen (1962), Stohler (1965), Jochimsen (1966), and Frey (1972). All these authors apply criteria in order to separate 'public' from 'private' capital that can be reduced to elements inherent in the two Musgravian categories of nonrivalness and of nonexcludability. However, as these notions are difficult to quantify, the list of resources labelled 'social overhead capital' or 'infrastructure' differs between authors. Sometimes a narrow, sometimes a broad, definition can be found. One of the broadest definitions is due to Jochimsen (1966) who includes almost all types of public services, even general administration, as institutional infrastructure. Such an extended notion, unfortunately, is much closer to that of 'public' *goods* in general than to 'public' *capital*. As already mentioned, the present approach starts from the idea that infrastructure is a part of the overall capital stock. The combination of 'capitalness' with 'publicness' is considered to be the main characteristic of infrastructure. From this point of view, infrastructure categories comprise transportation networks; energy supply networks; water supply and sewage systems; education and health facilities; social, sporting, and cultural facilities. Some of them may be offered by governments or government agencies, others by regulated private or public enterprises, and others by public or private associations. The types of supplying organisation observed in reality should, therefore, not be taken as a decisive criterion as the preferences for certain types of organisation, and the conditions may differ between countries. What is important is that all these types of organisation differ in one respect, or in several respects, from a typical private market or enterprise organisation. Even if a private enterprise is used as an organisation, it will at least have to work under public regulation or benefit from public protection of its markets. In some cases, there will also be differences as to taxation or subsidy.

Defining infrastructure by relying on 'capitalness' and 'publicness' implies that there may be an optimal relationship between the private and the public elements of the overall capital stock of a national or regional economy. Take, for example, the case of a road network. It would be extremely inefficient if each car-owner had to construct his or her own road in order to be able to travel from A to B. A road network has such a large capacity that many other users can be accepted at almost zero marginal cost. Even in the case of toll roads that are built and financed by private companies, this is only a profitable business if, first, the government grants the monopoly right to provide the road network between important nodal points in space, and, second, the company is not obliged to provide for access at any point of the system. The first condition excludes competition, the second reduces the cost of collecting fees and avoids crowding. Nevertheless, the two conditions seem to be realised only for highway systems and not for normal local and regional roads. Some countries do not make use of toll roads, Germany for example, because the density of population and car ownership, on the one hand, imply an extremely high number of access and exit points, and on the other, would lead to overcrowding of the nontoll roads if the highway system were to be subject to tolls. However, whatever the combination of public versus private supply of roads—it is clear that the other possible extreme situation, exclusive *private* supply of roads, would be totally inefficient. On the other hand, the cars needed in order to make use of a road system are always *private* capital goods, at least in developed mixed economies. Thus, if transportation is considered as the service in question, it is provided by an optimal combination of public and private elements of the overall capital stock. This is true independently of whether infrastructure provides *consumer* services (for example, using roads for pleasure trips) thereby increasing real consumer income, or it provides *producer* services that increase the productivity of private capital or decrease private production cost.

However, given that such a network represents a very large capacity, but will also have to be provided even if, because of low density of population, there are only a few users, a network cannot grow proportionally to demand or need. Typically, there will always be strong differences in rates of utilisation. Rates of utilisation will differ in space and in time. From a spatial point of view, highly agglomerated regions will already have overcrowded roads when there is still unused capacity in less populated regions. From the point of view of time, the rate of utilisation is low when the network is created, and it increases through time as utilisation continues to grow but capacity is no longer expanded. The larger the capacity of a given infrastructure category, the stronger will be the differences in rates of utilisation.

Despite these effects of indivisibility, in a first-best world, we would always have realised the optimal combination of private and public elements of our capital stock. In real life, unfortunately, we have both market failure and government failure, so that the optimal capital stock is not realised. Instead, market and government failure will be reflected in *additional* differences in rates of utilisation. There will be excessive underutilisation and excessive overutilisation existing side by side. Even if the private capital market worked efficiently, there is no guarantee that public investment decisions would also be optimal. In that case, we have to fear that suboptimal public investment decisions will distort private investment decisions, as private investors will react to costs caused by differences in rates of utilisation. All these effects will increase the difficulties encountered when trying to quantify infrastructure capacities and rates of utilisation.

Nevertheless, if we accept these unavoidable difficulties, we can formulate the general proposition that a better infrastructure endowment increases the productivity of private investment and correspondingly reduces private cost. A region that is well endowed with infrastructure will consequently have an advantage compared with a less well endowed one. This will show up in a higher regional GDP per capita or per employed person and/or also in a higher employment. The first proposition derived from the approach presented here is that regional productivity, regional income, and regional employment are an increasing function of regional infrastructure endowment.

This proposition applies first to the *potential* values of productivity, income, and employment. The values *actually realised* may differ, as there can be other factors that influence the rate of utilisation of infrastructure capacities. Potential and actual values will only coincide if the existing infrastructure capacities are optimally utilised. One reason for a suboptimal utilisation could be that labour costs per unit output are more or less equal among regions of the same country, but that infrastructure endowment differs. Under these conditions, the productivity-increasing, cost-decreasing effects of the better infrastructure endowment will not only represent a *comparative* or *relative* advantage in regional competition, but an *absolute* one.

This is illustrated with the aid of figure 1. In this figure, W represents labour cost, P productivity for the regions of countries A and B. In both countries, productivity increases with increasing infrastructure endowment, the labour-cost functions are, however, less steep than the productivity functions. As a consequence, all regions to the left of S_A and S_B are characterised by a labour cost/productivity ratio above 1, whereas the opposite applies for regions to the right of S_A and S_B. As these labour cost/productivity ratios can be interpreted as indicators of relative competitiveness of regional production, we will have less private investment and therefore fewer jobs and lower GDP per capita in those regions left of S_A and S_B, and will have more private investment, more jobs, and higher GDP per capita to the right of these points. With mobility of persons and capital, regions to the left-hand side will also show net out-migration and net private capital exports, whereas regions to the right-hand side have net in-migration and net private capital imports. It is assumed that there are also other factors at work that determine the different levels both of labour cost and of productivity in the two countries.

Given factor mobility, actual GDP per capita and actual employment measured in terms of activity rates may not necessarily be proportional to regional infrastructure endowment. It can, however, be expected that the left-hand side regions with the unfavourable labour cost/productivity ratios will tend to have a lower *actual* GDP per capita compared with their *potential* values, and that the regions at the right-hand side of S_A and S_B, with the favourable ratios, will show a tendency towards having higher actual than potential figures. The regions with favourable ratios will attract relatively more mobile factors of production from the regions with unfavourable ratios, so that the combination of private factors of production with public infrastructure tends to overutilisation in the regions with the favourable ratios and to underutilisation in the regions with the unfavourable ratios. It will have to be seen whether these predictions derived from the regional development potential approach will show up in the empirical analysis later on.

Up to now, we have dealt with infrastructure only as a determinant of regional development potential. However, as explained at the beginning of this section, we need to take into account that infrastructure is not the only determinant. The question is what other determinants may be relevant. In trying to answer that question we should remember that it is the high degree of publicness that allowed us to assume that investment in infrastructure is not determined by market processes, but the result of a political decisionmaking process that can be more or less independent of market decisions. We should, therefore, search for other types of resources that also possess high degrees of publicness and are also less dependent on private market activities.

In order to identify other 'publicness' resources, let us assume that 'publicness' can be divided into the following four subcharacteristics: *indivisibility*, *nonsubstitutability*, *immobility*, and *polyvalence*.

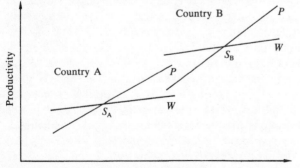

Figure 1. Relationship between productivity (GDP per capita) and infrastructure endowment.

Indivisibility has already been used in characterising infrastructure. If a resource has a high degree of indivisibility, it means that it has a large capacity that can be utilised in differing intensities. But in order to be able to derive even one single unit of service from it, the capacity has to be created first. Indivisibility also implies a long life cycle. As a result, marginal variable costs are low or even zero, and the investment risk is very high for a private investor.

Nonsubstitutability means that, if a specific resource is not available or is already fully exploited, it cannot be replaced at low cost by another resource, especially not by a private factor of production such as private capital. The extreme case is where production of a special good is impossible if the respective resource is not available, or is only possible to the extent that it still has unexploited capacity.

Immobility refers to the cost of mobilising a resource. A totally immobile resource cannot be moved from its location to another one. Again, a region that possesses such a resource is able to use it, whereas another one lacking it cannot specialise in production lines that require that resource.

Polyvalence is used in order to characterise a resource that can be an input in a large number of production processes. The opposite notion is mono-valence or full specialisation, meaning that the respective resource can be used as an input for one single production process only.

Each resource can now be characterised with respect to all four properties. Complete publicness means that all four properties are present at 100%. Lower degrees of publicness may be the result of a lower intensity of only one of these characteristics, or of two or more of them. 'Privateness' can then be defined as the extreme opposite properties: a completely 'private' resource or factor of production is one that is fully divisible, substitutable, mobile, and monovalent. To the extent that these characteristics are present, such a private resource is a low-cost resource for which investment risks are minimised so that private market decisions are fully efficient if adequate property rights also exist. On the other hand, nonexcludability of public resources can have two causes: First, non-excludability may be caused by a deficient system of property rights, so that there is market failure despite a good being sufficiently 'private' in character. However, as property rights are public goods, they cannot be provided by the market, or at least only at high cost. Second, non-excludability may be the result of the fact that the technical devices necessary in order to apply exclusion are too costly. This is the case if a toll road system is to be extended to a total road network, including local and regional roads. It would be extremely costly to allow entry to the road network at every connection point between a road and private land in villages and cities.

With the aid of this differentiation of publicness, we can identify *location, agglomeration,* and *settlement structure,* and finally *sectoral structure* as additional resources determining regional development potential.

Location means the relative closeness or distance of a region considered in relation to the main centres of continental or even world economic activities. It is a resource of high immobility, because geographical location cannot be modified, and economic location, measured in terms of transportation and communication costs can only be modified at the expense of large investments, for example in transportation infrastructure or improved private means of transportation. In addition, it has high indivisibility because all regional activities are affected by location. Substitutability can be high or low, depending on the cost of investment in transportation. Polyvalence again is high because a bad or good location does not necessarily restrict the range of possible production; this will depend on the relative prices of private capital and labour.

Agglomeration and *settlement structure* reflect the spatial concentration of population, producers, and consumers within a region. Their effects are similar to costs determined by distance. The more agglomerated a region, the lower the intraregional cost of transportation and communication. However, there is an optimal degree of agglomeration because increasing spatial concentration first reduces, but then increases, total cost, especially through negative external costs such as pollution, stress, time losses, etc. If measured in total real cost terms, there is an optimal degree of agglomeration per type of central place in the sense of Lösch (1940) and Christaller (1933). The different types of central places combine in order to represent a sort of optimal settlement structure. Again, a large agglomeration centre with its hinterland is highly immobile; it would be very costly to transfer it to another location. It is strongly indivisible, because all activities will be affected by spatial concentration, although there exists an optimal size of this capacity. Similarly, nonsubstitutability and polyvalence are high.

Sectoral structure means the relationship between the relative size of agriculture, industry, and service sectors on the one hand and level of development in terms of income per capita on the other. This idea is based on the three-sector hypothesis according to Kuznets (1971), Clark (1957), and Chenery et al (1975). The proposition is that there exists a typical pattern of development in the sense that low-income regions have a high share of agriculture, that income increases with increasing share of industry and decreasing shares of agriculture and traditional services, and that high-income regions are those with still declining agriculture, but with increasing services of the 'modern' types and either constant or decreasing industrial manufacturing. Although sectoral structure on the one hand is the *result* of regional development, it can also be a *determinant* of regional development for a medium-term horizon, as the problems of the 'old' iron and coal regions and the traditional agricultural regions in Europe demonstrate. Again, the causal impact of a given sectoral structure is higher, the higher cost of modifying this given structure, especially if an agriculturally dominated region is to be transformed into an industrialised one and an industrialised one into a region dominated by modern services. And the cost can be considered to be a function of the relative degrees of immobility, indivisibility, nonsubstitutability, and polyvalence.

If *infrastructure* is characterised from this perspective, it shows a large range of degrees of publicness. Network types of infrastructure such as roads, railways, waterways, communication networks, energy and water supply systems, have a relatively higher degree of immobility, indivisibility, nonsubstitutability, and polyvalence than point types of infrastructure such as schools, hospitals, and museums. Substitutability can be high for the different categories of transportation infrastructure (waterways can be substituted by railways and railways by roads), but is low if higher level infrastructure categories are considered such as transportation versus education or health. Infrastructure will, therefore, have to be considered as representing a holistic concept with important differences as to its internal structure. Obviously, a hierarchical model is needed in order to classify the different infrastructure categories and especially in order to measure its effects empirically.

Infrastructure, location, agglomeration, and sectoral structure are considered to be the four main determinants of the development potential of a region. Including the other three determinants in an empirical analysis provides for the requirement formulated at the beginning of this section. With an adequately specified regression function, there is no longer the risk that the influence of infrastructure is exaggerated.

These four resources represent the productive capacity of a regional or national economy. Private resources, the usual factors of production like capital and labour, are needed in order to exploit regional development potential, but they do not determine it. The reason is that they can easily be imported or exported if adequate market remuneration is offered to them. The fact that they are found to be less represented in a region with an unfavourable labour cost/productivity ratio does not imply that they are the factors limiting regional development. Limiting factors can only be resources with such a high degree of publicness that the cost of either attracting or creating these resources is considerably higher than that of attracting private factors of production. However, actual income and employment will always be lower than their potential if these private resources are not sufficiently represented in a region.

A number of important policy conclusions can be drawn from this approach:

(1) Whenever there is political concern about interregional income disparities, the first point to be analysed is whether actual income deviates more or less strongly from potential income. Given the expectation that better equipped regions will tend towards overutilisation and less well equipped towards underutilisation of regional development potential, actual income disparities will normally be larger than potential ones.

(2) Regions with relative underutilisation of productive capacity lack adequate quantities and qualities of private capital and labour. Their actual per-capita income can be increased if more and better qualified private labour is either 'produced' with the aid of educaton and training infrastructure on the basis of the domestic population or is attracted from other regions. Similarly, new investors have to be found within these regions or to be attracted into those regions. The fact that regions are not able to do this reflects their low endowment of public resources and their low potential productivity given the prices for private capital and labour. A strategy for the short and medium terms then is to subsidise private investors and qualified labour. A long-term strategy, however, requires that the endowment of public resources is improved. As long as potential productivity is low, because of the low resource endowment, subsidising private factors of production is not a sufficient condition for long-term improvement in those regions.

(3) Regions with relative overutilisation of their development potential have relatively too few public resources compared with their private ones. This implies that the cost of attracting, and using, private capital and labour in those regions is low compared with their productivity so that spatial concentration increases. As this increases the benefits from agglomeration, such regions can grow beyond their optimal degree of agglomeration measured in terms of social cost and benefit. As a consequence, capital and labour costs are too low as they do not include the increased cost of pollution, stress, time loss due to congestion, etc. Before deciding that these regions should receive an even better endowment, for example with public infrastructure, or should be subsidised in order to help them to reduce their social cost, it will have to be analysed whether or not a region really is overagglomerated. If it is, it should not be aided through increased public investment and subsidies. Instead, an inter-regional system of *Finanzausgleich* should be applied in order to tax away that part of the returns from resource use that are caused by noninternal-ization of social cost (Biehl and Muenzer, 1980).

(4) Among the four categories of public resources, only infrastructure represents a direct instrument of government policy. It is, for example, not possible to modify location directly, except through the improvement of transportation infrastructure. Also, agglomeration cannot be influenced directly, at least not under conditions of developed democratic societies where freedom of location and residence is one of the fundamental rights. Sectoral structure is more open to government influence, especially if investment and labour subsidies are used in order to attract more private resources into less developed regions. But as already mentioned, a long-term strategy always implies that the endowment with public resources is modified, and this basically always means using infrastructure investment. Infrastructure investment planning, decisionmaking and financing are therefore the most important instruments of regional policy.

3 An empirical approach to quantifying infrastructure endowment

An empirical application of this approach was developed originally for German regions by Biehl et al (1975) and later extended to the entire European Community by a multinational study group (Biehl, 1986). The results of this study are summarised here. At first sight, regional capital stock figures in monetary terms appear to be the best definition for quantifying infrastructure endowment. However, such figures do not exist for all regions of the European Community, and monetary figures do not provide unequivocal information on capacity. Take, for example, the case of a mountain region and a lowland region for which the road capacities are to be measured. As the mountain region will have to spend much more money on bridges, tunnels, road work in rocks etc., whereas the costs per km of roadbuilding are lower in the plain region, it could be the case that the monetary value of the roads in the first region are higher than in the second. Despite the high monetary value, however, the road system measured in terms of road km per unit area or per inhabitant can be lower. In addition, the roads can be smaller in the mountains than in the plain.

Therefore it seems advisable to look for another approach. Because the definition of capacity must be a simple one for which information can be obtained, the following approach was chosen. The objective was to identify that aspect of the capacity to be measured that determines its *bottleneck property* in physical terms. In the case of roads, this can be the total surface of the regional road system. With a given surface and assuming some average speeds for different categories of cars, trucks, and buses, taking into consideration also the properties of roads as to slope, curvature, number of exits and entrances, it is even possible to construct an index of performance. But again, this information is not available in all cases. Road surface nevertheless already contains two types of information: information about the length of a road network, and information about its quality, represented by the width. If two regions have the same road length, but the first has, on average, wider roads, this region also has a larger road capacity, allowing more traffic at average speed.

This idea was as far as possible applied to all infrastructure categories. Waterways, for example, were weighted by classes of admissible ship sizes; airports were characterised by the surface of their runways; for railways a distinction was made between single-track and double-track lines, weighted also with a technical coefficient for electrification; electricity transmission lines were weighted according to their voltage, etc. Compared with what would be desirable, these definitions of capacity are certainly very simple. Their advantage is that, in general, information is available and they allow a minimum degree of differentiation as to size and quality of capacity.

These measures of capacity are expressed in different dimensions. In order to be able to aggregate them, these dimensions have to be eliminated. This is done in the following way:

First, all indicators are expressed in relation to regional area and/or to regional population. Network infrastructures such as roads, waterways, and oil pipelines have a 'space-serving' character, whereas schools and hospitals are population-serving. Two variants are calculated: The first variant relates all network types of infrastructure to area and all point types to population or to age classes (for example in education). The second considers that the two properties of space-serving and population-serving are not either/or characteristics, but may be mixed. An attempt to quantify this mixture used the correlation between an infrastructure characteristic—say road surface—and regional area on the one hand and regional population on the other. These two measures are then weighted together with the aid of the correlation coefficients.

Second, each of these data series is standardised by dividing each single indicator by the maximal indicator value representing the best equipped region. This yields new data series for each infrastructure with values between 0 and 100, eliminating the different dimensions. These individual indicators are then aggregated in two stages. First the arithmetic mean is taken of the indicators for similar types of infrastructure to give an index for each main category of infrastructure. Second, the geometric mean is taken of these main indexes to give a single infrastructure index. This procedure was chosen in order to take account of the different degrees of nonsubstitutability. As roads, railways, waterways, airports, and harbours represent different modes of transportation, their services are substitutable to a certain extent. If transportation is aggregated with energy or education, substitutability is clearly substantially reduced. The geometric mean reflects this to the extent that geometric mean and arithmetic mean are identical if two indicators are equal, but deviate the more these values differ. The larger the difference in relative capacities, the smaller becomes substitutability.

Despite these simplifications, the approach chosen nevertheless proved to be very difficult to realise. The main reason is that many data series are not available from official statistics as these are mainly oriented towards flows, rather than towards stocks. It was, therefore, necessary to develop a special data-collection scheme and to ask the national experts of the study group to contact all those institutions in their member countries in order to obtain comparable data from those that were able to provide them. These were railway companies, harbour associations, airports, electricity companies, local governments, and so forth. Without their cooperation, the project would have failed.

An additional problem was to select the appropriate type of region. As infrastructure facilities have different servicing areas, it was not possible to start from any of these and to try to obtain comparable data for such a regional breakdown. The available data on the other hand were already related to sometimes very special regions like the telephone system networks or railway directorates. Official statistics are usually collected for administrative regions. An adequate approach would have been to start from 'functional' regions, that is a regional breakdown oriented towards labour-market criteria such as the travel-to-work-areas or *Arbeits-marktregionen*. Unfortunately, they exist in only a few countries. In addition, the Directorate General for Regional Policy of the European Commission which paid for the study was understandably interested in getting the desired information for the so-called level-II regions that are also used for the periodic reports on the socioeconomic development of EC regions. As these level-II regions in some member states correspond with the idea of a functional region (for example, in Italy and France), the final regional breakdown was as far as possible oriented towards this regional classification. In some cases, where at the start of the study no official level-II regions existed, data were sought for the national development planning regions or for approximate possible future regions as in the case of Portugal. In Spain, the autonomous regions were used, but their data had often to be aggregated from a provincial level or from other special types of regions.

Admittedly, there is still considerable work to be done in order to obtain time series of regional infrastructure endowment. The main reason why only cross-section information could be collected was that many sources do not provide yearly figures or that the work to be done in order to rebase the available data was too large. In spite of all these enormous difficulties it is nevertheless the first time that such a wealth of information for up to 168 regions of the Community of twelve has been made available on a satisfactory comparable basis. The statistical work will certainly have to be continued both in order to update the actual data series and to improve comparability. Given that in some cases, a larger number of sub-subcategories could be used in order to construct the indicators for the subcategories, and with their aid the main categories, there is also some sort of error compensation.

A first approach, for the years 1978–84 dealt only with the Community of ten. For the ten member countries, an aggregate infrastructure indicator was built on all data that were considered to be sufficiently comparable. Later on, the new member countries Portugal and Spain were included in the analysis. For this second approach, the two cross-section years chosen were 1980 and 1984, whereas the first study covered 1970 and 1980.

In addition, for the second study it was decided to deal only with those infrastructure categories that can be considered to be directly productive, such as transportation, communication, energy, and education. The reason was first, that the underlying theoretical approach relies heavily on the contribution of infrastructure to productivity; second, that many of the other infrastructure categories, from the findings of the first study, seem to reflect consumption rather than production influences, and third, that many of the indicators for these other categories are less comparable; in some cases they represent only *numbers* of facilities such as libraries,

Table 1. Productivity-oriented infrastructure indicator for 168 EC regions, correlation-weighted, 1980.

Region	Indi-cator	Rank	Region	Indi-cator	Rank
FRG (GE)			19 Auvergne	39.60	106
1 Schleswig-Holstein	42.23	122	20 Languedoc	42.22	121
2 Hamburg	100.00	168	21 Provence/Côte		
3 Braunschweig	39.72	107	d'Azur/Corse	48.44	141
4 Hannover	45.93	135	Total	47.12	
5 Lüneburg	35.34	82			
6 Weser-Ems	47.71	140	*Italy* (IT)		
7 Bremen	80.02	166	1 Piemonte	32.11	67
8 Düsseldorf	51.35	150	2 Valle d'Aosta	41.85	118
9 Köln	53.21	152	3 Liguria	56.09	155
10 Münster	50.43	147	4 Lombardia	35.28	79
11 Detmold	37.80	90	5 Trentino-Alto Adige	29.67	57
12 Arnsberg	41.47	116	6 Veneto	31.44	61
13 Darmstadt	44.67	131	7 Friuli Venezia Giulia	33.95	74
14 Giessen	30.84	59	8 Emilia Romagna	36.20	86
15 Kassel	36.01	85	9 Toscana	31.14	60
16 Koblenz	34.23	75	10 Umbria	26.34	52
17 Trier	37.43	89	11 Marche	24.44	47
18 Rheinhessen—Pfalz	44.86	132	12 Lazio	32.46	69
19 Stuttgart	38.06	91	13 Campania	21.14	36
20 Karlsruhe	51.31	149	14 Abruzzi	21.89	39
21 Freiburg	40.51	110	15 Molise	12.59	21
22 Tübingen	35.31	81	16 Puglia	22.67	42
23 Oberbayern	45.76	134	17 Basilicata	14.85	26
24 Niederbayern	41.22	115	18 Calabria	18.21	31
25 Oberpfalz	33.67	71	19 Sicilia	31.56	63
26 Oberfranken	31.86	64	20 Sardegna	30.83	58
27 Mittelfranken	39.59	105	Total	31.04	
28 Unterfranken	38.88	101			
29 Schwaben	33.70	72	*Netherlands* (NL)		
30 Saarland	41.07	114	1 Groningen	76.59	165
31 Berlin (West)	69.86	164	2 Friesland	48.61	143
Total	44.31		3 Drenthe	38.25	92
			4 Overijssel	47.07	138
France (FR)			5 Gelderland	43.60	126
1 Île de France	66.55	162	6 Utrecht	51.68	151
2 Champagne	38.78	98	7 Noord-Holland	57.10	157
3 Picardie	34.95	78	8 Zuid-Holland	60.16	159
4 Haute-Normandie	63.18	161	9 Zeeland	54.28	154
5 Centre	38.98	102	10 Noord-Brabant	41.94	119
6 Basse-Normandie	40.77	111	11 Limburg	46.09	136
7 Bourgogne	42.63	123	Total	51.17	
8 Nord	44.16	128			
9 Lorraine	44.07	127	*Belgium* (BE)		
10 Alsace	57.21	158	1 Antwerpen	69.42	163
11 Franche-Comté	40.99	112	2 Brabant	61.82	160
12 Pays de la Loire	41.58	117	3 Hainaut	38.65	96
13 Bretagne	42.95	124	4 Liège	44.67	130
14 Poitou Charentes	35.65	84	5 Limburg (BE)	38.80	99
15 Aquitaine	50.67	148	6 Luxembourg (BE)	31.99	65
16 Midi-Pyrénées	47.02	137	7 Namur	38.50	94
17 Limousin	42.17	120	8 Oost Vlaanderen	53.31	153
18 Rhône-Alpes	48.60	142	9 West Vlaanderen	38.34	93
			Total	50.08	

Table 1 (continued)

Region	Indi-cator	Rank	Region	Indi-cator	Rank
Luxembourg (LU)	82.53	167	9 Islands of Eastern Aegean	15.06	27
United Kingdom (UK)			Total	20.70	
1 North	44.88	133	*Spain* (SP)		
2 Yorkshire and Humberside	35.31	80	1 Andalucía	25.39	50
3 East Midlands	39.83	108	2 Cataluña	33.87	73
4 East Anglia	38.85	100	3 Madrid	32.28	68
5 South East	44.54	129	4 Comunidad Valenciana	22.48	41
6 South West	36.99	88	5 Galicia	23.99	45
7 West Midlands	33.11	70	6 Castilla-León	34.50	77
8 North West	43.39	125	7 Pays Vasco	39.18	103
9 Wales	38.56	95	8 Castilla-La Mancha	24.56	48
10 Scotland	39.39	104	9 Aragon	40.34	109
11 Northern Ireland	26.58	53	10 Asturias	28.52	55
Total	38.76		11 Extremadura	21.28	37
Ireland (IR)			12 Murcia	22.30	40
1 East	31.49	62	13 Baleares	27.90	54
2 South West	34.35	76	14 Cantábria	25.00	49
3 South East	6.06	2	15 Navarra	19.70	34
4 North East	6.54	3	16 Rioja	28.90	56
5 Mid West	16.69	30	17 Canarias	25.66	51
6 North West/Donegal	5.88	1	Total	29.48	
7 Midlands	13.26	24	*Portugal* (PO)		
8 West	21.32	38	1 Aveiro	9.10	11
Total	27.04		2 Beja	7.76	6
Denmark (DE)			3 Braga	9.72	14
1 Hovedstads-Regionen	56.36	156	4 Bragança	11.99	19
2 Vestsjaellands Amt	49.84	146	5 Castelo Branco	11.07	17
3 Storstroms Amt	36.52	87	6 Coimbra	15.52	28
4 Bornholms Amt	32.07	66	7 Évora	6.81	4
5 Fyns Amt	35.57	83	8 Faro	8.26	8
6 Sonderjyllands Amt	38.65	97	9 Guarda	7.12	5
7 Ribe Amt	49.14	144	10 Leiria	8.86	9
8 Vejle Amt	49.16	145	11 Lisboa	24.33	46
9 Ringkobing Amt	18.57	32	12 Portalegre	13.58	25
10 Århus Amt	41.00	113	13 Pôrto	15.79	29
11 Viborg Amt	18.75	33	14 Santarém	13.17	22
12 Nordjyllands Amt	47.27	139	15 Setúbal	13.19	23
Total	46.86		16 Viana do Castelo	10.17	15
Greece (GR)			17 Vila Real	11.81	18
1 Eastern Continental Greece/Islands	22.94	44	18 Viseu	9.41	13
2 Central/Western Macedonia	22.91	43	Total	15.19	
3 Peleponnese	19.90	35	EC total	37.95	
4 Thessaly	10.69	16			
5 Eastern Macedonia	9.13	12			
6 Crete	12.54	20			
7 Epirus	8.99	10			
8 Thrace	8.22	7			

theatres or old persons' homes, but do not allow differences in capacities or size to be characterised.

For the purposes of this chapter an updated and improved version of the total infrastructure indicator, IGSF, was selected, based on the four main directly productive categories: *transportation* (with roads, railways, waterways, airports, harbours), *communication* (telephones, telexes), *energy* (electricity networks, power stations, oil pipelines, oil refineries, gas network), and *education* (university education, and vocational training for the second cross-section year 1980). 1980 is also the first year for which a complete data set for the 168 level-II regions of the Community of twelve is available. These data are presented in table 1. They represent the normalised and correlation-weighted indicators described above for the four directly productive infrastructure categories mentioned. The best equipped region is Hamburg which accordingly is given the value of 100, all other regions being expressed in percentages of the Hamburg endowment together with their rank order.

As can be seen from table 1, the choice of level-II regions, and by that the choice of the German city-states as 'regions' has the consequence that Hamburg is the best equipped region, and that the two other city-states Bremen and Berlin (West) rank very high. This causes a certain bias because these city-states do not correspond to functional regions, given that they are only the narrowly delineated cities without their hinterlands. This implies that a considerable part of the infrastructure capacity of these cities that serves producers and consumers of the hinterland is now fully attributed to the city area and population. If these city-states had been defined as functional regions, presumaby Luxembourg would have been on the highest rank.

If one neglects this special problem, a ranking of the 168 regions yields an intuitively plausible picture. Most of the highly developed, densely populated, and centrally located regions are to be found in the higher ranks, and the less-developed mainly rural areas with peripheral locations are situated at lower ranks. The least equipped regions are in Ireland, Portugal, and Greece, and have only roughly 6–10% of the Hamburg endowment. The Spanish regions rank between 34 and 109, the least endowed one being Navarra with 19.70 and the best equipped one Aragon with 40.34. Madrid scores at rank 68 with 32.28 slightly below the EC average of 37.95.

Even if Hamburg is not included in an EC-wide comparison, the maximum–minimum ratio between the best and the least equipped regions amounts to roughly 10:1. This single figure illustrates the long way the Community has to go in order to have more convergence and more economic and social coherence. Although convergence does not mean equalisation, it is certainly not compatible with the actual disparities between European regions.

4 An estimation of the development potential of EC regions
As already explained, the regional development potential approach (RDPA) is based on the hypothesis that, besides infrastructure, there are three other determining factors: regional income, regional productivity, and regional employment. If similar simple indicators are used in order to quantify location, agglomeration, and sectoral structure, it should be possible to obtain a reliable estimate for these development indicators. A regression function based on this hypothesis can be considered to be a sort of production function or *quasi-production function* (QPF) where location, agglomeration, sectoral structure, and infrastructure represent the exogenous variables and one of the development indicators represents the endogenous variables. If one chooses GDP per capita as the endogenous variable, the general form of such a QPF is as follows:

$$RDP = f(I, L, A, S), \tag{1}$$

where RDP is the regional development potential in terms of GDP per capita, I is infrastructure, L is location, A is agglomeration, and S is sectoral structure.

For *infrastructure*, the indicator developed in the preceding section could not be used, because the results with this new correlation-weighted productivity-oriented infrastructure indicator are not yet available. Instead, an earlier variant will be used which yields subindicators related to area in the case of network infrastructures and subindicators related to population in the case of point infrastructures. In addition, the list of infrastructure categories is larger and also includes *environmental* infrastructure (sewage water systems, waste composting and incinerating), *health* infrastructure (acute treatment hospital beds), *social* infrastructure (children's homes, kindergartens, old persons' homes) and *cultural* infrastructure (libraries, theatres, concert halls). Unfortunately, it has not always been possible to obtain data for all these subcategories in all countries. The number of subindicators aggregated in order to yield the main indicators, therefore, differs between countries. Given the special procedure applied to calculate the total infrastructure indicator as an aggregated geometric mean of the main categories, this should not have caused a substantial bias.

The infrastructure data series have been normalised in the same way as those presented in section 3 with the aid of the following formula:

$$S_{ir} = \frac{a_{ir}}{a_i^{\max}} \times 100, \tag{2}$$

where a_{ir} are the indicators per infrastructure subcategory i and per region r, $a_i^{\max}$ is the indicator for the region with the maximal endowment, and S_{ir} are the normalised indicators per subcategory and region.

As already explained, these indicators have also been aggregated to obtain an arithmetic mean for the respective main categories, j:

$$M_{jr} = \frac{1}{n} \sum S_{ir}. \tag{3}$$

Given that main categories are more or less nonsubstitutable, they are aggregated via the geometric mean in order to obtain the total infrastructure indicator, IGES:

$$\text{IGES}_r = \prod M_{jr}. \tag{4}$$

A more detailed description of the whole approach and the results of it can be found in Biehl (1986). This study presents figures for the beginning and the end of the 1970s (approximately 1970 and 1980). In what follows, the results for the second cross-section year 1980 and for 139 regions of the European Community of ten are reported.

Location is measured in terms of the sum of distances between each individual region and all others. This sum is expected to have minima for centrally located and maxima for peripherally located regions. It is based on air-line distances calculated with a special program that takes into account geodetic properties. The variable is labeled ENTGKM.

Agglomeration is defined as simple density indicators [for example, population density (POFL) or employment density, the number of active persons per square km (EOFL)].

Sectoral structure is measured with the aid of the percentage share of industry and services sectors in total GDP or in total employment (BPG% and E%IS, respectively).

As the theoretical proposition is that infrastructure is but one of the determinants of RDP, it follows that a QPF based on infrastructure only is underspecified and will presumably yield regresssion coefficients for infrastructure that are too high, because the influence of the excluded variables will be partially captured by IGES. The so-called fully specified QPF with I, L, A, and S plus dummies will therefore give unbiased coefficients. However, it is possible that these coefficients are too low for infrastructure if one of the other exogenous variables tends to be a so-called dominant variable. In such a case in the extreme, 'weaker' explanatory variables will become insignificant because of the presence of such a dominating variable. As sometimes agglomeration and sectoral structure seem to be close to being dominant variables, it cannot be excluded that this decreased the influence of infrastructure in the full specified QPF, even if only QPF are considered that have significant regression coefficients. A large number of possible combinations of exogenous and endogenous variables has been estimated in order to make sure that the relationships to be tested do not only appear in a few regressions.

In general, the results for the fully specified QPF are as good as modified Cobb–Douglas functions with a similar number of dummies, in some cases even better. The $\bar{R}^2$ ranges between 0.62 and 0.99.

BPRO12 is the relative rate of utilisation of infrastructure capacity (IGES), defined as $(BEPO_a - BEPO_{f(IGES)})/BEPO_{f(IGES)}$. $BEPO_{f(IGES)}$ is estimated with the aid of the following double-log QPF:

$$BEPO_{f(IGES)} = 2.864 + 0.500\,IGES - 0.174\,DUMYIT - 0.177\,DUMYGR$$
$$\phantom{BEPO_{f(IGES)} = }{}_{(17.38)} \quad\quad {}_{(8.43)} \quad\quad\quad {}_{(6.82)}$$

$$+ 0.101\,DUMYDE + 0.112\,DUMYGE - 0.160\,DUMYUK$$
$${}_{(4.13)} \quad\quad\quad {}_{(5.27)} \quad\quad\quad {}_{(6.47)}$$

$$- 0.061\,DUMYNL + 0.029\,DUMYFR , \tag{5}$$
$${}_{(2.18)} \quad\quad\quad {}_{(1.31)}$$

$$\bar{R}^2 = 0.9125 , \quad F = 180.94 .$$

The independent variables are as defined above plus country dummies, DUMY followed by two code letters for a country as defined in table 1. All variables except DUMYFR are significant at the 95% level. Values in parentheses are t-statistics; the critical t-value is 1.66.

BPRO22 is the relative rate of utilisation of all potentiality factors (PF), defined as $(BEPO_a - BEPO_{f(PF)})/BEPO_{f(PF)}$. $BEPO_{f(PF)}$ is estimated with the aid of the following fully specified double-log QPF:

$$BEPO_{f(PF)} = 2.682 + 0.191\,IGES - 0.444\,ENTGKM + 0.986\,BPG\%$$
$$\phantom{BEPO_{f(PF)} = }{}_{(3.28)} \quad\quad {}_{(5.48)} \quad\quad\quad {}_{(4.02)}$$

$$+ 0.037\,POFL + 0.132\,DUMYGE + 0.040\,DUMYFR$$
$${}_{(1.83)} \quad\quad\quad {}_{(8.95)} \quad\quad\quad {}_{(2.15)}$$

$$- 0.114\,DUMYIT - 0.142\,DUMYUK , \tag{6}$$
$${}_{(6.14)} \quad\quad\quad {}_{(5.84)}$$

$$\bar{R}^2 = 0.9315 , \quad F = 199.17 .$$

All variables significant at the 95% level; critical t-value is 1.66.

As expected, the regression coefficients and the t-values per IGES are lower in equation (6) compared with the infrastructure-only function in equation (5) and the Cobb–Douglas functions. As the regression coefficients in a double-log QPF can be interpreted as production elasticities, this means that the relative contribution of infrastructure is reduced if the full set of potentiality determinants is considered. However, IGES remains significant in a large number of cases. Particularly as far as GDP per capita and GDP per employed person are concerned, infrastructure is a strong explanatory variable.

When assessing these results, one must take into account that the RDPA is subjected to a severe test. First, the explanatory variables are not derived from time series, so that the usual trend factor that often improves time-series regressions is absent. Second, all infrastructure indicators are purely physical capacity indicators which excludes the possibility that price or monetary values increase correlation. And, third, there are many problems with the databases that normally weaken correlation.

Given the very good fits of the QPF, it seems appropriate to use these results in order to test for the over/underutilisation hypothesis. As private capital and labour are excluded from the fully specified QPF, the residuals contain not only the usual influences of the error term and measurement and comparability problems, but also the influence of these explicitly excluded factors. One can therefore interpret the difference between the RDP-values obtained with a QPF and the actual observed values for GDP per capita (BEPO) or GDP per employed person (BEEM) as indicators of relative over or underutilisation. If $BEPO_f$ is markedly higher than $BEPO_a$ (where $BEPO_f$ is the predicted value and $BEPO_a$ is the actual value), this indicates that the respective region gets a lower return than 'normally' could be expected with a similar resource endowment, and vice versa. If this interpretation is applied to the fully specified QPF, it refers to total public resource endowment, that is, the relative underutilisation can consist of an underutilisation of location, of agglomeration, of sectoral structure, or of infrastructure. This interpretation can also be used to draw some additional conclusions about the influence of infrastructure.

As already mentioned, the contribution of infrastructure tends to be exaggerated if its influence is measured with the aid of a QPF that contains only infrastructure as an exogenous variable (plus dummies). In a fully specified QPF, the contribution of infrastructure is closer to its 'true' importance; in addition, such a QPF also accounts for the influence of the other potentiality factors. Assume now that it is infrastructure only that represents the bottleneck in a region, that is, that infrastructure is in minimum supply whereas the capacities of other resources are not yet fully used. We can then expect that the potential income to be obtained with the actual infrastructure endowment of that region will tend to be below its true value. If, on the other hand, infrastructure was in maximal supply, and if all other determinants were restricting the chance of a region reaching a higher level of BEPO, then the singular infrastructure QPF would yield a $BEPO_f$ beyond the $BEFO_f$ derived from the fully specified QPF. This interpretation again implies a certain optimal structure hypothesis: there is an unknown relationship between the endowment with the four potentiality factors; whenever this is realised, both the singular infrastructure QPF and the fully specified QPF will tend to produce the same potential BEPO estimate.

As far as the relationship between infrastructure and the three other potentiality factors is concerned, four possible cases can be distinguished:
(a) Both infrastructure and the other resources are overutilised and, therefore, represent bottlenecks (cell 1).
(b) Both categories of resources are underutilised and have excess capacities (cell 4).

(c) Infrastructure is underutilised, but the other resources are overutilised (cell 2).

(d) Infrastructure is overutilised and the other resources underutilised (cell 3).

The regions falling within each of these cells can be identified if the results for relative overutilisation and underutilisation derived from the best-fit infrastructure-only function and the best-fit fully specified function are compared. The main conclusions of this comparison can be summarised as follows if the additional distinction is made as to whether utilitisation is constant, decreasing, or increasing (see table 2):

(1) The majority of regions are to be found in cells 1 and 4 and their subclasses, if a band of ± 1.5 percentage points is used to separate regions with roughly 'normal' capacity utilisation according to both QPFs, and if a difference of 3.0 percentage points is used to identify regions with constant rates of over or underutilisation. This implies that the majority of regions are characterised by overutilisation or underutilisation independently of the QPF considered. However, the over/underutilisation can be constant, higher, or lower depending on the QPF.

(2) Only very few regions (that is, 15 of 118) fall in cells 2 and 3, that is, are underutilising their capacity according to the singular QPF and overutilising according to the fully specified QPF or vice versa.

(3) The clear majority of regions characterised by overutilisation represent the highly developed, agglomerated, well-structured, and infrastructurally well-equipped regions, whereas the opposite is true for the majority of underutilised regions. This lends support to the proposition that the better the infrastructure endowment in particular, and endowment with potentiality factors in general, the higher potential productivity and the higher the attractiveness of those regions for private capital and labour.

(4) The largest subgroup is the one with decreasing under or overutilisation (41 of 118). As the first column of figures in table 2 is based on the infrastructure-only QPF and the second on the fully specified QPF, this means that on the basis of infrastructure alone, both underutilisation and overutilisation are more pronounced than on the basis of all potentiality factors. As there are some of the least developed regions among those highly underutilising their infrastructure, but underutilising their total resource endowment to a lesser extent, they represent examples where a better infrastructure endowment seems to have been used in order to compensate for a disadvantage as to location, agglomeration, and sectoral structure. The opposite then applies to those regions showing a decrease in overutilisation; they belong mainly to the highly developed regions having an infrastructure equipment that is relatively smaller than their endowment with the other potentiality factors.

(5) Other less developed regions are to be found in the subgroups of cell 4, constant rates of underutilisation and increasing underutilisation. In the first subgroup, all potentiality factors together would allow a higher actual

Table 2. Comparison between regional rates of utilisation (source: Biehl, 1986).

Code [a]	Area	Relative rate of utilisation [b]	
		infrastructure only	fully specified
Regions with roughly normal capacity utilisation (deviation ±1.5% from 0)			
GE25	Mainz-Wiesbaden	−1.34	−0.12
GE18	Köln	−0.64	−1.08
UK3	East Midlands	1.46	−0.99
Regions with approximately constant rates of overutilisation (cell 1)			
GE29	Oberrhein-Nordschwarzwald	2.13	3.24
FR14	Poitou Charentes	2.60	3.24
UK2	Yorkshire and Humberside	2.85	0.35
NL7	Noord-Holland	3.64	1.92
IT11	Marche	4.26	2.57
GE28	Rhein-Neckar-Südpfalz	7.13	8.27
NL8	Zuid-Holland	5.61	2.75
FR18	Rhône-Alpes	5.62	4.90
GE10	Hannover	3.04	6.45
BE9	West-Vlaanderen	6.45	6.33
GE31	Ansbach-Nuernberg	10.26	6.98
GE5	Bremen	10.09	11.11
GE24	Frankfurt-Darmstadt	15.04	14.02
FR4	Haute-Normandie	14.04	11.05
GE30	Neckar-Franken	16.41	15.18
BE1	Antwerpen	22.86	22.44
GE3	Hamburg	41.59	43.08
Regions with approximately constant rates of underutilisation (cell 4)			
GE12	Göttingen	−18.31	−15.06
GE14	Dortmund-Siegen	−12.69	−14.81
GE13	Kassel	−11.45	−9.16
GE8	Münster	−6.40	−6.11
GE23	Aschaffenburg-Schweinfurt	−4.40	−7.56
NL3	Drenthe	−6.03	−6.79
GE32	Regensburg-Weiden	−8.69	−4.27
GE15	Essen	−5.79	−8.38
BE7	Namur	−5.60	−6.72
IT10	Umbria	−5.45	−3.10
FR6	Basse-Normandie	−5.13	−4.21
NL4	Overijssel	−4.44	−5.05
GE33	Landshut-Passau	−3.36	−0.45
UK6	South West	−2.64	−3.90
FR19	Auvergne	−2.01	−4.16
Regions with increasing underutilisation or overutilisation (cells 4 and 1)			
GE17	Aachen	−19.54	−23.78
GE26	Saarland	−10.47	−14.55
GE21	Mittel-Osthessen	−10.96	−14.33
BE3	Hainaut	−10.31	−15.91
GE20	Koblenz	−9.02	−14.06
GE27	Westpfalz	−8.44	−13.33

Table 2 (continued)

Code [a]	Area	Relative rate of utilisation [b]	
		infrastructure only	fully specified
IT13	Campania	−8.95	−16.98
GE19	Trier	−7.59	−11.94
GR7	Epirus	−7.65	−12.96
UK8	North West	−6.93	−12.16
NL11	Limburg	−5.80	−17.35
FR10	Alsace	−3.13	−10.50
NL5	Gelderland	−0.54	−7.58
UK4	East Anglia	−0.21	−5.51
BE8	Oost-Vlaanderen	−0.04	−3.58
FR12	Pays de la Loire	0.74	5.12
GE36	Alb-Oberschwaben	2.33	6.19
UK10	Scotland	4.55	20.79
LU1	Luxemburg	5.16	17.90
GR3	Peloponnese	5.33	15.97
GE35	Kempten-Ingolstadt	8.35	10.23
FR5	Centre	6.11	11.25
GE11	Braunschweig	8.48	13.36
GR5	Eastern Macedonia	9.80	13.40
IT8	Emilia Romagna	13.27	19.04
GE1	Schleswig-Holstein	15.11	22.05
GE34	München-Rosenheim	19.43	23.38

Regions with decreasing underutilisation or overutilisation (cells 4 and 1)

GR9	Islands of Eastern Aegean	−32.77	−26.62
GR8	Thrace	−28.42	−18.03
FR20	Languedoc-Roussillon	−25.32	−9.78
IT18	Calabria	−23.12	−12.89
IT19	Sicilia	−21.39	−14.82
FR16	Midi-Pyrénées	−20.83	−7.38
NL2	Friesland	−19.42	−11.40
BE6	Luxemburg (BE)	−18.08	−9.47
IT14	Abruzzi	−16.92	−8.16
FR13	Bretagne	−16.91	−6.81
UK9	Wales	−15.08	−6.23
FR17	Limousin	−14.03	−9.50
FR21	Provence-Alpes-Côte d'Azur	−13.52	−3.45
IT16	Puglia	−9.52	−4.24
IT3	Liguria	−9.19	−4.08
GE4	Luneburger Heide	−8.15	−5.45
IT20	Sardegna	−8.07	−1.42
GE7	Ems	−6.33	−2.74
GE37	Oberrhein-Südschwarzwald	−5.35	−2.56
IT7	Friuli Venezia Giulia	−5.50	−2.56
GE9	Bielefeld	3.06	0.06
IT5	Trentino-Alto Adige	4.57	0.47
FR11	Franche-Comté	6.03	2.03
GE6	Osnabrück	6.64	2.03

Table 2 (continued)

Code [a]	Area	Relative rate of utilisation [b]	
		infrastructure only	fully specified
UK7	West idlands	8.47	5.16
IT12	Lazio	9.25	5.30
IT17	Basilicata	14.21	8.45
UK11	Northern Ireland	14.79	4.21
GE16	Düsseldorf	13.67	7.79
IT4	Lombardia	15.62	7.72
FR3	Picardie	17.91	6.14
GR4	Thessaly	22.95	11.74
FR2	Champagne-Ardennes	23.33	15.41
IT1	Piemonte	23.75	12.24
BE4	Liège	25.47	11.00
GR2	Central/Western Macedonia	25.56	1.94
GR1	Eastern Continental Greece/Islands	26.40	5.05
NL9	Zeeland	32.19	27.85
BE2	Brabant	37.27	23.84
IT2	Valle d'Aosta	40.55	32.47
FR1	Île de France	42.93	26.10
Regions with changes from negative to positive utilisation rates (cell 2)			
UK1	North	−10.63	4.32
FR15	Aquitaine	−6.86	5.81
IT9	Toscana	−2.05	0.15
CR6	Crete	−0.29	24.20
GE2	Mittelholstein-Dithmarschen	−0.23	8.13
Regions with changes from positive to negative utilisation rates (cell 3)			
NL6	Utrecht	0.43	−5.37
FR7	Bourgogne	0.71	−2.16
NL10	Noord-Brabant	1.51	−9.73
BE5	Limburg (BE)	1.72	−1.25
FR9	Lorraine	2.04	−10.27
IT6	Veneto	2.34	−2.09
GE22	Bamberg-Hof	0.74	−1.94
IT15	Molise	4.33	−6.05
UK5	South East	7.26	−2.55
FR8	Nord-Pas de Calais	9.11	−13.13

[a] See table 1.
[b] Relative rate of utilisation calculated as $(BEPO_a - BEPO_f)/BEPO_f$ on the basis of infrastructure only [equation (5) in the text] or fully specified [equation (6) in the text].

income; in the second subgroup, regions are relatively less well equipped with infrastructure compared with all resources. This raises the issue of whether there is not a sort of minimum equipment with potentiality factors below which a region will not be able to compete effectively with other, better endowed regions both within its own markets and especially in export markets. If regional labour costs are not in line with regional productivity, but instead reflect national average productivity or are even out of line with national average productivity, it is plausible that this will, above all, negatively affect employment in the less well endowed regions: because of their low endowment with public resources, they are not capable of competing successfully with other, better endowed regions where the same or even a higher level of labour cost is compensated by the productivity-increasing public resources.

Although in the majority of cases, the results obtained fit well with the theoretical proposition outlined above, there are a number of exceptions or deviations. They may be partly the result of statistical data problems, but may also arise because a region is considered to be a meaningful entity to which the type of analysis developed here can be applied. If a region is too close to being a purely administrative area, so that forward and backward linkages are cut through, the analysis may allocate a given infrastructure capacity to an inadequately delimited region. Furthermore, an ideal definition of a region for the purpose of the analysis developed here is that the intensity of spill-ins and spill-outs of infrastructural services are roughly equal. This has also to do with the size of a region: there may already be an optimal regional size for analysis. Such an ideal region could be a labour-market area where the decision about what hinterland to link with a central place depends on the intensity of commuting. Again, different labour markets may exist for different labour-market qualifications than for the relative range of commuting distances. A better solution may therefore require a system of hierarchical labour markets as already inherent in the Christaller–Lösch theories of market networks and central places.

5 Conclusions for regional policy in the 1990s
The Cecchini report and the many studies on which it is based clearly demonstrate that the Commission's programme to complete the internal market up to 1992 will significantly increase welfare and employment in the European Community. There is, however, also a fear that the predicted benefits will mainly accrue to the regions within the EC which are already highly developed and competitive. This has been certainly one of the reasons that the member states, when negotiating the Single European Act of 1986, finally agreed to double the structural funds and to attribute a stronger role to regional policy in order to contribute to convergence.

This strategy is basically supported by the findings of the regional development potential approach. In the long run—and regional development is a long-run phenomenon—reducing interregional disparities requires that

the economic consequences of peripheral location, both of underagglomer-
ation and of overagglomeration, of distortions in the sectoral structure and
especially of deficits in regional infrastructure endowment, are paid due
attention and that an appropriate regional development strategy is realised.
Such a strategy should differentiate between regions that underutilise and
those that overutilise their development potential. In the first case, traditional instruments like subsidies to professional training and to private
investment can be used in order to reduce the gap between potential and
actual income and productivity. In those regions, however, where even full
utilisation of existing productive capacities will not significantly reduce the
income gap, because the endowment with public resources is too low, a
long-term strategy will have to improve the resource endowment. In those
regions that are significantly overutilising their economic capacity, it has to
be checked whether these are at the same time overagglomerated regions.
If this is the case, policies to internalise the social cost of overagglomeration will have to be realised. Apart from instruments of environmental
policy, a well-designed system of *Finanzausgleich* has also to be applied. It
should consist in transferring a part of those regional tax revenues that are
due to excessive agglomeration to the structural funds in order to be
channeled towards the significantly less endowed and less agglomerated
regions. Such a strategy does not require bureaucratic regulation like a
licensing of private investments in agglomerated areas or a taxing of
private investments in those areas. The strategy would be much more
compatible with a market economy approach and would basically not
interfere with private decisionmaking. Its essential elements are a more
progressive system of financing Community activities and clear preferences
for investments in human and in material capital in the lagging regions.

Such a strategy will only be successful if trade unions also understand
that their decisions substantially affect the productivity/labour cost ratio in
each region. If they try to obtain equal pay for equal work in all regions of
a country, or even worse, throughout the whole Community, without taking
into account the differences in regional resource endowments, they will
reduce employment in the less endowed regions and increase it in the well
endowed regions. This will create out-migration in underendowed and
in-migration, and therefore overagglomeration, in well endowed regions.
Such a strategy would be counterproductive and would increase the
tensions between agglomerations and rural areas in the Community. The
pressure of the trade unions would be very welcome if they would also
insist that public infrastructure investments have to play a crucial role in
reducing the resource endowment disparities between leading and lagging
regions. This does not involve an extra burden for trade unions—it only
involves an assessment of problems and policies that are oriented more
towards medium-term and long-term goals and less towards short-term
ones—and this is what both entrepreneurs and governments will also have
to do in order to survive and be successful.

References

Biehl D (Ed.), 1986 *The Contribution of Infrastructure to Regional Development* 2 volumes (Office for Official Publications of the European Communities, Luxembourg)

Biehl D, Hussmann E, Rautenberg K, Schnyder S, Suedmeyer V, 1975 *Bestimmungsgründe des regionalen Entwicklungspotentials: Infrastruktur, Agglomeration und sektorale Wirtschaftsstruktur* (J C B Mohr, Tübingen)

Biehl D, Muenzer U A, 1980, "Agglomerationsoptima und Agglomerationsbesteuerung—Finanzpolitische Konsequenzen aus der Existenz agglomerationsbedingter sozialer Kosten", in *Ballung und öffentliche Finanzen* Ed. H Zimmermann, Forschungs- und Sitzungsberichte der Akademie für Raumforschung und Landesplanung, Hannover, pp 113-150

Cecchini Report, 1988 *Research on the 'Cost of Non-Europe', Basic Findings. Volume 1: Basic Studies, Executive Summaries* (Office for Official Publications of the European Communities, Luxembourg)

Chenery H, Syrquin M, 1975 *Patterns of Development, 1950-1970* (Oxford University Press, Oxford)

Christaller W, 1933 *Die zentralen Orte in Süddeutschland* (Gustav Fischer, Jena)

Clark C, 1957 *The Conditions of Economic Progress* 3rd edition (McGraw-Hill, London)

Frey R L, 1972 *Infrastruktur, Grundlagen der Planung öffentlicher Investitionen* 2nd edition (J C B Mohr, Tübingen; Polygraphische, Zürich)

Hirschman A O, 1958 *The Strategy of Economic Development* (Yale University Press, New Haven, CT)

Jochimsen R, 1966 *Theories der Infrastruktur, Grundlagen der marktwirtschaftlichen Entwicklung* (J C B Mohr, Tübingen)

Kuznets S, 1971 *Economic Growth of Nations* (Harvard University Press, Cambridge, MA)

Lösch A, 1940 *Die räumliche Ordnung der Wirtschaft* 1st edition (Gustav Fischer, Jena)

Musgrave R A, Musgrave P B, 1984 *Public Finance in Theory and Practice* 4th edition (McGraw-Hill, New York)

Stohler J, 1965, "Zur nationalen Planung der Infrastruktur" *Konjunkturpolitik* **11** 279-308

Tinbergen J, 1962 *Shaping the World Economy* (The Twentieth Century Fund, New York)

Transport Infrastructure in the European Community: New Developments, Regional Implications and Evaluation

R W Vickerman
University of Kent at Canterbury

Introduction

Currently there is much interest and activity in the development of new transport infrastructures in Europe: the Channel Tunnel, a North European High Speed Rail Network, fixed links in Scandinavia, and new trans-Alpine base tunnels. Coincident with this is the desire to complete the Single European Market by 1992. In this chapter I discuss some of the background to these developments and the problems of developing a coherent policy framework. I discuss an outline methodology for appraising the integrational effects of transport, through its impact on regional development.

At the European Community level transport was recognised in the Treaty of Rome as one of the two key sectors on which a common policy was required. What has never been entirely clear is what should constitute the main elements of such a Common Transport Policy and progress towards this state has been painfully slow. Three main areas have been tackled: competition, harmonisation of standards, and infrastructure, but here we shall concentrate on the role of the last of these.

Clearly one of the main aims of the European Community is to secure greater economic integration between its member states and their various regions. Economic integration implies a convergence of levels of welfare in the various economies. That integration should come about partly by an increase in trade between the countries, such that their economies are more closely tied together in terms of specialisation, and partly through a movement of factors of production, labour, capital, etc between the countries seeking the highest reward. Either way transport is clearly involved. The process of integration requires the reduction of barriers to trade. These are usually thought of as being either tariff or nontariff barriers of which the first are more directly visible and easily removed, the second probably the most important. Nontariff barriers affect transport widely through such direct features as border delays for customs examination or less directly through a failure to integrate transport networks either side of an internal frontier within the Community.

New infrastructure can alter the transport costs of users and potential users and hence patterns of location and trade. These effects on trade and other transport flows will affect both the aggregate level of economic activity in the Community as a whole and the distribution of benefits and costs between regions and member states. This will apply obviously to international infrastructures, of which the Channel Tunnel is the clearest example, but it will apply equally to many national links which can have a significance well beyond the region in which they are located. The argument will offer some insight into the role which the European Community as a whole, as opposed to its individual members, should be playing. This is of crucial importance now, given the role which infrastructure will need to play in the reconstruction of Eastern Europe and in ensuring that this reconstruction is not at the expense of Europe's western periphery.

2 Transport and economic integration
Considerable interest has been shown in the past in the role which transport plays in the process of economic development (for example, Gwilliam, 1979). Although transport, like any infrastructure, is clearly associated with economic growth as part of the public goods resource input, in the way discussed in chapter 1, it is not unambiguously the promoter of such growth. It is perhaps better to regard the absence of good transport links as being a constraint on the economy of a country or region, but that for development to occur other favourable circumstances must be present (Blum, 1982). Usually the analysis is carried out from the standpoint of one region, typically a lagging region in terms of economic development, of the effect of improving transport links to or within the region. Increasingly, however, this is becoming an inadequate approach to understanding the potential importance of transport in a national or international situation.

This point is discussed in more detail in chapter 5, but briefly the argument is that transport infrastructure relates to transport within a given region as part of the costs of production faced by firms in that region and to access to and from the region, which enters into cost of acquiring inputs and of selling outputs. It can also be of primary relevance to flows through the region, producing an implicit corridor effect. This point is particularly significant because it implies an impact on regions away from the location of the new infrastructure and this will be a major factor in the process of integration.

The Common Transport Policy recognised the strategic role of transport in building the Community and aimed to ensure the development of transport consistent with that of the economy of the Community as a whole. There has been periodic reaffirmation of the importance of transport and the need to widen interests from inland transport (road, rail, and waterways) to include shipping and airlines as the Community expanded from the original six members to include more peripheral nations with different direct transport needs and greater involvements in external trade. However, little real progress on the development of a Common Transport Policy was made. This was recognised by the European Parliament which brought an action against the Commission and the Council of Ministers in the European Court in 1983 for their failure to implement the requirements of the Treaty of Rome (CEC, 1985a; 1985b).

Some progress was made in this time, on three basic fronts (for general discussions of the development of transport policy see Erdmenger, 1983; Gwilliam, 1983; Whitelegg, 1988). Considerable efforts have gone into studies to coordinate the way in which major infrastructure investments are appraised in the transport sector, partly because of the need to compare projects for the award of infrastructure grants. Second, the harmonisation of technical and social standards in the industry has been achieved as a means of promoting a freer market, covering such items as vehicle weights and drivers' hours. Third, attempts were made to develop an appropriate policy on competition in transport, initially by an elaborate system of regulation through both quantity licensing (for example, of road haulage) and price controls (for example, through bracket rate tariffs). It is in competition policy where the least success has been achieved, mainly through a rather outdated restrictionist regulatory approach to transport problems. In the emergent policy proposals for the role of transport in the Single European Market, proposed for completion by 1992, a critical distinction has emerged between the completion of a single market in transport itself and the role of transport in achieving the Single Market in the Community as a whole. It is this second area which is the most important for this paper.

2.1 The meaning of economic integration
Before discussing the role of transport, it is necessary to discuss more precisely what is meant by economic integration. Economic integration can be thought of both as an end result and as a means to that end. The end result is the achievement of a degree of convergence in the economic performance of a set of economies as a consequence of removing all restrictions on the movement of goods, services, and factors of production between them. Ultimately this might imply a full economic and monetary union where all macroeconomic decisions are taken jointly, but many commentators feel that this is a consequence of the achievement of full integration rather than a means of achieving it (Delors, 1988). The means to this end has more to do with processes and microeconomic policy decisions. The lack of convergence in the economies of the European Community has much to do with the latent protectionism of nontariff barriers such as divergent technical standards. The programme of reforms towards 1992 is concerned with removing the remaining barriers to mobility within the Community. There are two routes to this reform: the regulatory route, which implies replacing national standards and restriction with agreed supranational ones, which for many could imply regression towards the lowest common denominator rather than progress to the best available practice, and the liberalising route, in which the emphasis is placed just on the removal of controls and allowing competitive forces to produce the best set of rules.

There is, however, no clear evidence as to the ability of free movement of goods and factors of production to secure, on its own, a convergence in the economic performance of regions within a single country. Indeed, much work on regional economics has emphasised the lack of any such process and the need to explain what has usually been called a process of cumulative causation by which rich regions become richer and poor regions relatively poorer (Myrdal, 1957). The question is then whether cumulative causation is endemic or only happens because of latent barriers to a true single market. One of these latent barriers is transport, or rather the lack of it in an appropriate form.

2.2 The role of transport

A full understanding of the role of transport in economic integration requires an understanding of the microeconomic significance of transport as a factor in the location of industries and of their competitiveness and growth through time. Transport is important both as a means of importing factors of production into, and finished products out of, a production process and as a factor of production itself within the production process. Hence transport should not just be regarded in the conventional way as a derived demand, but as a factor which can be substituted for other factors of production. Location theories typically assume a given technology of production and level of output to determine an optimal location. The process of integration implies a search for change in both of these dimensions and hence a more fluid set of location principles is needed.

An earlier analysis of this question has suggested two important concepts which will have a bearing on the way transport may affect the development of a region: the economic shadow effect of national frontiers and the corridor effect of improving transport infrastructure through a region (Vickerman, 1989a; 1989b). The shadow effect involves a depressing of the natural level of economic activity in a region because of the way national frontiers constrain market areas. It is akin to the conventional notion of peripherality in regional economics (Friedmann, 1966). Despite the existence of a Common Transport Policy in the European Community and the several studies on coordinating at least the appraisal of infrastructural investment (CEC, 1973), national frontiers are still very clearly defined by transport networks. National transport policy has tended to reinforce national frontiers and preserve the shadow effect.

New international infrastructures could clearly have a role in breaking down the economic effects of frontiers, linking regions which are peripheral in a national context, but less peripheral in a wider European context. The danger to these frontier regions is that the new infrastructures just provide a convenient transport corridor through the regions without creating any lasting economic effect. The nature of these infrastructures is that they are more likely to connect major centres of population and could thus be seen as an instrument of increasing centralisation in the Community.

On the other hand, to the extent that these existing major centres act as bottlenecks in the transport system, corridor improvements which bypass such areas could lead to a better integration of peripheral areas into the Community's economy (Vickerman, 1990).

3 Infrastructure bottlenecks in the European Community

The development of European Community thinking on infrastructure has gone through a number of phases, but with the basic objective of securing a greater coordination of investment between national transport programmes. Initial ideas were largely confined to the need to establish common guidelines for investment appraisal (CEC, 1973). If investments in transport infrastructure were being evaluated differently in different member countries, especially if investments in different types of infrastructure were receiving different treatment, this could lead to major distortions in the allocation of resources and to implicit nontariff barriers between countries.

The emphasis has gradually changed towards a greater awareness of the need not just to coordinate natural appraisal policies, but also to think more seriously about the appropriateness of the transport network for the Community, recognising the rapidity of growth in international traffic (CEC, 1979). Such an emphasis has highlighted the existence of critical bottlenecks in the Community's transport system (CEC, 1980). Three categories of project were identified as being of particular significance:
(a) projects on congested sections of the network through which traffic from various international routes must pass (particularly projects to ease the crossing of natural barriers);
(b) projects on links carrying a large volume of combined transport traffic which may have a large influence on modal split;
(c) projects to open up peripheral areas.
These bottlenecks occur both between countries and within individual member countries. The first case includes improving communications to the Community's islands by building fixed links, such as the Channel Tunnel or the Great Belt Link in Denmark, and across the major mountain barriers such as the Alps and Pyrenees. Bottlenecks within countries affect transit traffic, particularly to more peripheral parts of the Community, such as links across the United Kingdom to Ireland or across Spain to Portugal, but may also involve the need to improve infrastructure in nonmember countries such as Austria and Yugoslavia through which traffic passes to reach Greece.

Identifying a network and bottlenecks on it is one thing, providing the finance for a series of major projects is quite another. The 1980 report suggests that a combination of guarantees, loans, subsidies, and interest rate reliefs could be used. The cost of guarantees and loans is difficult to assess, but subsidies and reliefs to the amount of 60 million units of account per annum (the amount included in the Budget) could provide help for projects totalling 2 billion units of account over five years. But this would only scratch the surface of the problem.

During the 1980s the Commission developed its view of infrastructure needs further. Following an initial proposal for a medium-term infrastructure programme in 1984 (CEC, 1984), a revised proposal for a general regulation to provide the Community with a permanent facility to offer a financial stimulus to projects was submitted in 1986 (CEC, 1986a). Alongside this programme was a specific report on the possibilities of a European High Speed Rail Network (CEC, 1986b). This identified in particular the problems of interdependence between neighbouring sections such that a careful analysis of incremental rates of return on different links would be needed, the frontier effect on international links and the question of connections between modes. A further proposal detailed possible new means of financing major infrastructure projects of Community significance (CEC, 1986c).

There was no substantive agreement on these proposals. The larger countries, the United Kingdom, France, and Germany, generally argued against the principle of funding infrastructure specifically, as aid to such projects could be given from other sources. There was support from the European Parliament, however, and a revised proposal for a Community Regulation was made in 1988 (CEC, 1988a). This identified five main aims of such a programme:

1 the elimination of bottlenecks,
2 the integration of areas which, geographically, are either landlocked or situated on the periphery of the Community,
3 the reduction of costs associated with transit traffic in cooperation with any nonmember countries concerned,
4 the improvement of routes which use land–sea connections,
5 the provision of high-quality links between the major urban centres, including high-speed rail links.

Some thirty-three projects were listed for inclusion in an initial 1988/89 action programme, grouped into ten main areas:

1. combined transport network, widening of loading gauge in United Kingdom, Benelux, and Italy, and links Belgium–Dijon, Amberieu–Modane (1),
2. road and rail links to Spain and Portugal (2–13),
3. infrastructure associated with the Channel Tunnel (14–19),
4. the Northern European High Speed Rail Project (20),
5. transit routes in Ireland (21–22),
6. inland waterways between Netherlands, Belgium, and France (23),
7. the Scandinavian Link (24–25),
8. transit routes between Southern Germany and Italy and Greece (26–29),
9. international links in frontier regions, Germany–Netherlands, Pyrenean crossings (30–32),
10. Alpine links to Italy (33).

A five-year action programme was proposed for the period 1988 – 92 with an estimated total cost of 5 to 6 billion ECU (European Currency Units). The proposed regulation implied the use of social cost – benefit analysis as an indicator of the need for any particular piece of infrastructure, plus its consistency with other Community or national policies. Community financing would be available for between 15% and 30% of the total cost of a project. Higher rates of assistance would be given to projects with lower financial profitability, with the degree of specific Community benefits and specific problems encountered by individual states in meeting their obligations. This implied Community funding of around 630 million ECU over the five-year period.

Against opposition from the larger member states in particular, the Council of Ministers failed to reach agreement on the proposed Regulation in December 1988, although a minimal list of projects was agreed upon (including assistance to Channel Tunnel road links in Kent and Nord – Pas de Calais) over a two-year period. This was finally approved with a budget of 90 million ECU in June 1989.

In June 1989 the Commission proposed a modified version of the 1988 Regulation (CEC, 1989). This would restrict the Action Programme from that in the 1988 proposals to the following:

(1) two high speed rail axes: Paris – London – Brussels – Amsterdam – Cologne; Lisbon – Seville – Madrid – Barcelona – Lyon,

(2) the Alpine transit axis (Brenner route),

(3) improving European air traffic control,

(4) the 'Irish Landbridge' transit route (A5/A55 road route in North Wales),

(5) completion of the Scanlink routes to Scandinavia,

(6) reinforcing land links in Greece.

Money would be available on the usual basis from the European Regional Development Fund (ERDF) and the European Investment Bank (EIB) and from line 580 of the Budget (infrastructure projects of Community interest). This proposal reinforced three principles for the use of line 580 in the Budget for such purposes, that such projects: present the greatest utility for the Community; present particular difficulties for financing; cannot be executed by national and regional powers alone.

There has still been considerable opposition to this proposal on two basic grounds. One is that the EIB and ERDF already provide substantial support to transport infrastructure and that a further expansion of the Community's so-called Structural Funds was already taking place, rendering such a further expansion with a new Infrastructure Fund undesirable. In fact some 43% of ERDF expenditure for infrastructure projects went to the transport sector in the period 1983 – 87 and 15% of EIB loans in the same period, a total of about 9.6 billion ECU. However, the 4.8 billion ECU of EIB loans went typically to the financially most profitable ventures rather than to those most needed from a Community perspective.

The second objection is that national planning was a better way of achieving coordination rather than the introduction of yet another tier of decisionmaking on transport infrastructure. This was certainly the view expressed by the UK Department of Transport (House of Lords, 1989). This argument may be valid in terms of the way national governments treat EC decisionmaking, but seems untenable on the evidence of the effectiveness of national governments in providing a Community infrastructure. This may be particularly so in the case of the United Kingdom because of the resistance to the principle of additionality in transport expenditures. Despite the considerable evidence both from transport providers and users and from regional interests, the House of Lords Select Committee on the European Communities (1989) came to the conclusion that the proposals for financing should not be recommended, principally because the Commission's proposals for a European network did not go far enough and that member governments would be tempted to take out as much as they contributed.

This discussion demonstrates clearly the lack of understanding of the role of the transport network. Transport is seen as beneficial only if it is being provided directly to or within one's own territory. If there is any chance that the return from a new instrument will not be at least as great as the contribution, then it is seen as not acceptable, and from the UK perspective it is viewed as recycled government money anyway which does not increase the total contribution to a scheme.

In a wide-ranging plan for transport submitted to the Commission at the end of 1989, Karel Van Miert, EC Transport Commissioner advocated harmonisation and coherence throughout the Community, regardless of national frontiers, in both infrastructure and organisation of transport. Particularly controversial was the suggestion of the separation of infrastructure and operation, especially for railways, a policy already followed by Sweden, Switzerland, and Austria. This had also been advocated by the Round Table of European Industrialists (1989) in a proposal for expenditure of 32 – 40 billion ECU a year to be coordinated by a European Infrastructure Authority, which would be responsible for coordinating plans and their finance from EC, national governments, and the private sector. Van Miert's plan offers the possibility of a genuine 'Europeanisation' of a transport 'system' which, for too long, has been neglected at Community level.

There is still much to be done in achieving the ambitious plans of the Round Table or of the Community of European Railways (1989) for a high speed network of 19000 km costing 90 billion ECU, or indeed those laid down by the European Commission itself in 1986. However, the key links are still contained in the 1989 plans which were finally approved by the Council of Ministers in 1990. Under this, 60 million ECU are being allocated in 1990 with a further 188 billion ECU in 1991, a total of 240 million ECU by 1992, less than 40% of the original 1988 proposals.

Seven specific programmes are being backed:
1. high-speed rail links: Paris–London–Brussels–Amsterdam–Cologne, Seville–Madrid–Barcelona–Lyon–Turin–Milan–Venice–Trieste, Oporto–Lisbon–Madrid,
2. Brenner Pass Alpine route,
3. road and rail connections with Ireland: A5/A55 North Wales Coast road, Dublin–Belfast railway,
4. rail and road links with Scandinavia,
5. rail and road links with Greece,
6. trans-Pyrenean road links,
7. combined transport network.

It is relevant to note the synergy between major European plans to eliminate missing links and also the interest in the use of private-sector capital. As the private sector often has the most to gain in terms of reductions of costs and time imposed by these missing links and bottle-necks, it is reasonable to expect the private sector to bear some of the costs. The question is whether it should bear all of the cost given the presence of wider social benefits which cannot be captured in tolls. Perhaps more significant is whether the private sector should bear any or all of the risk, particularly during construction, or whether the protection of the private sector from risk by government guarantee would remove the possibility of efficiency gain. So far it is only the Channel Tunnel of the major projects which is being entirely privately financed without any guarantee under a fifty-five-year concession agreement from the United Kingdom and France (Vickerman, 1991). A more common form of orga-nisation is the establishing of a specific public–private joint venture organisation to develop the project—here construction companies are induced to take some equity share in the project as they will gain benefits from the construction itself. Variations on this are found in the fixed link projects for the Great Belt in Denmark (see Illeris et al, 1990, and chapter 6) and the Strait of Messina in Italy (see Secchi, 1990, and chapter 7).

However, these schemes cannot be considered or appraised in isolation from each other. In particular, the emphasis on rail in many of these schemes will enhance rail's competitiveness both because of the elimina-tion of model changes or bottlenecks and because of the way it facilitates long-distance rail haulage where rail has the economic advantage. This has particular significance for the more peripheral EC countries such as Italy, Spain, and the United Kingdom. Each of these links depends therefore on each of the other links to enhance its financial and overall economic viability. From a European perspective incremental appraisal is ideally required to prioritise between such investments. What is certainly clear is that they are too important to be left either to individual governments or to the private sector. It is significant that the only body able to take any real part in this development at a European level has been the EIB. The EIB significantly sought a major role in the finance of the Channel Tunnel despite the fact that it had to adopt unusual rules for both the initial loan of £1 billion (secured on commercial bank letters of credit rather than government guarantees) and the further loan of £300 million (secured on the existing assets of Eurotunnel). This makes EIB loans the largest single financial stake in the Channel by a substantial margin.

In December 1990, EC Commissioner Karel Van Miert presented a master plan for a 25 000 km network of new and upgraded railways to the EC Council of Ministers. This was costed at 150 billion ECU of which 60 million ECU would be found from the EC Budget, the rest would be shared between member states and the private sector. Particularly relevant is the focus on fifteen 'key links' mainly located in border regions which link together national plans for high-speed lines and which feature strongly in the infrastructure programmes agreed earlier in 1990. These are Hamburg–Copenhagen, Belfast–Dublin–Holyhead–Crewe, Utrecht–Arnhem–Emmerich–Duisurg, France–Germany via Saarbrücken, France–Germany via Strasbourg, London–Channel Tunnel, Brussels–Luxembourg, Rhine–Rhône, Lyon–Turin, Madrid–Barcelona–Perpignan, Milan–Basle, Brenner Pass, Tarvisio–Vienna, links to and within Greece.

This may indicate a quickening of the pace towards a genuine Community infrastructure, and certainly a consensus as to the main priority areas. However, the Community as a whole does not have the financial power to ensure that any of these links are built without the support both of member governments and of the private sector. EC interest may increase the commitment of the latter, but not without some form of financial inducement in the form at least of guarantees. Successive Commission proposals have recognised the difficulty of assessing the cost of such guarantees and the presence of financial guarantees reduces the risk pressure on those committing equity stakes to such projects to improve efficiency (see Vickerman, 1991, for a further discussion of this point).

3.1 Evaluating a transport infrastructure programme
The proposals for an Action Programme accepted in 1990 confirm the specific interest of the Community in projects which break down physical or frontier barriers to trade. This interest arises from the externalities present in major infrastructure schemes which affect regions away from the location of the infrastructure. However, it is necessary to set these in context before concluding that if implemented this programme would immediately lead to a great increase in integration within the Community. Although it is clear that considerable gaps have existed in the international transport network, the delays imposed by these have probably been much less significant than those imposed by frontier controls which have been estimated to add up to around 2% of the value of products crossing frontiers (CEC, 1988b). This cost may underestimate the loss to the Community's economy by a considerable margin because it only allows for the costs imposed on goods which are actually traded and omits the loss of

welfare from those which are deterred by this extra cost. It is often believed that this cost falls disproportionately on small and middle-sized firms which do not have specialised export staff and which may be less able to negotiate favourable terms with transport operators.

Infrastructure can only promote economic integration by increasing the trade in goods and the specialisation in resource use which promote economic welfare. The main way this will be done is by reducing the cost of carrying goods and thereby promoting competition in the larger Community market between goods produced in a wider variety of locations. However, transport costs only account for some 3 to 4% of value added for most goods and services traded internationally, a reduction of even 40% in the cost of a short section across an international frontier will possibly reduce overall transport costs by only 10% for goods carried across that frontier. Hence goods would need to be very price elastic to occasion much increase in trade from this route. Furthermore, many of the schemes in the proposed Action Programme represent improvements to passenger traffic only, such as high-speed rail links, and thus may have no direct effect on the carriage of goods.

The traditional response to the argument on the relative unimportance of transport costs is that as these costs are the main variable costs between locations and that as average profit rates may be well below 10% of costs, variations in the figure of 3–4% could be a highly significant determinant of the performance of individual firms or locations (Tyler et al, 1988). Furthermore, although data are not easy to find to demonstrate it, it is also likely that transport costs become much more significant when selling to more distant, and particularly foreign, markets. Hence, in the absence of easy international transport, firms may be less willing to trade. Much of this lack of willingness may be as psychological as it is based on objective analysis, but this could nevertheless lead to substantial increases in trade as a result of fairly minor changes in the infrastructure.

Improvements in rail infrastructure aimed at passenger traffic may have significance for freight traffic where the main constraint on higher speed operation has been congestion of usage, particularly that caused by the incompatibility of traffic operating at different speeds. Because freight traffic typically has lower priority on European railways this lowers the average speed of freight and the creation of new dedicated passenger lines will allow for higher effective operating speeds on existing infrastructure to the benefit of freight.

All of these arguments point to the importance of identifying bottlenecks in the infrastructure acting as constraints on traffic growth; removal of such constraints will usually have disproportional effects on traffic growth.

4 Towards a methodology for evaluation

In chapter 5 I discuss in more detail a way of evaluating the wider impact of infrastructure than is incorporated in the more usual regional study. There are two basic elements in this framework. The first is to isolate the purely transport impacts from the wider economic impacts on other activities. The second is an identification of the differential responses of different sectors and the locational impact of these.

The pure transport impacts concern the way in which a new infrastructure changes transport usage in terms of route and mode choice. The concern here is first of all a redistribution of existing flows to cheaper, faster, or more reliable means of transport, and second any increase in those flows arising from lower costs (for a detailed discussion in the case of the Channel Tunnel see Vickerman and Flowerdew, 1990). These can have direct and indirect effects on local economies. A fixed link across a strait previously served by ferries will have a direct impact on employment in port and ferry industries in those regions either side of the strait. In extreme circumstances this could lead to the closure of the ferry service (as is expected in the case of the Great Belt) with serious consequences for ports whose whole raison d'être is the ferry service (Illeris et al, 1990; Waagstein, 1989).

It will also have an impact on ferry services on alternative routes. The Channel Tunnel may concentrate more traffic, both by tunnel and ferry, via French ports and away from Belgian ports, given the longer crossing across the Belgian Straits and the investment in rail and road infrastructure in France. Other ferry routes in Denmark will be affected by the Great Belt Link, including the Fehmarn route between Denmark and Germany. This effect may diminish fairly rapidly with distance from the new link, except where mode changes become possible. Hence any development of rail freight, including intermodal traffic, between the United Kingdom and the continent, could have greater impact on long sea routes such as Hull – Rotterdam or Portsmouth – St Malo than would be implied just by the opportunities of a new route for lorry traffic. Again, however, the regional consequences are only serious where small ports depend heavily on the ferry trade.

There is one further dimension to this pure transport effect on routes, the impact of any change in access to ports or airports within the Community on the choice of point of entry to the Community for passengers or freight. Hence the Channel Tunnel could have an impact on Britain's West coast ports, making them more competitive for deep-sea trade with continental ports such as Rotterdam or Antwerp, although the economics of this do not look promising. The development of high-speed rail networks serving major international airports, such as Paris – Charles de Gaulle or Amsterdam – Schiphol, could affect the development of a deregulated airline industry in Europe.

The wider economic effects are concerned with the way in which transport changes affect different sectors of the economy differentially and, through changes in the optimal structure of those industries and their choice of technology, lead to a changing pattern of location. Such changes clearly affect all regions potentially, not just those close to the infrastructure. Some of these changes will relate simply to a redefinition of market areas and changing competitiveness. Here much of the argument concerns the centripetal and centrifugal forces involved in improved transport (Vickerman, 1990). Understanding of this requires a consideration of transport alongside other changes affecting competitiveness, and protection from competition, inherent in the 1992 programme for a Single European Market. The benefits would seem to favour larger firms with greater scale economies in faster growing regions towards the centre of the Community. This is the type of effect picked up in the studies of economic potential by Keeble and his colleagues (1981; 1988).

More fundamentally, however, a changing use of transport as an input, rather than just as a means of carrying finished products or people, could lead to a major restructuring of certain industries across existing frontiers. This will depend not just on the relative importance of transport costs in the sector, but more on the way in which transport is actually used. Where scope for process specialisation occurs, regional location advantages can be exploited, but linked together by a reliable and efficient transport system. Such effects need to be identified at the industry level, not just at an aggregate regional level. Some results from a study of six contrasting sectors: textiles; automobiles; a high-technology sector; food, drink, and tobacco; financial services; and tourism will be available shortly.

5 Some conclusions

In this chapter I have outlined the development of thinking on the key links in a transport infrastructure strategy in Europe. I have argued that the proper role of transport in the process of economic integration in the European Community has not been understood. Thus short-term and national interests have dominated and prevented the emergence of a coherent policy framework for evaluating projects of Community significance. National transport policies have reinforced existing barriers to integration. The main problem has been the lack of an adequate way of demonstrating both the aggregate benefits from a particular project and the distribution of those benefits. This would appear to be to the disadvantage of smaller and more peripheral countries.

Some elements for such a framework have been presented above from work which is still in progress. The importance of this is twofold. One is that allowing national evaluation of the worth of projects to be the major arbiter of which projects are undertaken, even where EC finance is used, does not necessarily produce the best list of projects, even for the individual state. We have, for example, no means of knowing whether Irish interests are best served by investing in improvement of the road and rail links between Holyhead and the Channel Tunnel or of the longer sea routes directly between Ireland and the continent. Use of private finance for projects does not overcome this problem. Second, and perhaps of more crucial long-term importance, is the integration of transport and regional concerns as part of the central economic decisionmaking process of the EC. This is being shown to be the major issue in the restructuring and integration of Eastern Europe, but it has to be recognised that such restructuring does have implications for all regions of the Community which require a better understanding than we have at the moment.

Acknowledgement. The research in this Chapter was partly funded by an ESRC Research Grant (YD00250018) to the Channel Tunnel Research Unit, University of Kent.

References
Blum U, 1982, "Effects of transport investment on regional growth" *Papers and Proceedings, Regional Science Association* **49** 169–184
CEC, 1973 *Coordination of Investment in Transport Infrastructures* Studies, Transport Series No. 3, Commission of the European Communities, Luxembourg
CEC, 1979, "A transport network for Europe" *Bulletin of the European Communities* supplement 8/79, Commission of the European Communities, Luxembourg
CEC, 1980 *Report on Bottlenecks and Possible Modes of Finance* Document COM-(80)323, Commission of the European Communities, Luxembourg
CEC, 1984 *Broad Outlines of a Medium Term Transport Infrastructure Policy* Document COM-(84)709, Commission of the European Communities, Luxembourg
CEC, 1985a *Official Journal of the European Communities* 13 June, C 144, Commission of the European Communities, Luxembourg
CEC, 1985b *Bulletin of the European Communities* 9-1985, point 3.4.1, Commission of the European Communities, Luxembourg
CEC, 1986a *Medium Term Transport Infrastructure Programme* Document COM-(86)340, Commission of the European Communities, Luxembourg
CEC, 1986b *Towards a European High-speed Rail Network* Document COM(86)341, Commission of the European Communities, Luxembourg
CEC, 1986c *The Financing of Major Infrastructure of Community Interest* Document COM(86)722, Commission of the European Communities, Luxembourg
CEC, 1988a *Proposal for a Council Regulation for an Action Programme in the Field of Transport Infrastructure with a View to the Completion of an Integrated Transport Market in 1992* Document COM(88)340, Commission of the European Communities, Luxembourg
CEC, 1988b *The Economics of 1992* European Economy No 35, Commission of the European Communities, Luxembourg
CEC, 1989 *Communication from the Commission to the Council regarding a Transport Infrastructure Policy: Concentration of Efforts and Means* Document COM(89)238, Commission of the European Communities, Luxembourg
Community of European Railways, 1989 *Proposals for a European High Speed Network* Community of European Railways, rue de France 85, B1070 Brussels
Delors J, 1988, "Programme of the Commission for 1988" *Bulletin of the European Communities* Supplement 1/88, Commission of the European Communities, Luxembourg
Erdmenger J, 1983 *The European Community Transport Policy* (Gower, Aldershot, Hants)

Friedmann J, 1966 *Regional Development: A Case Study of Venezuela* (MIT Press, Cambridge, MA)

Gwilliam K M, 1979, "Transport infrastructure investment and regional development", in *Inflation, Development and Integration* Ed. J K Bowers (Leeds University Press, Leeds) pp 241–262

Gwilliam K M, 1983, "The future of the Common Transport Policy", in *Britain within the European Community* Ed. A El Agraa (Macmillan, London) pp 88–107

House of Lords Select Committee on the European Communities, 1989 *21st Report: Transport Infrastructure* House of Lords papers, Session 1988–89, HL84 (HMSO, London)

Illeris S, Jakobsen L, Madsen P, 1990 *Storebaeltforbindelsens Indflydelse på den Langsigtede Regionale Erhvervsudvikling: Edb-Branchen som Eksempel* (AKF, Copenhagen)

Keeble D, Owens P L, Thompson C, 1981 *The Influence of Peripheral and Central Locations on the Relative Development of Regions* Department of Geography, University of Cambridge, Cambridge

Keeble D, Offord J, Walker S, 1988 *Peripheral Regions in a Community of Twelve Member States* (European Communities, Luxembourg)

Myrdal G, 1957 *Economic Theory and Underdeveloped Regions* (Gerald Duckworth, London)

Round Table of European Industrialists, 1989 *Need for Renewing Transport Infrastructure in Europe* European Round Table of Industrialists, Brussels

Secchi C (Ed.), 1990 *Elementi per un 'Analisi degli Effetti Economici di un Attraversamento Stabile dello Stretto di Messina* (Edizioni Scientifiche Italiane, Napoli)

Tyler P, Moore B, Rhodes J, 1988 *Geographical Variations in Costs and Productivity* Department of Trade and Industry (HMSO, London)

Vickerman R W, 1989a, "After 1992—the South East as a frontier region", in *Growth and Change in a Core Region: The Case of South East England* Eds M Breheny, P Congdon (Pion, London) pp 87–105

Vickerman R W, 1989b, "Measuring changes in regional competitiveness: the effects of international infrastructure investments" *Annals of Regional Science* **23** 275–286

Vickerman R W, 1990, "Whither the core of Europe in the 1990s?", in *Proceedings of Seminar E: Land Use Planning in Europe* PTRC 18th Summer Annual Meeting, Brighton, September (PTRC, London) pp 67–79

Vickerman R W, 1991 "Financing the Channel Tunnel" *Journal of Transport Economics and Policy* forthcoming

Vickerman R W, Flowerdew A D J, 1990 *The Channel Tunnel: The Economic and Regional Impact* special report 2024 (Economist Intelligence Unit, London)

Waagstein E, 1989, "The Great Belt Link in a European Context", in *European Transport Planning Colloquium 1989: European Transport in 1992 and Beyond* Ed H G Smit (Infotrans, Delft) pp 37–46

Whitelegg J, 1988 *Transport Policy in the EEC* (Routledge and Kegan Paul, Andover, Hants)

Investment in Transport Infrastructure and Regional Development

B Gérardin
European Investment Bank

1 Introduction

The commissioning of the Channel Tunnel and the Northwest European TGV will coincide with the opening of the single European market in early 1993. The region affected, directly or indirectly, by these new transport infrastructures are concerned about their positive or negative consequences. This concern among local decisionmakers goes hand in hand with that of researchers who, in spite of many more or less fruitful studies into the subject, are still short of necessary information.

These two large-scale projects offer an exceptional area for observation and experiment. Before setting up observation and survey tools, it is worth taking stock of what has already been acquired in theory and in terms of empirical data, from research in this area.

In this chapter I will present an overview of existing theoretical thinking together with the main elements of the problems involved and the methodology which will guide theory and empirical work in following up the impact of the Channel Tunnel and North TGV on regional development as the basis for a research design.

2 The theoretical background

Before one begins a research project, it is worth looking at one's toolbox and examining with a critical eye the main concepts on which thinking is implicitly or explicitly based. It is a matter of taking stock of things as they stand, of the state of the art.

2.1 Space and economy

Classical and neoclassical economists have long neglected the spatial dimension. The basic concepts of a market economy are aspatial. When we talk in terms of supply, demand, market, price, optimum, general equilibrium, etc, the question of the localising of economic activities is not clearly posed. This might appear to be paradoxical when we consider the slowness and difficulty of means of transport for goods and people until the recent past, as underscored by Braudel (1979).

Implicitly, space is assumed to be isotropic, that is its physical properties are identical in every direction. Space is characterised by individual 'locations' which are organised by relations of distance (Moran, 1966). This 'rational', 'mathematical', geometrical conception is very remote from those prevailing in the life sciences where it is preferred to talk in terms of territory, ecological nooks, biotopes, etc. Thus spatial economy introduces space through distance. Space is a Euclidean transport surface. For economists, this distance is translated into cost; it is a constraint, a function of resistance, of attenuation of flows. From then on, the principal function of transport systems will be to reduce this distance with the unspoken dream of eliminating it.

The current craze for telecommunications, telematics, in addition to the power of the tools, probably resides ostensibly in this Promethean dream of ubiquity. How powerful to be able to transport oneself to another place even if time travel and the elimination of death are not yet here. It is the myth of the jet society. Systems of persons and goods do not have the capacity of electrons to move at the speed of light. This often makes them a mere accessory "which is going to follow" and above all "is going to make itself forgotten". But why move and travel other than to exchange, that is to find elsewhere what cannot be found on the spot?

Accordingly, these abstract points are not all identical. They are characterised by their potentials. They concentrate resources and different activities. From that point on, there are resultant concepts due to regional disparities and local specialisation. Because economy is fundamentally based on the logic of exchange, these locations will become locations for exchange, production, consumption, etc. Once again, we find the traditional notion of a market.

Transport systems which make these exchanges materially possible require support: infrastructure. More often than not, these are costly investments which have a long life span and which leave a profound mark on the land. Like spiders, they tend to weave their webs and to form a network structure to serve an area, sometimes even imposing order and layout on it.

2.2 From plane space to polarised and hierarchical space
As soon as this happens, the 'plane' space loses its homogeneity. Perroux (1954) introduced the concept of the polarisation of space which refers back to the notions of polarised growth and of centre–peripheral relations. Boudeville (1969) has defined polarised space as "a heterogeneous space the different parts of which are complementary and which maintain one another, in particular with dominant poles with more exchanges than with the neighbouring region".

This functional hierarchy of space had already been introduced by Christaller (1933) with his theory of central places, then by Lösch (1940) with his theory of market areas. In addition to Central Germany which served as an experimental basis for the genesis of this theory, many other experiments have confirmed the relevance of these concepts. Braudel refers to the case of Chinese markets in the Setchouan region near the city of Cheng Tu (Skinner, 1964–65).

The best known example is that of Mecklenburg which is at the origin of von Thünen's work (1826). Von Thünen demonstrated the part played by a market located at the centre of a uniform plane amid different types of cultures and methods of production. His concentric circles are the basis of a spatial economy which, from the outset, contrasted with the dominant economic theories of the time, in particular that of Ricardo. More particularly, it was based upon vegetable gardening and agricultural activities, but is not particularly pertinent in the industrial area. The Weber locational model (1909) and its subsequent developments by Isard (1956), Moses (1958), and Alonso (1967) was an attempt to determine the optimum location of the firm as a function of the localisation of production factors, demand, and the transport system.

On these bases, mathematically minded economists have attempted to reaffirm and improve abstract models but, unfortunately, without trying to make any experimental verification of their hypotheses; this considerably limits their influence. It is one of the weaknesses of spatial economy.

2.3 The system space

The introduction of the system-space concept, while making allowance for influences of market area and central place theories, contributes to a dynamic vision of a spatial economy. Economic space is not isotropic as has already been discussed, but neither is it fixed and immobile. As defined by MacLoughlin (1972), it is "a set of independent elements but each element can be considered itself a system and the entire system can be perceived as an element of a more vast system".

This approach, based on the polarised space and plane space concepts of Perroux, emphasises the dynamics of economic forces in terms of market economy and the disparities and interdependence they generate. As affirmed by Aydalot (1976), "space is not neutral, homogeneous, isotropic; growth is not identical, harmonised, balanced at all points of spaces". We encounter the problems facing Perroux when he wrote (1954)

"Growth does not appear everywhere at the same time; it appears at poles of growth with variable intensities and is spread through different channels with variable levels of effect for the overall economy."

These ideas were truly innovative in the 1950s, but have been rethought, enriched, and developed by many researchers: especially Boudeville (1969), Lajugie et al (1985), Piatier (1979), Paelinck (1985), and Nijkamp and Paelinck (1975).

Among the factors influencing the diffusion of growth, transport infrastructures play an important part, even if, a priori, their significance in the whole communication network should not be overestimated.

2.4 Territorial networks

Before I continue the analysis of relations between development and transport infrastructures, it is essential to introduce the concept of a network in order to complete the conceptual toolbox.

Curien (1988, page 212) has put forward as a general definition:

"Any infrastructure permitting the transport of matter, energy or information, falling within a territory where it is characterised by the topology of its access points or terminal points, its transmission arcs, its forking or communication nodes."

If we compare this definition with the theories mentioned above, the hypothesis that infrastructure networks will play a strategic part in the structuring of space-systems and more particularly in their functional hierarchisation can be put forward. This hypothesis is at the centre of research within the 'Réseaux' group of the CNRS headed by Dupuy). The territorial network is first and foremost a topology of locations, a framework for development (Rouge, 1953). But this framework has to be associated with a "circulatory machine". From then on the network "becomes the privileged mode of circulating and processing information within a deeply adaptive and evolving systemic organisation" (Dupuy, 1988, page 13).

Analysis of the structure of these networks draws on contributions made by graph theory, whereby nodes, arcs, and cycles can be quantified and elements of measure can be added to notions of hierarchy and mesh structures of networks, which form the core of such thinking. Thanks to the introduction of concepts of articulation and isthmus points (Flament, 1968; Kuntzmann, 1972), this theory makes it possible to understand more adequately the part played by missing links in the integration of infrastructure networks. Accordingly, for instance, the Channel Tunnel will endow the land transport networks of England with a property of connectiveness to the European continent (Gérardin, 1990).

Network connectiveness is an essential dimension guaranteeing the fluidity of flows and which limits its fragility. De Gennes (1988), as part of a physical theory of 'percolation', reveals a percolation threshold within which the connectivity of infrastructure arcs is insufficient to ensure fluid circulation of the transmitted flows. The network only really comes into being once this threshold has been crossed. This concept can be applied to European transport infrastructure networks. Connectiveness between national networks remains weak because there is a border effect and insufficiently tight meshing of national networks with one another. The provision of missing links is designed to ensure a new stage in European integration by enabling land transport infrastructure networks to go beyond the percolation threshold and thus achieve true interconnection of European infrastructure networks.

Beyond the indispensable physical links needed, this interconnection calls for compatibility of networks and therefore harmonisation of dimensions but also of information, management, trading, signalling, and of course pricing systems. Only when such conditions are satisfied will interconnection lead to real synergies linked with what it is now considered appropriate to call 'network effects'.

In a network, of course, it is impossible to join all the nodes directly two by two. This would require $\frac{1}{2}n(n-1)$ links, which would represent an exorbitant investment cost and have negative indirect external effects; consumption of space, nuisances, etc. For a network connecting 100 cities, 4 950 links would be needed!

This is the logic used to ensure natural orientation toward network hierarchies, much like the functional hierarchies of economic space.

2.5 Territorial networks and functional hierarchies in space

This centralising logic, combining hierarchies of axes and hierarchies of nodes, in some extreme cases leads to a 'Napoleonic' and Jacobin logic, the excesses of which are still being felt in France. The Legrand railway star system, defining the railway master plan decided upon by the monarchy in July 1842 is a clasical illustration. We might speculate how far the recent TGV masterplan proposed for the regions by the government really breaks away from this logic.

The functional hierarchy of the network, built in the image of a pyramidal or 'barycentric' design, consists of having everything work its way to the summit, converging on a central node. The node of the Paris RER at Chatelet is the best illustration of this. In strict application of this principle, whether knowingly or unknowingly, the network designers have caused millions of suburban commuters to converge on the centre of Paris. They now have to live with the unpleasantness of making connections in a hostile environment.

Theoretically this centralising logic is justified when connections are slow and difficult, as demonstrated by Claval (1988). When connections improve, the optimum structure does not imply a dominant pole but may be based on a network of regional metropolises which can play a directional role without constantly having to refer back to the capital. Large cities like these try to make the most of the congestion, one might even say asphyxia, of the overburdened capitals. They are attempting to develop their immunities by making a play for Europe in order to break free from the excessively tight grip of the national capital. Infrastructure network nodes may contribute directly to this evolution by reinforcing effects of regional polarisation. They can also play the part of a diffusing node for economic development. The problem is then that of knowing under what conditions the node in a network of infrastructures may be an open distributing node rather than a closed node, facilitating growth and regional development. Today there is no clear answer to the question.

This thinking is at the centre of research currently being carried out in Nord – Pas de Calais but is relevant to many other European areas, such as Catalonia, Kent, and also Rhône-Alpes or Lombardy. But how do we go beyond the stage of hypotheses and reach that of true modelling which combines theoretical reflection with experimental work?

This is what I shall examine in the following section.

3 From theoretical modelling to experimental verification

I have already underlined the predilection of space economists for mathematical abstraction. This is not a weakness in itself, quite the contrary;
mathematicians' conceptual tools can be used as a basis for many physical
and economic theories. Through a kind of strange communication
between physical reality and mathematical abstractions, these theories
enable us to understand better the operation of what is going on around
us, as long as there is real confrontation between observation and modelling.

Conversely, empirical observation is essential to validate experimentally
the hypotheses resulting from more general thinking. This dialectic
approach between theory and experiment has been described at length by
epistemologists, but the impossibility of establishing a 'constructed experience' in the field of human sciences considerably complicates the exercise.

Beyond these particular cases, corresponding to single and nonrepetitive
experiments, is there any way of defining general rules, tendency laws, like
those used by physicians? Is it possible to find points in common between
observations made of structuring effects along the motorways of the Rhône
Valley, the alpine motorways, or the new TGV lines? Each of these infrastructures has its particularities and exists in a network with specific
characteristics. But beyond particular cases, thinking is on the move.

Constant confrontation between theoretical thinking and empirical
observation provides a heuristic approach but it is sown extensively with
pitfalls. Fieldwork has the double advantage of highlighting cul-de-sacs (at
least provisional) or naïveties. They may also suggest new ways to people
who know how to look for them. This is the framework under which the
current work of exploring the economic and social impact of European
infrastructures like the Channel Tunnel and the North European TGV is
taking place.

I outline a few of the current lines of research in the general perspective
of study into relations between transport infrastructures and regional
development.

4 The observation of the impact of the Channel Tunnel and the North TGV

The commissioning of these two transport infrastructures during the 1990s
is going to be a major event at a time when the process of European
integration is on the move. Accordingly, it is an outstanding opportunity
to attempt to bring together the conditions of a constructed experiment,
that is, one within which a certain number of parameters can be mastered.

The first condition for controlling the conditions of the experiment
consists in properly characterising the ex-ante situation and current trends.
Ideally, it would be good to be able to identify a reference zone not
concerned with the impact of the infrastructures so as to compare the
ex-post evolution of the observed zone against the evolution of the
reference zone. In this way a differential balance can be established. This
process, an everyday process in biology and medicine, is very difficult to

implement here for at least two reasons: (1) the difficulty of defining a priori a pertinent observation zone, (2) the even greater difficulty of selecting a reference zone which is strictly comparable.

However, the twofold principle of this approach will be used. It is not necessarily just by attempting to measure the positive effects of development near a transport infrastructure that pertinent results are reached. The 'negative' effects in areas which are not served and which are barely accessible may be more revealing, better able to highlight by contrast the effects of development linked with infrastructure. Previous studies (Gérardin, 1981) into the analysis of localising factors have revealed that the infrastructure is often a necessary but insufficient condition for establishing an industrial or commercial organisation. These studies have also demonstrated the part played by the nodes of the infrastructure networks in the decision to locate new activities and in the distribution of regional development.

Accordingly, detailed analysis of the creation of industrial enterprises along the Lyon–Chambéry and Lyon–Grenoble motorways (Gérardin, 1980) has revealed a strong concentration of new projects near motorway interchanges. This is designed to meet a need for logistic organisation. On the other hand, areas badly served by 'autoroutes' and by other land transport networks did not experience any significant setting-up of businesses during the period studied. Surveys made among company managers clearly confirmed the part played by transport infrastructures in the decisionmaking process.

The location of new set-ups falls within the framework of global organisation of the firm, itself based on a principle of 'functional disjunction'. It reproduces at its own level an organisation based on the functional hierarchisation of economic space. The company headquarters must be located near the economic, political, and financial decisionmaking centres, that is, in the directorial centres of the capital (for example la Defense or the 8th district of Paris) or in some cases in large provincial cities. The people in charge of production establishments, when choosing between locations, take into account factors related to manpower (quantity, price, qualification). Commercial establishments have to organise themselves in networks in order to get closer to clientele. Therefore each type of establishment has its own localising criteria. But for the system to operate efficiently, the flows of information exchanges, of people, and of materials, must be managed within the framework of efficient logistic organisation.

The part played by transport infrastructure can be analysed in this context. The part played by airport infrastructure in relations between company headquarters and other establishments has often been noted. As observed by Claval, "the plant must be within one hour of an airport by car if a journey made within a day is to be cost-effective" (1988, page 147). A motorway connection between the establishment and the airport is therefore an appreciable advantage. The same type of thinking can be applied to a TGV connection because this method of transport cannot be compared with conventional rail transport but rather with air transport, with which it is a direct competitor. In the case of the North TGV line, this phenomenon will play a very important part in the spatial diffusion of development effects. Emphasis has often been placed on the privileged position of the future Lille TGV station which will put Lille at the intersection of the connections between the major European cities: London, Brussels, Paris, but also Amsterdam (and the Dutch Randstadt) and the Ruhr.

Accordingly, a major effort of observation should be undertaken in the Lille area to detect in real time the setting-up and investment decisions made. This work has already begun with precise identification of sources of information available concerning real estate transactions, building permits, company creations, etc. If it succeeds in reaching the critical size in terms of the higher tertiary industrial area, services to companies, banks, etc, the Lille area could become a European metropolis. Obviously the TGV alone will not be sufficient to guarantee this development, but it could play a part as catalyst for private and public initiatives. In this way, it could contribute to changing the image of the city. Investment decisions are obviously based on objective and rational criteria, but if all things were otherwise considered equal, they could be affected by image criteria. Whatever the case, the images tend to modify the psychological universe of choices made by decisionmakers. Of course, this will need to be filled out with precise observations, then quantified and validated by comparing the results of surveys against the data supplied by economic indicators. The analysis of the impact in terms of development will also affect other transport nodes likely to become development poles (Gérardin, 1990).

The selection of observation zones will lead to in-depth surveys and will be based on a system of indicators incorporating access modifications related to the advent of the North TGV line and the Channel Tunnel (transport supply); and evolution or anticipation identified on the basis of overall indicators produced from existing statistics. These analyses will be essentially related to changes which are themselves related to the evolution of passenger transport supply.

Specific analysis will be carried out in parallel of goods transport chains and evolution. The logic of 'functional disjunction' of the establishments of a company, as mentioned above, is based on effective logistic organisation of transport chains. These chains bring into relation: sources of production of raw materials and intermediate goods; production plants; and distribution, fan-out, and transit centres.

The Channel Tunnel will lead to great modifications in the organisation of chains of transport between Great Britain and the Continent. But their importance should not be exaggerated in view of the relatively modest share of trans-Channel goods transport that the Tunnel would handle. The road and motorway plan accompanying the Tunnel will contribute to connecting the Northern France autoroute network more densely, by improving connections with the Benelux and German networks. The coastal strip appears as an element of the future Atlantic 'arc' which will connect Northern Europe to Gibraltar. Completion of the Calais–Dijon A26 will connect the Tunnel directly to the Rhône Valley without transit via the Paris region. The A6 autoroute will connect Calais to Paris via Amiens.

The exchange nodes of this network will be privileged intersections for setting up transport exchange platforms and, possibly, production plants; consider, for example, the privileged position of the Arras region.

The observation and analysis methodology will combine better knowledge of the logistic chain organisation; analysis of the relations between the various operators: loaders, carriers, transport auxiliaries; and an observation of the locations of new establishments and the extensions of existing establishments.

If the Nord–Pas de Calais region is a privileged field of observation, analysis of the logistic chains should fall within a European context, in particular integrating the strategy of the main European ports concerned. This part of the research project is probably one of the most innovative because traditional analyses in the fields of goods transport are more often than not based either upon studies of logistic organisation cases which are the subject of hasty generalisation; or on quantitative flow analyses which, although useful, are insufficient to understand the logic of the players involved and the decisionmaking processes.

5 Conclusion
The forthcoming commissioning of a very important group of new transport infrastructures—the North European TGV, the Channel Tunnel, the accompanying highway plan—is an outstanding opportunity to recommence theoretical and empirical thinking into the relationships between transport infrastructure and regional development.

Existing theoretical knowledge is rich, diverse, and insufficient. The contributions of spatial economics, the theory of graphs, and network analysis are all pieces of a puzzle which has to be assembled and examined in an effort to locate the synergies between complementary approaches, but this approach can only be validated by observation and experimental 'verification'.

The ambition of this research is not to develop a unique theory for universal application to the spatial and aggregate economy. It is more modestly aimed at contributing to the relaunching and stimulation of research in an area where the stakes are important for territorial development and regional development in a European setting. Finally, it is a question of contributing to renewing traditional methods of evaluating infrastructure projects and of giving them the real status of decisionmaking tools.

References
Alonso W, 1967, "A reformulation of classical location theory and its relation to rent theory" *Papers of the Regional Science Association* **19** 23-24
Aydalot P, 1976 *Dynamique Spatiale et Dévelopement Inégal* (Economica, Paris)
Boudeville J R, 1969 *Les Espaces Économiques* (Presses Universitaires de France, Paris)
Braudel F, 1979 *Les Jeux de l'Échange—Civilisation Matérielle, Économie et Capitalisme XVᵉ - XVIIIᵉ s* (Armand Colin, Paris)
Christaller W, 1933 *Die zentralen Orte in Süddeutschland* (Gustav Fischer, Jena)
Claval P, 1988, "Réseaux territoriaux et enracinement", in *Réseaux Territoriaux* Ed. G Dupuy (Paradigme, Caen)
Curien N, 1988, "D'une problématique générale des réseaux à l'analyse économique du transport des informations", in *Réseaux Territoriaux* Ed. G Dupuy (Paradigme, Caen)
De Gennes, 1988, "Continu et discontinu, l'exemple de la percolation" *Encyclopaedia Universalis* (Universalia Éditions, Paris)
Dupuy G (Ed.), 1988 *Réseaux Territoriaux* (Paradigme, Caen)
Flament L, 1968 *Théorie des Graphes et Structures Sociales* (Gauthier-Villars, Paris)
Gérardin B, 1980, "Créations et délocalisations d'établissements industriels dans le Bas Dauphiné de 1972 à 1978", note de travail LET 80-9, Laboratoire d'Économie des Transports, Lyon
Gérardin B, 1981, "La création de locaux dans le Nord Isère de 1975 à 1980", rapport LET-CNRS, Laboratoire d'Économie des Transports, Lyon
Gérardin B, 1981, "Système permanent d'observation du triangle Lyon – Chambéry – Grenoble", ATP changement Social—LET CNRS—Région Rhône-Alpes, Laboratoire d'Économie des Transports, Lyon
Gérardin B, 1990, "How to evaluate the impact of missing links on the development of European integration", in *Proceedings of Seminar A: Current Issues in European Transport* (PTRC, London) pp 151-162
Isard W, 1956 *Location and Space Economy: A General Theory Relating Industrial Location, Market Areas, Land Use, Trade and Urban Structure* (John Wiley, New York)
Kuntzmann J, 1972 *Théorie des Réseaux-graphes* (Dinod, Paris)
Lajugie J, Delfaud P, Lacour C, 1985 *Espace Régional et Aménagement du Territoire* (Dalloz, Paris)
Lösch A, 1940 *Die räumliche Ordnung der Wirtschaft* (Gustav Fischer, Jena)
MacLoughlin J B, 1972 *Urban and Regional Planning. A Systems Approach* (Faber and Faber, London)
Moran P, 1966 *L'Analyse Spatiale en Science Économique* (Cujas, Paris)
Moses L N, 1958, "Location and theory of production" *Quarterly Journal of Economics* **72** 259-272
Nijkamp P, Paelinck J H P, 1975 *Operational Theory and Method in Regional Economics* (Lexington Books, Lexington, MA)
Paelinck J H P, 1985, *Éléments d'Analyse Économique Spatiale* (Éditions Régionales Européennes, Genève)
Perroux F, 1954 *L'Europe sans Rivages* (Presses Universitaires de France, Paris)
Piatier A, 1979 *Radioscopie des Communes de France—Une Recherche pour l'Action* (Economica, Paris)
Rouge M F, 1953, "L'organisation de l'espace et les réseaux", in *Éventail de l'Histoire Vivante, Hommage à Lucien Febvre* (Armand Colin, Paris)
Skinner G W, 1964-65, "Marketing and social structure in rural China" *Journal of Asian Studies* **24** 3-43; 195-228
Von Thünen J H, 1826 *Die isolierte Staat in Beziehung auf Landwirtschaft und Nationalökonomie* (Puthes, Hamburg)
Weber M, 1909 *Über den Standort der Industrien* (Verlag A Mohr, Tübingen)

Other Regions' Infrastructure in a Region's Development

R W Vickerman
University of Kent at Canterbury

1 Introduction

A major theme of this volume is that, although it is known that new transport infrastructures have important implications for economic development, it is extremely difficult to predict accurately in advance what those consequences may be. Hence, in the United Kingdom, for example, wider economic consequences for regional development arising from new roads are excluded from the approved highway appraisal exercise and British Rail is only allowed to include benefits which can be turned directly into revenue in its appraisal of new investment. Nevertheless, that there is an association between infrastructure and economic development is well documented in Europe as shown in chapter 2. More particularly there is clear evidence that the lack of good transport will act as a constraint on local economic development (Blum, 1982).

Infrastructure can have substantially different effects according to its context. Figure 1 shows us three basic ways in which transport might affect the economic development of a region (Plogmann, 1980). Type-A effects are where the infrastructure simply passes through the region, without having much impact. This would be the case of motorways with few access points or high-speed railways with no stations. This could be termed the *pure corridor effect*. Type B concerns the improvements of communication into and out of the region. This could be in just one direction, typically for a peripheral region, or in several directions in which case a *crossroads effect* will be felt. Type C involves improvement of communications within the region. Unlike type B which implies changes in the costs of supplying inputs and providing outputs to markets, type C will affect the internal efficiency of the region.

In practice, A, B, and C will not usually represent separate infrastructures, but, rather, different flows along a given infrastructure. Understanding the

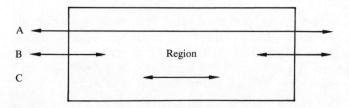

Figure 1. Three ways in which transport might affect the economic development of a region.

interrelationship between these flows will be critical to understanding the possibilities for development in the region.

The purpose of this chapter, however, is to go somewhat beyond this stage of identifying links between infrastructure and the economic development of that region in which the infrastructure is located. Infrastructure in one region will also affect the economic performance of other regions, possibly quite remote from it, both directly and indirectly.

2 Indirect and direct effects

The indirect effects will derive from changes in the relative competitiveness of regions brought about by that infrastructure. Hence the creation of a new link into a peripheral region enhances the potential of that region relative to a similarly located region which is left without such a link. This effect is clearly thought to be significant by regions as witnessed by the clamour to be part of the TGV-network in France (CEDRE, 1990). Similarly, lack of investment in urban infrastructure, leading to congestion is being held out as having a depressing effect on competitiveness and economic performance in Greater London relative to equivalent metropolitan regions in Europe (CBI, 1989; Corporation of London, 1990).

The direct effects are perhaps the more interesting here—this is the impact which remote infrastructure can have directly on activities within a region. There are two sorts of impact which need to be discussed:
(1) objectively measurable impacts on transport costs faced by particular industries for the transport of their inputs or outputs;
(2) changes in subjective views about the relative position of particular regions, and the advantages and disadvantages of locations within them.

The measurable impacts depend on the changes in transport costs for specific routes and the more difficult to assess response to these changes. These depend on the initial perception of the change and the response to that perception. What is important here is to assess not just the direct impact of new infrastructure on likely overall costs and transit times, but also the effects on access routes to that infrastructure. Hence a major infrastructure such as the Channel Tunnel, new Alpine tunnels or a high-speed rail route could have major impact in regions well away from those where the infrastructure is built. This may include the reductions in costs associated with the new infrastructure and the potential increases in costs associated with greater congestion on key access routes.

However, the extent of perception of these changes is more difficult because evidence from previous transport improvements seems not to be entirely relevant to the rather more fundamental changes implied by these major infrastructures. We do have some knowledge of both shipper and passenger response to price and quality changes—the difficulty is in knowing how these can be transferred.

In addition to the changes in transport costs and the evaluation of these as an input to an individual firm's assessment of locations, markets, and sources of inputs; assessments of regions as a whole may be altered by a major project. It is likely, for example, that costs of crossing the Channel will not change that much as a result of the Channel Tunnel, but the Tunnel clearly has had an impact on people's views of the relative isolation of the United Kingdom within the EC. This could easily be transferred to concrete decisions. It is clear from some research already carried out (Henley et al, 1989) that perceptions of the characteristics of a region are better determinants of location decisions than actual values of the same set of variables.

The major impacts to be identified are on the logistic structure of product and transport chains and the implications of this for the location of activities. Major changes in infrastructure have the potential to change the geographical distribution of economic activity in Europe, leading to greater concentrations towards core regions. This process would start with the distribution sector. The counterview is that improved communications will benefit lower cost peripheral regions and enable new activities to locate in these without a loss of logistic coherence. The balance between these will depend on whether current investment decisions in certain regions involve mainly the expansion of indigenous firms, new inward investment involving either branch plants or relocation, and the relation of the new plant's activities to other plants in the same organisation, and whether the new investment is using different technologies from existing plants in the same industry (that is, what particular economic advantage is it exploiting?).

The expected pattern of change is that some regions will be potential gainers and some potential losers. But which regions will gain and which lose? This involves a closer look at a typology of regions.

3 A typology of regions
A typology of regions for understanding the impact of new infrastructure needs to reflect three key issues:
1. the geographical distance from the new infrastructure, and hence the size of the immediate impact;
2. the functional position of the region within both its own national context and any wider EC context;
3. the eligibility of the regions for assistance from national regional policy or from the Community's Structural Funds.

This leads to the definition of five basic regional types which would need to be used for most studies (although there may be a direct overlap between some of these in some cases). The five regional types are (figure 2):
1. Those nearest to the new infrastructure, which receive the direct impact of construction and of changes in accessibility.
2. The main conurbation areas in the economic and geographical core of Europe, cities such as London, Paris, Frankfurt, Köln, Düsseldorf, Amsterdam, Rotterdam, and Brussels.

3. Regions which lie between these main conurbation areas of northwest Europe (Greater London, Île de France, Rhein–Main, Rhein–Ruhr, Randstad). These include Kent, Nord–Pas de Calais, most of Belgium (excluding Brussels and Antwerp), Limburg and Noord-Brabant.

4. The fast growing new industrial regions of Europe which lie in the main just outside the core regions of Europe, including some of those which have benefitted the most from the growth of new technologies. These include East Anglia, East Midlands, Rhône-Alpes, Franche-Compté, Stuttgart, and Lombardia.

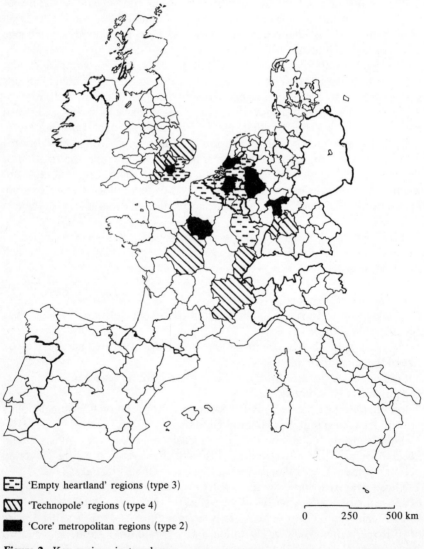

□ 'Empty heartland' regions (type 3)

▨ 'Technopole' regions (type 4)

■ 'Core' metropolitan regions (type 2)

0   250   500 km

Figure 2. Key regions in typology.

5. The peripheral regions which will include the generally poorer regions of the Community, but regions which may benefit from any general improvement in transport provision across the Community as a whole. These can be divided into two groups according to their degree of peripherality and level of development. In the less peripheral and less backward group are regions such as Wales, Scotland, Bretagne; in the more peripheral and backward group are Republic of Ireland, regions of Central and South Italy, Spain, Portugal, and Greece.

Although economic status and distance from the infrastructure are clearly factors in this typology, it is important to note that neither of these is either the sole or indeed the major factor determining the likely impact. It is more the functional position of the region both in national and in European regional systems which is critical. It will be as important to understand economic interactions between regions as to understand the economy of each region in turn. It is the failure to allow for this which can be seen as one of the main limitations of more conventional approaches. However, this also requires us to examine extremely carefully the role of transport on a more microeconomic level.

Type-1 regions will have a specific direct impact of the new infrastructure, but will otherwise have the functional characteristics of one of the other types of region outlined below. This means that the direct effect of construction will be felt here, affecting the local labour force and local industries according to the existing industrial structure of the region. If the region has no heavy industrial or construction bases, this implies a major inflow of labour, with potential effects on local wage rates, etc. This may affect two adjacent regions joined by a new infrastructure differentially; for example, the Nord–Pas de Calais region of France was much better placed to benefit from the construction of the Channel Tunnel than was Kent. In the longer term the impact of operation of a new link will depend much more on the position and existing economic structure of the region.

The conurbation regions of type 2 are core regions of the European economy, the main generators of growth, and have shown increasing interdependence. This interdependence makes them reliant on fast and efficient transport, especially passenger transport, given the dominance of service sectors in their economies. Most other regions are functionally dependent on these regions, usually within a national context. The question is then whether the removal of internal frontiers after 1992 will change this dependency. Although the proportional significance of any new infrastructure built outside these regions on the economy of these regions may be small, relative to other types of region these may be the regions which in absolute terms almost always benefit the most. A critical policy question may be how to divert some of the potential benefits away from these regions to other types of region. For example, by improving accessibility across or around the major cities, their typical dominance over internal communications may be reduced. As new transport infrastructure reduces the importance both of national frontiers and of physical barriers to communication, such as the Channel or the Alps, the conurbations may become more obvious as bottlenecks to traffic. The growing concern is whether these regions can all maintain their current status against this background, as some of the research discussed in chapter 13 of this volume shows; the position of London is particularly relevant in this context.

Regions of type 3 are a particularly interesting group because they lie within the geographic core of Europe without being fully part of the economic core. They are essentially functionally dependent regions within their own countries. The nature of this dependency differs in nature and degree between regions and national contexts, being determined by industrial structure, location relative to neighbouring conurbations, etc. Kent is, for example, much more dependent on London, or Hainaut on Brussels through daily economic interaction, than Nord–Pas de Calais is on Paris. The dependency of Nord–Pas de Calais results more from the impact of decline in its basic industries. These regions are relatively close to one another geographically, but have little interdependence between their economies—such relations are hampered by the proximity of national frontiers. Hence Nord–Pas de Calais, for example, would be seen to interact with Paris, London, and Brussels rather than with its immediate neighbours. Some of these regions are partially eligible for assistance under Objective 2, declining industrial regions, but Kent is not designated at all.

Type-4 regions are in many respects the most successful regions in terms of growth, and in particular the growth of new, especially high-technology, industries. This growth has tended to release the regions from former functional dependence with the conurbation areas into more equal interaction and into greater interaction with each other on the basis of their technologies (for example, see Plassard and Cointet-Pinell, 1986). Locationally these regions are often similar to type-3 regions relative to the major conurbations except that they suffer less from the border region effects of internal frontiers. They stand to benefit from improved communications integrating them further into the 'core' of European regions. These regions are in the main not eligible for assistance, although they include some areas which are partially eligible both under Objective 2 (declining industrial regions) and under Objective 5B (rural problem regions).

The peripheral regions of type 5 are likely to show dependency both at national and at European levels. They are a much less homogeneous grouping than the other region types, including industrial peripheral regions in countries such as the United Kingdom and poor agricultural regions in Spain and Italy. These regions already suffer from peripherality, although the degree of peripherality (and of the intensity of the regional problem) differs within this group between, for example, Northern England, Ireland, and the more remote parts of Portugal or Greece. The question is then whether improved communications will reduce or intensify this peripherality. Regions in the United Kingdom, for example, already fear an intensification as a result of the Channel Tunnel, but there is an alternative which takes into account a more dynamic view (see, CLES, 1989; Vickerman and Flowerdew, 1990). These regions generally have lower unit costs than the other types of region and this could lead to their use as low-cost production centres by decentralising activities from core regions of the Community. This, however, will depend on the improvement of transport links, the lack of which will act as a constraint on their growth potential even if the provision of new transport infrastructure is not in itself a promoter of regional growth. There is already evidence of this tendency for Wales and some Spanish regions. Obviously sectors involved in this are process and assembly industries such as automobiles and foodstuffs. An interesting corollary of this is that within the Single European Market context after 1992 our type-3 regions are likely to be in competition for similar industrial developments as type-5 regions. Type-5 regions are all eligible for assistance, variously under Objectives 1 (structurally deficient regions), 2 (declining industrial regions), and 5B (rural problem regions). This illustrates the heterogeneity of such peripheral regions including industrial regions in the United Kingdom, structurally backward regions in Ireland and Southern Europe, and predominantly rural regions in France, the United Kingdom, and parts of Germany and Denmark.

4 Infrastructure and traffic flows

Transport infrastructure typically serves a range of different flows which compete for the available capacity; international, national, regional, and local. The relative balance of these will differ according to the geographical location of the region. Thus a remote peripheral region will have a greater emphasis on local and regional flows, a border region in the geographical centre of Europe will have a much higher proportion of international flows. The real significance of this is the extent to which one type of flow will impose costs on another. Hence in a border region the provision of capacity for international traffic imposes environmental and financial costs on the region, and the congestion caused by inadequate capacity imposes additional costs on local users of the infrastructure. For the remote region it is the lack of capacity in other regions which imposes costs on its national and international traffic.

Different types of traffic will have different valuations of using a given piece of infrastructure. This can be taken into account in any evaluation of new investment if the proportions of different types of traffic can be forecast. However, it is typically not taken into account when allocating given road space, because even if road pricing were available this would tend to charge according to vehicle type and not to journey purpose or

ultimate destination. For example, the average unit value of exports from
the United Kingdom in 1987 was £426 per tonne, but that through the
ports of Felixstowe and Harwich was £1814 per tonne, and through Dover
was £3543 per tonne. For traffic through Dover, that destined for West
Germany had an average unit value of £4113 per tonne, whereas that for
France was only £2948 per tonne. As the average daily number of heavy
goods vehicles handled by the Port of Dover in 1987 was about 2500
(inward and outward) and the average daily total flow of goods vehicles on
one of the two main routes to the port was 5700, this shows the significance of high-value traded goods. In addition, we know that 80% by
volume of nonfuel exports from the United Kingdom to the continental
EC are generated from outside the South East region, of which 15% pass
through the Thames and Kent ports, principally Dover. This traffic, 12%
by volume but over 30% by value of British exports, has to pass by or
through London to reach the ports.

The role which access points to networks play in determining their
regional and local impact is well known for the case of motorways
(Bonnafous et al, 1975). More recent evidence from the French TGV
confirms the fact that it is not just access to a network which is important
in determining whether it has any impact, but also the way in which
supporting infrastructure and local policies complement this (Plassard and
Cointet-Pinell, 1986). Taking into account the mix of traffic, however, is
also of interest. A comparison of French and British motorways, for
example, reveals that, although there are not very dissimilar densities of
networks in terms of km of motorway per km^2 of area, and the number of
vehicles is slightly higher in France, the density of vehicles km^{-1} is nearly
twice as high in the United Kingdom, and the level of traffic on UK motorways
much higher (Bendixson, 1989). Although tolls on French motorways may
act to restrict usage, it is also the case that access points are also much
less frequent (Quinet and Morancay, 1989)—this reduces the incidence of
short distance traffic on major interurban sections.

For peripheral regions in the United Kingdom the concentration of
high-value international traffic on a single route where it conflicts with
national traffic to the major conurbation, London, and with regional and
local traffic in and around that conurbation, has become a source of
increasing concern. Congestion imposes delays which have a major impact
on firms' costs and hence, for exporters, on their competitiveness.

5 Infrastructure and changes in urbanisation
There is a wider issue here, however. Transport changes also lead to
changes in settlement patterns and the structure of urbanisation on both a
local and a wider scale. Improved rail services in the United Kingdom
have led to a massive increase in long-distance commuting, compensating
the rapid rise in house prices in the London area. Similar effects can be
identified in the Paris region as a result of the expansion of the RER

regional rail network. This enabling of a city to expand through infra-structure helps to contain rising costs in the city. This prevents the equilibrating effect which these costs would otherwise have through the diversion of economic activity to other regions. To some extent the lack of investment in London's transport system can be seen as a deliberate policy attempt to secure a regional policy effect. But it has a negative conse-quence too. Although rising costs may make London less attractive vis-à-vis say Newcastle within the United Kingdom, they also make it less attractive than Paris or Frankfurt. The real competition is thus between cities or regions of the same type or functional significance and not between cities within a functional hierarchy. If London becomes less competitive at a European level, then not only London, but also all of the cities and regions which are functionally dependent on it will become less competitive.

The link through infrastructure to competitiveness and the way it is transmitted through a spatial hierarchy is a key linkage on which we have so far only patchy and partial evidence.

There is a further issue about access to networks and its critical role in regional development. Increasing transport, indeed whole logistical, systems are becoming multimodal. The traditional argument about the economic development of major ports was because they serve as transshipment points. This is no longer the case, with unitised freight dominating, partic-ularly in intra-EC trade. Little or no economic development has been associated with Britain's two fastest growing ports, Dover and Felixstowe. What multimodal transport systems do is create miniports at strategic locations—the term 'freight villages' has been coined in the United Kingdom. Access to these multimodal termini is seen as critical in regional development terms because absence of such access will reduce the reliability which any service can give.

Such transport systems are important not so much for the carrying of finished goods, but as part of the production process itself carrying inter-mediate goods and raw materials. Here reliability is of utmost importance to ensure just in time delivery of inputs to users; often only a fully integrated transport system can achieve this. However, the more peripheral a region is, the more it relies on the efficiency of the system in other regions to ensure this reliability. Peripheral regions are attractive to potential investors because they have lower costs of inputs other than transport which can overcome the greater transport cost. Indeed the higher direct costs of transport which arise through greater distances may also be offset by lower congestion levels on access to the primary network and ability to use more efficient transport systems for long hauls. This is one way in which peripheral regions (type 5) may also be competitive with more central but nonmetropolitan (type 3) regions.

6 Measuring the impact of infrastructure

The discussion in the preceding sections has shown the great complexity of assessing the wider impact of infrastructure. In this section I outline an initial approach to making that assessment. It depends on the two basic principles discussed above, a set of regional relationships and an understanding of the microrelationships determining usage. For ease of exposition I shall use as a case study the Channel Tunnel, as it represents a major infrastructure project which will have a fairly widespread effect (for a fuller discussion see Vickerman, 1987; 1989; Holliday et al 1991).

First we need to separate out the purely transport effects from the wider economic effects. The opening of the Tunnel will lead both to mode changes and route changes and to new trip generation. These pure transport impacts relate to the existing distribution of activities and will affect, in particular, regions with ports and airports in the United Kingdom and on the continent through which trade passes. Such changes will not have a profound knock-on effect on other employment in these regions because most trade is unitised and passes straight through. They will also have minimal effects on more distant regions.

However, the creation of a new link with different characteristics from the existing links can affect production and location decisions over a much wider area, making the.impact of the Tunnel much more significant. We need to distinguish changes which do not affect location, only market areas, and those which lead to relocation. Changes which affect market areas are about the changes in competitiveness which result from differential changes in transport costs (Vickerman, 1989). These are likely to benefit dynamic firms in fast growing (type 4) regions and those with substantial existing scale economies in the major metropolitan (type 2) regions. The proportional impact on these regions in aggregate may be small, but in absolute terms could be substantial. This would imply a diversion of activity from firms in peripheral regions. This centralising effect is one of the most feared impacts of such infrastructures.

However, this is only part of the impact because relocation may also be brought about by the new opportunities offered by the Tunnel. Such relocation is unlikely to be induced solely by the transport changes, but these changes enable a desired relocation to take into account a wider range of potential destinations and be more likely to get close to an optimal location. This reorientation may particularly affect small and medium-sized enterprises (SME) which currently trade much less than larger companies because they face proportionately greater costs from cross-border trade. Much of these higher costs arises from administrative barriers to trade, but inefficiencies in transport are clearly related to these. New transport opportunities in multimodal transport which help to minimise these factors may make such firms much more open to change than existing traders. The SME sector is also believed to be that where many of the impacts of the 1992 programme will be most significantly felt (see Cappellin, 1990).

The interrelationship between infrastructures is important. New investment in rail in Alpine tunnels and in Spain, as well as improvement in East–West links may all have an important synergy with a project such as the Channel Tunnel as discussed in chapter 3. Hence regions well connected by rail will be able more quickly to become part of a multiregional network.

It will also be crucial to take into account changes already in progress in the regions, independently of any changes in transport provision. This is particularly true of restructuring occasioned by the move towards the Single European Market scheduled for completion in 1992. 1992 changes may prove to be much more significant per se than transport infrastructure, though there is likely to be an important synergy between the two. In this context particular attention should be paid to those sectors where transport delays and other border costs currently appear significant or where significant regional restructuring as a result of scale economies or other dynamic changes to industry are likely to occur.

Certain key sectors may be much more affected than industry in general. These sectors include major growth sectors and sectors where transport is either a significant part of total costs, for example, transport of bulk materials, or reductions in transport time could lead to significant gain, for example, transport of perishable foodstuffs.

Three types of sectoral response can be identified. First, we need to consider the extent to which changes in transport provision induce a relocation of economic activity between regions. Such activities will be footloose and be sensitive to changes in the transport sector. They will therefore have either relatively high levels of transport costs to total costs and be seeking to reduce these, or will be sensitive to the need to relocate relatively close to markets. Some traditional manufacturing industries might fall in the first group, although few industries have transport costs greater than 10% of total costs. The second group could include most service-sector industries including high-technology related services, business and financial services, where it is the movement of people rather than goods or materials which is relevant.

Second, locally based industries which serve wider markets, will be affected by the changes, inducing, for example, a faster rate of growth in sectors already important in the local economy.

The third type of activity is the primarily locally oriented activity. Each of the first two types will depend on trade with groups outside the local region; this third type of activity depends entirely on the local market and is therefore dependent on the so-called primary or economic base activities. Retailing and local business services fall into this group, but it can also include small and medium sized construction companies, transport, public utilities, and some manufacturing. These groups depend on the success of the base sector for their success, but are also vulnerable to some extent to competition from outside. Hence local retailing stands to face competition from new out-of-town developments by large multiples, local construction firms face competition from national firms for larger contracts, and the nature of urban development in the area may change.

However, we must recognise that transport costs account for a very small fraction of the total costs (value-added) of most manufacturing firms, typically less than 4%. Hence a very large change in transport costs would be required to have even a 1% effect on total costs of production. Furthermore, the larger the haul in question the less will be the impact of any reduction in costs on one part of the haul. For example, the cost of the cross-Channel element will be typically between 15% and 40% of the cost of moving a lorry-load between the United Kingdom and most continental destinations. Since Eurotunnel claim a possible average 10% cost reduction in real terms for the cross-Channel leg this would give an average 0.01% reduction in total costs.

This would suggest that infrastructure like the Tunnel will be insignificant as an agent of relocation, but this might be an oversimplification. Three main factors account for this. First, transport may be a more variable cost between locations than other costs and hence a substantial contributor to variations in profits. This is unlikely to lead to firms wishing to relocate in itself, but those seeking relocation or expansion may take transport factors into account when choosing between alternative locations. Second, the absolute level of transport costs may be less important than the reliability of transport. If transport costs are 4% of total costs they may be as much as 40% or more of profits and thus even a 10% variation in transport costs is effectively a 5% variation in profits. Lack of reliability in transport may cause greater costs than just the financial impact because lost or late deliveries can halt a production process or lead to lost future orders. The size of costly inventories may reflect transport unreliability. The Confederation of British Industry (CBI, 1989) has suggested that transport congestion alone is costing £15 billion a year in the United Kingdom (probably two thirds of which occurs in London and the South East) and one extra week's inventories in the retailing sector cost some £200 million a year.

7 Conclusion: some policy implications
The best way of drawing out the main issues from this chapter is in terms of the implications for policy. Four main issues have been identified:
(1) that infrastructure has effects beyond the region where it is located;
(2) that adequate assessment of infrastructure requires an understanding of a complete network;
(3) that a common typology of regions is needed for use in infrastructure appraisal in order to be able to identify the extent to which particular types of region may receive cumulative benefits or cumulative disbenefits from otherwise separate projects;

(4) that traditional static regional assessments are inadequate when major changes in infrastructure occur because a fuller analysis of the way transport can be used by relevant sectors of the economy is necessary.

These wider and often unpredictable impacts imply the need for a wider appreciation of policy than can be achieved by regional or even national authorities, whether or not private-sector capital is used. The asymmetry between regions incurring costs and regions enjoying benefits requires either that major infrastucture should be provided only at the highest level where all these factors can be taken into account (for example, at the EC level) or by a formal procedure for introducing interregional factors such that appropriate compensation could be determined.

Examples of the need for this approach can be seen in the failure to cope with the problem of London vis-à-vis the situation of Northern British regions; the need for improved infrastructure to benefit Irish traffic across the United Kingdom; or compensation for regions like Hainaut in Belgium or Picardie in France which must suffer the construction of a high-speed rail line without gaining adequate access to this network. Although the EC has attempted to define necessary infrastructure improvements of Community importance (see chapter 3 for a full discussion), it has not been possible to get widespread agreement on the financial instruments necessary to implement a policy at the Community level. Before such policies can be introduced, a much more fully developed and robust methodology for measuring wider impacts is needed. This is illustrated by the work on the impact of such projects as the Channel Tunnel, the Great Belt crossing, and Strait of Messina crossing reported in this volume.

Acknowledgement. The research in this Chapter was partly funded by an ESRC Research Grant (YD00250018) to the Channel Tunnel Research Unit, University of Kent.

References

Bendixson T, 1989 *Transport in the Nineties* Royal Institution of Chartered Surveyors, London

Blum U, 1982, "Effects of transportation investments on regional growth: a theoretical and empirical investigation" *Papers and Proceedings of the Regional Science Association* **49** 169–184

Bonnafous A, Plassard F, Soum D, 1975 *Impact of Infrastructural Investment on Industrial Development* Round Table 25 (European Conference of Ministers of Transport, Paris)

Cappellin R, 1990, "The European internal market and the internationalisation of small and medium-sized enterprises" *Built Environment* special issue "1992 and regional development in Europe", Ed. R Vickerman, **16** 69–84

CEDRE, 1990, "Transports à grande vitesse, développement régional et aménagement du territoire", rapport de synthèse, Centre Européen du Développement Régional, Strasbourg

CLES, 1989 *Channel Tunnel: Vicious Circle* Research Studies Series No. 2, Centre for Local Economic Strategies, Manchester

CBI, 1989 *Transport in London: The Capital at Risk* Confederation of British Industry, London

Corporation of London, 1990, "London's transport: a plan to protect the future", a report by Segal Quince Wicksteed in association with The MVA Consultancy, London; copy available from City of London, PO Box 270, Guildhall, London EC2P 2EJ

Henley A, Carruth A, Thomas A, Vickerman R W, 1989, "Location choice and labour market perceptions: a discrete choice study" *Regional Studies* **23** 431–445

Holliday I M, Marcou G, Vickerman R W, 1991 *The Channel Tunnel: Public Policy, Regional Development and European Integration* (Belhaven Press, London)

Plassard F, Cointet-Pinell O, 1986 *Les Effets Socio-économiques du TGV en Bourgogne et Rhône-Alpes* produced by Laboratoire d'Économie des Transports, Lyon, and Interalp; published by DATAR, Institut National de Recherche sur les Transports et leur Sécurité, Observatoire Économique et Statistique des Transports, and SNCF, Paris

Plogmann F, 1980 *Die Bedeutung der Verkehrsinfrastruktur für das regionale Entwicklungspotential* Beiträge zur Siedlungs- und Wohnungswesen und zur Raumplanung 64, Institut für Siedlungs- und Wohnungswesen, Universität Münster, Münster

Quinet E, Morancay G, 1989, "The toll system on French motorways", in *Systems of Road Infrastructure Cost Coverage* Round Table 80 (European Conference of Ministers of Transport, Paris) pp 107–142

Vickerman R W, 1987, "The Channel Tunnel: consequences for regional growth and development" *Regional Studies* **21** 187–197

Vickerman R W, 1989, "Measuring changes in regional competitiveness: the effects on international infrastructure investments" *Annals of Regional Science* **23** 275–286

Vickerman R, Flowerdew A, 1990 *The Channel Tunnel: The Economic and Regional Impact* Special Report 2024 (Economist Intelligence Unit, London)

The Effects of the Fixed Link Across the Great Belt

S Illeris, L Jakobsen
Ruskilde University, Denmark

When the two halves of Denmark, until now separated by the sea, are connected by a fixed link, the consequences for economic development of the various regions must be enormous. That is the general opinion which we intend to scrutinise in this paper. Our conclusion is that these great expectations should be reduced, since the conditions will not change much for competition between differently located firms or for regional economic development.

1 The project of a fixed link across the Great Belt

Denmark is made up of the Jutland peninsula and roughly one hundred inhabited islands. This configuration was the very reason for the creation of the kingdom in the tenth century AD, at a time when sea transport was better developed than land transport. The sea was a linkage, not a separating element.

That is not the case any more. Today, because of the sea crossings, it takes a considerable number of hours to get from one end of the country to the other by surface transport, though the total surface is only 43 000 km². The construction of bridges developed early in Denmark. Many bridges were built, especially in the 1930s. For instance, in 1935 Funen and Jutland were connected by a bridge across the Little Belt, and in 1937 a bridge of 3 km was opened between Zealand and Falster (figure 1).

The effect of these works was that 99% of the Danish population lived in two major regions, each consisting of several parts connected by bridges: Jutland–Funen with 55% of the present population, and Zealand–Lolland–Falster with 44%. These two major regions are separated by the Great Belt and the Kattegat which are crossed by a number of ferry lines. The most important line is the shortest one, between the two small towns of Korsør and Nyborg.

The possibility of a bridge or a tunnel across the Great Belt was already being discussed in the middle of the 19th century. Since then, innumerable committees have studied the question. However, only in 1987 did the Danish parliament decide that a fixed link should be constructed. The work began in 1988. The fixed link will comprise a railway, to be completed in 1993, and a motorway which will be opened in 1996. The eastern part of the Great Belt is up to 70 m deep and is used by the heavy traffic between the Baltic Sea and the oceans. It will be crossed by a railway tunnel and a high motorway bridge. The western part, between the tiny island of Sprogø and Funen, will be crossed by a combined railway and motorway bridge. The costs are estimated at 18 billion Danish kroner or 2.25 billion ECU.

The government has established a company to construct and manage the fixed link. The company will remain national property. The costs will be covered by national and international loans. A passage toll will be levied, corresponding to the current price of ferry tickets, and in this way the loans will be repaid. At least two of today's ferry lines will be maintained, one crossing the Kattegat, and the other across the Langeland Belt.

Many problems have been encountered. In particular, the exchange of water between the Baltic Sea and the oceans must be maintained, because of the heavy pollution of the Baltic. The reduction which the bridge pillars will cause must be compensated by digging the bottom deeper elsewhere.

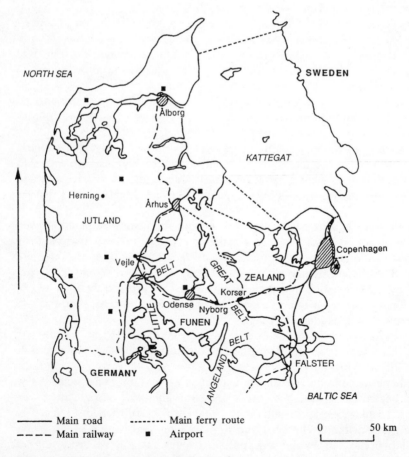

Figure 1. Main transport routes in Denmark.

2 Regional consequences

Normally, it is the purpose of transport investment to create economic benefits in the areas concerned. After all, it is recognised that transport improvements form a fundamental condition for the division of labour and for economic growth. Thus the purpose of the fixed link across the Great Belt, as expressed by the political authorities, was to enhance general economic growth.

However, the local and regional governments most concerned by the fixed links needed more precise predictions. What will be the consequence if the ferry lines, which are major local employers, close down? Will these job losses in the long run be compensated by increased employment in other sectors? Furthermore, local governments in Northwest Zealand and North Jutland wish to know if their economic development will be weakened by the possible closure of some of the ferry lines across the Kattegat.

That is why a number of local and regional governments commissioned the Local Governments' Research Institute to study the effects of the fixed link. The Fixed Link Company and the National Council for Social and Economic Research have cofinanced the study. The total study will comprise several parts: the construction of an econometric model and a local study of the small town of Korsør. In this paper, we shall present the results of a project dealing with the long-term effect of the fixed link on the development of economic activities in different regions of Denmark.

3 Transport investments and location of economic activities

Classical industrial location theory, as founded by Weber (1909), attributes a decisive influence on location to the costs of goods transport. Where these costs are minimised is the optimal location. According to the economic base model, service activities then have to follow the location of manufacturing industries in order to serve them and their personnel.

Modern location theories have modified this point of view substantially (Gwilliam, 1979; Scott, 1988; Vatne, 1987; Vickerman, 1987). Today, the costs of transporting goods are insignificant, apart from some sectors which deal with very heavy or perishable objects. The remaining transport costs are difficult to reduce by transport investments, as they are largely incurred at each end of a haul in terminal costs. Therefore, goods transport costs have only modest effects on the location of firms.

However, the costs of personal travel—business travel—have in a way replaced the costs of goods transport. For modern firms, and especially for advanced and innovative firms, close contact is very important with customers, suppliers, consultants, institutions of education and research, public administration, etc. Some of these contacts can be maintained via telecommunications. But personal meetings remain necessary, whenever orientation, discussion, and negotiation is on the agenda—that is, whenever the questions are complicated, difficult to foresee and to standardise.

The costs of travelling to meetings are not only the direct costs of tickets, hotels, etc. Often, lost working time forms the heaviest cost.

Location theories do not tell us who benefits most from transport infrastructure investments. If a project will be used by firms located everywhere—which the fixed link across the Great Belt will be—transport costs will be reduced for everybody.

In order to highlight this question, we must use models of the distribution of transport, for instance, the gravity models. According to these models, the accessibility of a place—which expresses to costs of coming to and going from the place—varies in the following way:

$$P_i = \sum_{j=1}^{n} \frac{M_j}{D_{ij}},$$

where

P_i is the economic potential (or accessibility) of area i,
M_j is the economic production of area j,
D_{ij} is the distance between areas i and j.

4 Empirical studies on situations similar to the fixed link across the Great Belt
Only a few studies (Illeris et al, 1990) have been performed under conditions more or less similar to the ones which exist for the Great Belt Link. Clearly, it is impossible to draw parallels to our countries from, for example, Third World countries with little transport infrastructure, where an investment may have important consequences.

Dodgson (1974; as quoted by Tapper, 1985) studied the effects of a motorway between Liverpool–Manchester and Leeds–Sheffield. The reduction of goods transport costs amounted to roughly 0.33% of the firms' total costs. The employment growth was calculated to be a maximum of 2000 in a city of two million people such as Manchester.

Plassard et al (1985) studied the effects of the high-speed train between Paris and southeast France, which in 1983 reduced the passenger travelling time from Paris to Lyons from over four to two hours. They found that the consequences for economic activities in the Burgundy and Rhône-Alpes regions were very modest.

Apart from these ex-post studies, the ex-ante studies of the impact of the Channel Tunnel must be mentioned. The general impression is that the regional effects in the adjacent regions will be limited and will depend very much on other measures to improve economic performance (Keeble et al, 1982; Vickerman, 1987).

Toft (1985) calculated the effect of the reduced goods transport cost caused by the link across the Great Belt. If the level of the bridge toll—as planned—corresponds to the present cost of ferry tickets, the cost reduction will be insignificant. But even in the case of almost free passage, the cost reduction would only create 200 jobs in Funen—which is the region with maximum advantage from the fixed link.

The conclusion of the theoretical discussion and the empirical studies is that in our societies, large transport projects will only have modest consequences for regional economic development. In particular, the effect of goods transport improvements seems to be limited. A reduction of passenger transport time (and thus of lost working time) should have more important consequences, according to modern theories. Even if the experience of the French high-speed trains does not confirm this hypothesis, it led us to focus on firms which are very dependent on personal contacts, when we planned our limited-budget study.

5 Computer firms

Therefore, we decided to focus the study on computer firms. This sector is growing, but it is not representative of all economic activities. We shall return to this question later.

In the spring of 1989, we carried out interviews with the managers of thirty Danish firms in the computer sector. They were spread over different size brackets, different types, and different locations. We asked the managers to explain the location of their firm and to discuss the advantages and disadvantages, compared with the locations of their competitors. We also asked them to tell us about their business travel and how they expected that the link across the Great Belt would influence the performance of their firms.

Five types of computer firms could be distinguished:

1. Computing bureaux, which make routine calculations (for example, of wages) on mainframe machines for their clients, which may be local or national. Often they are daughter firms of large corporations which remain their most important clients.

2. Providers of total computer solutions. This type of firm has specialised in providing everything necessary for an in-house computer system to their clients, which are often small and medium-sized enterprises in selected sectors: They sell hardware, they offer advice on the purchase and use of computers, they sell software and adapt it to the needs of the individual clients, they instruct the staff of the client, they find and remove errors, etc. These firms need to be in frequent contact with their clients, which are normally found within a distance of 50 – 100 km.

3. Software houses and consultants. These firms have specialised in highly qualified tasks. Their personnel, apart from a few secretaries, are all university trained. For this work, distance is unimportant, and clients are found everywhere in the country—or other countries. When a new computer system is to be developed, the firm and its client often set up a special team which may work anywhere on the problem for months or even years.

4. Multifunctional firms, which offer more of, or all, the above-mentioned services. These firms are big and in many cases daughter firms of transnational corporations, intending to penetrate the Danish market.

They have clients all over the country, and they have established local branch offices in order to offer services which require frequent contacts and proximity.

5. Manufacturers of electronic hardware. The size of these firms varies. Often they have originally developed their products for Danish customers, but now most of the production is exported.

6 The location of computer firms

Statistical information on the location of computer firms is not good, because the traditional classification of activities is not adapted to this sector. However, it is certain that the sector—as in all countries—is more concentrated in the capital region than economic activities are in general. This is especially the case of the most highly qualified firms.

The geographical dynamism seems to vary between countries. Kelly (1987) reports that in the United Kingdom, the computer industry concentrated its R&D activities in the South of England. In France, on the other hand, Moulaert et al (forthcoming) observe a decrease in the dominating position of Paris. In Denmark, about 60% of the employment in computer services is found in the Copenhagen region. However, in the 1981–87 period a certain shift away from the major metropolitan regions has taken place. Thus computer service firms are now found in local areas all over the country.

Our survey showed that when the computer firms were created, the founders did not think much about the location. Firms which were founded by one or a few persons were always located as near as possible to where they lived. Firms created by large mother firms were located in their proximity or—if the latter were foreign—near the international airport of Copenhagen.

Relocations do not occur outside the urban area where the firms were originally located. Behind this fact lies the decisive necessity of keeping the staff—a question we shall come back to.

Thus the advantages and disadvantages of different locations of existing firms is a more interesting question than the motives of the original location. Geographical shifts do occur in the total distribution of the sector, and this dynamism depends on the competitive performance of firms in different locations.

According to our interviews, the *possibility of recruiting and keeping qualified staff* is the most important factor of advantages and disadvantages of different locations. This is especially true for firms employing highly skilled personnel. Recruitment is easiest in cities where engineers, econo-mists, computer scientists, etc are educated. In Denmark, that means Copenhagen, Århus, Odense, and Aalborg. However, there is also a need for staff with medium-level educations, which are offered in a number of medium-sized towns. According to the interviews, it is possible to attract qualified persons elsewhere, too, but only under certain conditions.

First, the local labour market for these kinds of people must be big enough to offer a certain choice between different jobs. Such a choice is offered in the medium-sized towns of Herning and in the Vejle – Kolding – Fredericia area. Second, the local urban, cultural, landscape, and leisure environments must be attractive. The stability of the staff is an essential factor—it may take 6, 12, or 18 months before a new staff member has become sufficiently acquainted with the job. In this respect, provincial computer firms have a clear advantage over their Copenhagen competitors. *Proximity to clients* was mentioned by many firms as an important factor, especially by firms which offer total computer solutions and by multi-functional firms. By contrast, distances were unimportant for software and hardware manufacturers. Some of the latter types of firms mentioned that good *accessibility for business travel* was an important factor, but more often than not they added that this was no problem. At least in Denmark, low accessibility does not seem to be a significant disadvantage anywhere.

In the interview survey, other factors of location were rarely mentioned, and they have only secondary importance. A *local professional milieu* where inspiration can be obtained was mentioned in a few cases—usually as a disadvantage of small and medium towns. But other firms denied that this should be important—in contrast to the many statements to that effect in modern location theories. Most firms got their professional inspiration, apart from journals, from their suppliers and from specialised fairs, conventions, and conferences. *Local possibilities of supplementary training* were also quoted in a few cases—in particular firms in small and medium towns complained about this. However, most of this need was covered by courses organised by suppliers and by professional institutions in the major metropolitan areas or abroad—which did not cause inconveniences. *Geographical differences in salary levels* exist, up to 10% for the least skilled workers. But the computer firms considered these differences negligible. *Price differences between premises* were considered unimportant, too. *Prestigious locations* were quoted by some of the best-known firms, but usually in an intraurban context and thus irrelevant for this study.

7 The travelling and communication pattern

As already mentioned, we selected the computer sector because we assumed that personal meetings and business travel play a big role there. This assumption was fully confirmed. Nothing is known about travelling intensity in other sectors, but it is unlikely that there are sectors with more travelling. The direct travelling costs (tickets, hotels, etc) of the interviewed firms varied between 1% and 4% of the turnover, to which lost working time must be added. The highest costs were found in highly qualified firms working on national and international markets.

We focused on business travel as a factor of location. But first, the travelling pattern must be described. Local travel is almost exclusively carried out by car. We were specially interested in journeys between

Eastern and Western Denmark which must cross the Great Belt or the Kattegat. Most of the interviewed firms normally flew, but sometimes went by car. In particular, for the highly qualified firms travelling time was decisive, whereas the direct costs were of no importance. If they went by car, it was because of the greater flexibility, for instance in order to combine visits to several clients. Journeys abroad were made by plane, except between Jutland and Northern Germany where cars were used.

Goods transport only played a small role for computer firms and posed no problems that could influence their location.

The importance of telecommunications is increasing rapidly, and the possibilities of on-line communications are steadily improving. For instance, computer firms are increasingly able to search for, find, and repair errors in the systems of their clients via telecommunications. The outputs of computing performed for clients are more and more transmitted electronically to them, instead of being printed out and sent by post. On the other hand, nothing indicates that personal meetings should be substituted by video-conferences in the foreseeable future.

None of the firms in Denmark thought that the infrastructure for telecommunications was insufficient, or that telecommunications could be a factor of location. They are making it easier for firms east of the Great Belt to serve markets in Western Denmark, but also the opposite.

8 How will the fixed link change accessibility?
The fixed link across the Great Belt will change one of the factors which influence the competitive power of firms with different locations, namely their accessibility. As already mentioned, we limited our study to the accessibility for personal travel and calculated the accessibility changes due to the fixed link for forty-three places spread all over Denmark.

We did not take international accessibility into account, because the Great Belt is not and will not be crossed by much international passenger travel. The main routes are Germany – Jutland – Scandinavia or Germany – Zealand (Copenhagen) – Scandinavia.

Accessibility can be measured in various ways, for instance using economic potential as mentioned above. We decided to use an expression which is more easily comprehensible: *The number of people that can be reached within one, two, or three hours' travelling time*. Accessibility can be measured separately for each traffic mode. Or it may be assumed that the traveller in each case will choose the most rapid means of traffic. For business travel—especially for highly qualified computer firms—this assumption is realistic, according to our interviews. So it is the basis of the following calculations.

For 1989 and 1996—before and after the construction of the fixed link—we have calculated the accessibility for the forty-three places by plane (plus car), by car, and by train, as well as by the most rapid means of transport. The calculations show that Copenhagen has the highest accessibility in Denmark, which is no surprise. From Copenhagen, 4.8 million Danes can be reached in less than two hours (places west of the Great Belt by plane). The second highest accessibility is found in Eastern and Central Jutland as well as Central Funen, from which 3.5 – 4 million Danes can be reached in less than two hours (places east of the Great Belt by plane). The least accessible places are islands and remote places without air services.

The accessibility changes due to the fixed link across the Great Belt and the possible ferry line closures will be considerable, if one looks at the road or railway traffic alone: increased accessibility in Western Zealand, in Funen, and in Southern Jutland. But if the most rapid means of transport is taken into account, the improvements are small and concentrated in a few areas of Western Zealand and Eastern Funen (see figure 2). The explanation is that planes will remain the most rapid means of traffic

Additional number of persons (in thousands) that can be reached within two hours' travelling time.

| no change | 1 – 150 | 150 – 300 |
| 300 – 500 | 500 – 1 000 | |

Figure 2. Accessibility changes after the opening of the fixed link across the Great Belt, by most rapid means of transport.

between Eastern and Western Denmark, or that the fixed link only makes cars and trains slightly more rapid than planes. On the other hand, the possible closure of ferry lines across the Kattegat will not reduce the accessibility of any place by the most rapid means of transport, because ferries are in almost all cases slower than planes.

9 The impact of the fixed link on firms in different regions

If it is true that the competitive situation of places to some degree depends on their accessibility for business travel (using the most rapid means of traffic), the conclusion of the calculated accessibility changes is that the regional distribution of economic activities will be only slightly modified by the fixed link.

This conclusion can be compared with the expectations of the computer firms themselves, as regards the impact of the fixed link and the possible ferry line closures on their competitive situation. Clearly such expectations are rather uncertain. At the time of the interviews (spring 1989), the opening of the fixed link was a matter of a very remote future. The predictions should only be regarded as a check on their statements as regards factors of location and the calculations of changed accessibilities.

A large majority of the interviewed firms expected no perceptible changes in their competitive situation, because of the fixed link and the possible closure of ferry lines. This was very clear for the software houses and the hardware producers. For the providers of total computer solutions (and for the similar branch offices of the multifunctional firms) which serve a local market, it is possible that West Zealand and East Funen firms will become competitors on their own separate markets. In these cases one has to keep in mind that bridges lead in both directions: it is not easy to foresee whether the firms east or west of the Great Belt will gain from the increased competition.

It should be added that several firms thought that the fixed link may reduce psychological barriers that exist today. Such a reduction will reinforce the reduction of time and cost barriers and will increase competition between East and West Danish firms.

10 Conclusion

Location theory as well as the survey of the effects of other major transport projects both indicate that today, improvements in goods transport only have a modest influence on the location of economic activities. Such improvements reduce the total costs of firms only marginally. Sectors which deal with very heavy or perishable goods may be exceptions.

Changes in passenger transport may have a greater impact, because personal contacts and thus accessibility for business travel are becoming more and more important. This was why we chose to study in more depth a sector with intensive personal contacts, namely the computer sector. The result of this study is that neither the fixed link across the Great Belt, nor the possible closure of ferry lines across the Kattegat are likely to influence the competitive situation between firms located in different regions much. However, the computer sector is not representative of all economic activities. In other sectors where personal contacts are less important, the effect must be expected to be even more modest. On the other hand, in sectors which less often travel by plane, the time cost reduction for road and railway transport may count more.

These results do not exclude the possibility of psychological effects. For instance, places near the bridge and the access routes may acquire a dynamic image which in itself may make these locations more attractive and contribute to a symbolic effect.

References
Gwilliam K M, 1979, "Transport infrastructure investments and regional development" in *Inflation, Development and Integration* Ed. J K Bowers (Leeds University Press, Leeds) pp 241–262
Dodgson J, 1974, "Motorway investment, industrial transport costs and sub-regional growth: a case study of the M62" *Regional Studies* **8** 75–91
Illeris S, Jakobsen L, Madsen P, 1990 *Storebaeltsforbindelsens Indflydelse på den Langsigtede Regionale Erhvervsudvikling—Edb-Branchen som Eksempel* (AKF, Copenhagen)
Keeble D, Owens P, Thompson C, 1982, "Economic potential and the Channel Tunnel" *Area* **14** 97–103
Kelly T, 1987 *The British Computer Industry* (Croom Helm, Beckenham, Kent)
Moulaert F, Chickhaoui Y, Djellal F, 1991, "Locational behavior of French high tech consultancy firms" *International Journal of Urban and Regional Research* **15** 5–23
Plassard F, with Begag A, Bernadet M, Buisson M-A, Clusset J-M, 1985, "Les effets du TGV sur les agglomérations du Centre et du Sud-Est", Laboratoire d'Économie des Transports, Lyon
Scott A J, 1988 *Metropolis: From the Division of Labor to Urban Form* (University of California Press, Berkeley, CA)
Tapper H, 1985, "Regionala effekter i samhällsekonomiska bedömninger av transportinvesteringar", report 45, Expertgruppen för Forskning om Regional Utveckling, Stockholm
Toft G, 1985, "Regionaløkonomiske effekter af en fast Storebaeltsforbindelse", modelpapir 19, Institute for Graenseregionsforskning, Aabenraa
Vatne E, 1987 "Teknologisk utvikling, arbeidsdeling og lokalisering av naeringsvirksomhet Industriøkonomisk Institutt, Bergen
Vickerman R W, 1987, "The Channel Tunnel: consequences for regional growth and development" *Regional Studies* **23** 187–197
Weber A, 1909 *Über den Standort der Industrien* Tübingen

Economic and Social Effects of a Fixed Link on the Strait of Messina: A Preliminary Analysis

C Secchi, M Antonioli, A Pio, L Resmini
Università Commerciale Luigi Bocconi, Milan

1 Introduction

The crossing of the Strait of Messina by means of a fixed link which would join the Sicilian rail and road system to the Continent's has always been a captivating idea. As for all big infrastructural projects, there exist a number of anecdotes: in the year 250 BC, Lucius Caecilius Metellus built a pontoon bridge using wooden casks on which, as well as his troops, 106 elephants captured from Hannibal in Sicily were taken to the mainland. A more relevant proposal for a fixed link was that produced much later, in 1870, in a thesis by a graduating student at Turin's Politecnico, a certain C Navone, who titled his work "A tunnel under the Strait of Messina to create a fixed link between the Sicilian rail and road system and that of the Peninsula". From that date until after the Second World War no other relevant study was published.

The starting point of our research is the 1969 tender issued by ANAS (the state-owned road authority) and FS (the national railway authority), which produced a large number of projects. Two years later, law number 1158 was passed, for the construction of a bridge across the Strait by a specifically established company, actually founded in 1981, which was to "study, design, build and run a fixed road and rail link between Sicily and the Continent".

Two decades after the law was passed, the programme is still only on paper. The only step forward has been the completion of the feasibility study which, in 1988, favoured the construction of a bridge in preference to a submerged tube or a bored tunnel. At the moment the general project is being developed and, in 1992, it should be submitted to parliament.

In 1985, when the debate on the pros and cons of building a fixed link across the Strait was at its highest, the CNR (the Italian national scientific research council) founded a specific study group, coordinated, together with others on related aspects, by Luigi de Rosa of the Istituto Universitario Navale, Naples. The group started its activities in 1987 with the task of studying "the economic and social consequences of the construction of a fixed link across the Strait". Under the direction of Carlo Secchi, it had the task of ascertaining the potential costs and benefits of the project. This chapter gives a brief account of the results of this research, recently published in a book edited by Secchi (1990).

The research has been divided into three parts:
(1) Critical analysis of the methods for evaluating the project. Evaluating an investment project means comparing the different benefits obtainable from the alternative uses of limited available resources and choosing the best solution in terms of advantages for the community. Cost-benefit analysis (CBA) has some limitations: first, it is not always easy to evaluate costs and benefits in monetary terms and, second, it is not possible to take correct account of the distribution effects or the priorities of economic policy. For these reasons, two other methodologies, besides CBA, were used: multicriteria analysis (MCA), which makes it possible to appreciate noneconomic considerations expressed both in quantitative and in qualitative terms, and environmental impact assessment (EIA), which must unquestionably be taken into account in a thorough examination of a large-scale project.
(2) Analysis of some selected foreign studies on determining the social and economic effects of large transport infrastructures and the use of these methodologies to examine the state of the art of the subject. From this some methodological and practical expedients can be suggested for a preliminary appraisal of a fixed link across the Strait of Messina.
(3) Application to the Strait project of the findings of the preceding research work. During this introductory study, two aspects were considered: identification of the main investment options to implement the link and the definition of the social and economic effects to be appraised.

This paper is a compendium of the results of the last part of the study. As it is preliminary research it has only been possible to make some assumptions about the quality and size of the main effects of the construction of a fixed crossing. Those assumptions will be confirmed or revised as soon as detailed data are available.

2 Present situation and the alternatives examined
The connection between Sicily and the Continent can be made in two ways: by ferry service or by a fixed link. However, the difficulties of the connection between Sicily and the Continent, as with other natural barriers in Europe, are not solely caused by the physical division (the Strait of Messina) but also by the inadequate transport systems on both sides of the Strait. The motorway between Messina and Palermo is still incomplete and the railway network south of Naples is inadequate. These are conditions which hinder traffic of goods and passengers and can cause delays and costs exceeding those of the ferry crossing.

For this reason two types of investment have been envisaged. First, there are the 'main options', that is, the solution to the actual problem of the Strait crossing (by ferry, bridge, submerged tube, or bored tunnel). Second, 'complementary actions', by removing the existing transport problems on both sides of the Strait, can significantly increase the effectiveness of the investment. There are several such actions, which apply mainly to the railway system. Such actions (either for infrastructure or for service management) would improve the transport system regardless of the existence of a fixed link. Therefore, in the following pages we shall examine only the alternatives connected with a new Strait crossing. For a fuller examination of the complementary actions see the complete study mentioned above (Secchi, 1990).

2.1 The present situation
The connection between Sicily and the Continent takes place currently along two routes: Villa San Giovanni – Messina and Reggio Calabria – Messina, by means of ferries and hydrofoils. Sicily is also connected to the mainland by private shipping and air transport, mostly using the ports and airports of Catania and Palermo. For data on traffic in the Strait see table 1.

In the last decade there has been a significant increase in passenger traffic (40%) accompanied by strong growth in the number of cars (130%). This switch from rail to road also applies to the goods sector: the number of rail wagons ferried decreased by 10% whereas the number of lorries increased by 22%.

The adequacy of the current system may be evaluated according to two criteria: an analysis of demand growth and a comparison between supply and demand. Further analysis on the safety of the service, its reliability, and its impact on the areas surrounding the docks needs primary data which at present are not available.

The *crossing time* depends on ferry boarding and unloading operations and on the actual sailing time. In a 1985 article, crossing times of 100 minutes for trains and 60 minutes for cars are quoted, together with the remark that "during holidays or in case of bad weather ... [crossing time] ... increases by 100% or even 300%, and in exceptional circumstances waiting times can amount to tens of hours" (Polese, 1985).

Table 1. Traffic across the Strait of Messina (routes: Villa San Giovanni – Messina and return, Reggio Calabria – Messina and return; source: Ministero dei Trasporti, 1988, pp 487 – 491).

Year	Number of				
	crossings	passengers	railway cars	cars	lorries
1980	53380	10382360	414395	1106188	990530
1984	54841	14495142	381685	1903649	1023598
1985	55654	14085544	378796	1990819	1027952
1986	56521	14630400	385305	2149226	1067380
1987	58013	14716984	385931	2280053	1125778
1988	59499	14117300	368733	2379842	1165030
1989	62704	14589627	373333	2555542	1212455

With regard to *transport capacity*, the data show that available capacity is relatively large compared with demand (see table 2). It is, however, important to consider traffic distribution both on a daily and on a seasonal basis because, even though supply may be adequate on average, it may not be adequate during peak periods when waiting times may increase considerably. Once again, the situation does not, generally speaking, appear to be critical. The daily traffic peaks do not generate conditions of congestion and the increase in tourist traffic in summer is at least partially compensated by the simultaneous reduction in commercial traffic. To confirm these first impressions, one should study the phenomenon in detail by systematic and extensive sampling of the traffic flows in order to monitor accurately the demand changes in different hours and seasons.

We can conclude this analysis of the current situation by saying that the crossing system is at the moment adequate in terms of journeys offered, unless some congestion is found by monitoring the activity in certain hours or seasons. With regard to crossing time, there would seem to be room for improvement, particularly to the benefit of the local traffic, which represents one third of the total. The adequacy of the system has yet to be checked in view of future changes in the demand.

Table 2. Available ferry capacity in the Strait of Messina (route: Villa San Giovanni – Messina and return; source: Ministero dei Trasporti, 1988, pp 487 – 491).

	Passengers (thousands of seats)			Cars (thousands of seats)		
	supply	demand	%	supply	demand	%
1982	21 459	5 607	26.1	6 621	3 419	51.6
1985	25 305	6 128	24.2	7 532	3 743	49.7
1986	25 576	6 782	26.5	7 710	4 151	53.8
1987	25 814	6 721	26.0	7 869	4 174	53.0
1988	28 165	7 140	25.3	8 478	4 351	52.3
1989	31 466	7 735	24.5	9 386	4 628	49.3

2.2 The main alternatives

In addition to extensive analysis of the existing situation, we believe it is important to study a number of alternative technical solutions: improvement of ferry and hydrofoil services, construction of a road and/or rail bridge, construction of one or more submerged tubes, construction of a bored tunnel.

2.2.1 *The improvement of ferry services*

This option appears to be satisfactory in view of a gradual increase in demand, because it would solve some of the existing problems by moderate investment spread over a number of years and would make progressive adaptation of crossing capacity to changes in demand possible (costs would, however, increase in 'steps' equal to the cost of each shipping unit introduced). Nevertheless, this solution could be less effective than a fixed link in reducing crossing times and could prove inadequate in the long run given a considerable increase in traffic. Moreover, this solution could raise safety problems due to the frequent crossings of routes of ships travelling across the Strait with those of ships sailing through the Strait and is also subject to problems connected with bad weather. On the other hand, this alternative is not influenced by the physical and technical limits set by the geographical pecularities of the region, as shown in table 3.

Table 3. Physical and technical constraints of the Strait crossing.

	Improvement of ferry services	Single-span bridge	Multi-span bridge	Submerged tube	Bored tunnel
Physical conditions					
Winds		••	•		
Currents			•	••	
Earthquakes		•	•	•	•
Shipping	••		•		
Weather	•	•			
Limits to traffic					
Railway (load, vibrations)		••	•		
Road (pollution)				•	•
Impacts on the environment					
Aesthetic (access ramps)		•	•		
Aesthetic (overall)		•	•		
Disposal of excavation rubble					••

• Constraints which may be overcome.
•• Constraints which need particular attention.

2.2.2 The fixed link alternatives

Each of the three alternatives proposed for the fixed link would allow a shortening of crossing times; the savings vary only slightly, in the range of 30 to 40 minutes for road traffic and of 60 to 80 minutes for rail traffic, depending on the locations of access points on the two coasts. Depending on the fares applied, these savings in terms of time could be accompanied by a reduction of the monetary costs for the users. As a consequence, it is possible to forecast a considerable increase in road traffic because of the greater comfort of road transport and because of better accessibility, mainly for local traffic, within the integrated metropolitan area of Reggio Calabria–Messina. It should be noted that any type of fixed link would have to come to terms with the geophysical characteristics of the area and in particular with strong water currents both near the surface (5 to 6 knots, that is, 2.5 m s^{-1}) and beneath it (1 knot); strong winds which reach average speeds of 40 to 50 km h^{-1} and top speeds of up to 150 km h^{-1};

the area is also highly seismic and traffic through the Strait is heavy, amounting to approximately 80000 craft movements a year. Each of the proposed solutions therefore represents a technological challenge whose economic benefits clearly depend on whether the innovations developed can be applied to future projects and in different contexts.

3 Social and economic effects in the short and medium terms

The following sections are dedicated to defining all the main foreseeable effects of the infrastructure, effects which must necessarily be taken into account in an appraisal of the infrastucture itself. The three main areas affected by the link are: the transport system, economic activity, the natural and human environment. The effects have been summarised in table 4.

Table 4. Outline of the social and economic effects of a fixed link across the Strait of Messina.

The transport system	*Level and structure of economic activity*
Travelling time	During construction
Travelling costs	direct effects
Demand increase:	induced effects
diverted	possible disparity between demand
generated	and supply of labour and inputs
Accidents	effects on inflation and the
Comfort	balance of payments
Environment and structure of territory	Medium and long term boost of
Permanent changes in the landscape	production and interregional
Animal and plant life on land, in	commerce
water, and in air	induced economic activity
Pollution	agriculture
Metropolitan integration	industry
Increase in road traffic and bottlenecks	services
Moving of residential and industrial	Value of property in and around the
sites	Strait area
Problems related to the assignment	Technological progress and innovation
of contracts	

3.1 Objectives and effects of the transport system

The transport system is of paramount importance in the evaluation process for a number of reasons. First, the main objective is the removal of the bottleneck affecting the transport of goods and people between Sicily and the Continent. Second, the expected economic developments are based upon the improvement of such links.

The effects on the transport system can be summarised in five main categories:
1. time savings,
2. cost savings,
3. increase in transport demand,

4. reduction in the number of accidents,
5. improvement in comfort.

The most important effects are related to the first three categories. It is through these three that the benefits on the whole economic system may be measured: a reduction in the forwarding costs of goods frees resources which may either be employed by the producer or be transferred to the consumer in the form of a reduction in prices. In either case a surplus is produced which can be directed towards the consumption of goods and services of a different kind. It is easier to measure this surplus at the time when it is produced (through a reduction of the cost and time of transport), rather than in the form of an increase in final demand. For that reason we should not talk about 'the effects on the transport system', because what is measured already includes the more general effects on the economic system. Such a distinction will be kept in this paper for the sake of clarity.

3.1.1 *Time savings*
The construction of a fixed link or the improvement of ferry transport would unquestionably bring about a shortening of crossing time across the Strait. In order to measure the overall time savings, it is necessary to determine accurately the shortening of crossing time, T, the number of trips to which the shortening applies, N, and the value of the time saved, V. The total value of time saved may then be determined by simple multiplication:

$$\text{total value of time saved } = T \times N \times V.$$

This result is significantly different if referred to passenger rather than goods traffic, and road rather than rail. A difference should also be made between local and long-distance traffic. A 30-minute saving is in fact very relevant for local traffic, but much less so for long-distance traffic, which is influenced by a number of factors (for example, traffic conditions on the motorway network) that can cause much greater time savings or delays. This point should undoubtedly be considered when estimating demand. Therefore, it may well be reasonable not to take into account all traffic for which the time saving relative to improvements on the crossing accounts for less than 5% of total journey time.

In normal conditions, the construction of a fixed link could allow time savings of up to 30 to 40 minutes. Such savings would be insignificant for road or rail traffic travelling to Northern Italy and Europe, the length of similar journeys being 24 hours or more. With regard to rail transport, substantial shortening of journeys could be achieved through the speeding up of shunting operations on both sides, the real cause of delays.

Available data show that local traffic accounts for about a third of all crossings. For these, a shortening of crossing time of 30 to 40 minutes would be extremely significant, for it would mean a reduction of about 50% of the total journey time. Therefore, the most relevant positive effects would concern this type of traffic and would most likely bring about an increase in the volumes of traffic as well as significant forms of metropolitan integration.

3.1.2 *Cost savings*

Although as far as time savings are concerned, all of the alternatives considered produce a shortening of crossing time (in the case of an improvement of the ferry system related only to the waiting and loading and unloading operations), the effects on costs are a lot less clear. The costs that should be considered are of the following two types: (a) the toll or fare paid for the crossing by means of either a ferry or a fixed link; (b) the cost of running the link.

Even if it is widely assumed that the toll for a bridge or tunnel crossing would be equal to the present ferry fares, an in-depth analysis should consider the effect that different toll levels may have on the number of crossings, in order to make an accurate appraisal of the final benefits generated by the link. Paradoxically, lower prices would have a negative influence on the financial return of the infrastructure, but would improve its economic performance by extending the benefits of speedier crossings to a greater number of travellers. The net effect would also be dependent on diseconomies caused by the more intensive use of the transport system on land, road transport in particular, which would, as a consequence, produce even heavier congestion on the entire national road and rail network.

At present, crossing costs are only those related to the running of the ferry system, because vehicle costs (consumption, ageing, and other) during the crossing are nonexistent (depreciation being calculated on the basis of clocked mileage rather than age). The costs that increase if it is decided to improve the ferry alternative are only those related to shipping, whereas it becomes necessary to consider both the reduction in ferry crossing costs and the increase in running costs (fuel, depreciation, maintenance, etc) of vehicles crossing by bridge or tunnel, if the fixed link alternative is chosen. Because of the generally high levels of productivity on the ferries, the net balance for a fixed link may well be a cost increase, which would partly neutralise the benefits generated by quicker crossings.

3.1.3 *Increase in the demand for transport*

The benefits for existing and future traffic are given by the net savings in transport time and costs that the new alternatives bring about compared with the old one. Further thought should at this point be given to two other types of traffic. As far as diverted traffic is concerned (that is, traffic which presently travels on other routes but which would be diverted towards the Strait only in the presence of a fixed link), the net benefits should not be calculated on the basis of a comparison with the existing ferry services, but on the basis of the actual means used, for example, private shipping in the case of sea traffic diverted to road or rail as a consequence of the fixed link.

Finally, the focus should be put on generated traffic, that is, the increase in traffic induced by the improvement in accessibility. Increases in this type of traffic are caused by cost savings, the need for transport connected to the actual construction of the link, and, once the link is fully operational, the level of induced economic development.

3.1.4 *Other effects*
Accidents are an important element in the transport system: it is impossible to say what sort of impact the fixed link would have on these. It is likely that road accidents would be greater both in number and in seriousness than at present. The appraisal of each alternative should thus include an estimate of accident seriousness and costs.

Last, but not least, is passenger comfort, which would be substantially improved because tiring and time-wasting changes of mode would no longer be necessary. However, because time savings have previously been accounted for, and because quantification may turn out to be extremely difficult, we believe this particular aspect may be left out of the appraisal process.

3.2 Effects on the level and structure of economic activity
The improvement of the connection across the Strait of Messina can produce two kinds of effect on economic activity: short to medium term effects connected to the completion of the infrastructure or the improvement of the ferry service, and medium to long term effects resulting from easier travel between Sicily and the Continent. A third kind of effect can also be considered: technological developments connected to technical innovations of the work. These effects would be moderate in the case of an improvement in the ferry service or the construction of a bored tunnel, both alternatives being based on widely known technologies.

On the contrary, the effects would be substantial in the case of construction of a submerged tube or a single-span bridge. The development of these new technologies could improve the competitiveness, both domestic and international, of the companies involved in the project.

3.2.1 *Effects connected to the construction of the link*
The completion of a fixed link will have important effects on the levels of production and employment. These effects can be divided into direct effects (related to construction) and generated effects (the multiplier effects on the economy induced by the increase in aggregate demand produced by the construction activity itself). A further distinction can be made between short to medium term effects during the construction period and the minor ones related to the running of the link, once it has been completed.

In order to evaluate the direct effects, it is necessary to have precise information concerning the size of the workforce, various materials, equipment, and services to be used in connection with each of the alternatives considered. As regards the workforce, the main qualification levels must be identified; as regards the supply (input) of equipment and services, the quantities and sources must be known (steel industry, chemical industry, concrete and construction materials, machinery, transport and freight costs, other services such as insurance, planning, work management, etc). In considering these data, two analyses can be made: the first to check the adequacy, relative to the needs of the project, of the job market and of national and local industrial and service structure; and the second to evaluate the secondary effects.

Through the analysis of sector interdependences (input–output), it is possible to determine the total demand activated by the project and, consequently, its induced effects. For this reason, it will be necessary to adjust the technical coefficients of the matrices used. Such coefficients usually relate to highly aggregated sectors and may thus be very different from the actual effects produced by the demand for specific inputs of each of the considered alternatives. Once the total sectoral demand has been estimated and distributed through the construction period, it will be possible to examine the relation between national and local production capacity and such additional demand. This will, moreover, allow identification of the possible territorial distribution of economic activity induced by the construction of the fixed link and the possible unfavourable effects on the inflation rate or on the balance of payments produced by an excess demand which cannot be met by a programmed increase in national productive capacity.

A similar analysis of the labour market in the Strait area and the two contiguous regions will allow identification of the possible difference between demand and supply at each level of qualification, and evaluation of the social impact of migratory flows produced by the adjustment of labour supply.

3.2.2 Effects generated by improved accessibility
In the medium to long term the improvement of the accessibility between Sicily and the Continent can produce:
(a) an increase in traffic as a consequence of the reduced transport costs,
(b) the creation of new industrial companies in Sicily,
(c) an increase in the value of property in the Strait area.

From the point of view of general welfare, the increase in trade between Sicily and the Continent is noteworthy only if it is accompanied by a more efficient use of resources which means lower costs or higher production. Considering regional development, it has frequently been claimed that the reduction of transport costs would increase the competitiveness of Sicilian products on continental markets. But Vickerman (1987) remarked that bottlenecks in the transport system operate as a nontariff barrier. A non-central region with a weak economy can therefore find itself exposed to the competition of external companies as a consequence of the removal of transport difficulties.

The evaluation of the net result of improved accessibility therefore requires parallel assessments of regional imports and exports. Once the reduction of transport costs has been assessed, it is necessary to determine how important this is in relation to total production costs in order to find out the final reduction in the prices of the main products. Considering the relationship between import and export demands and price, the increase in external demand for regional products and in internal demand for imported goods can be worked out for each of the main sectors.

Such a result can be used as a basis for determining possible changes in employment figures related to the average productivity of the sectors considered. It is likely that the variations in imports and exports will apply to different economic sectors (for example, manufactured goods and agricultural products), and will then consequently result in a change of the sectoral structure of the economy. The existing literature seems to indicate that such effects will be moderate, particularly if the reduction in transport costs is inconspicuous.

On the other hand, with regard to the economic activity generated by a new connection (not including activity connected to the actual construction) some estimates can be made for the different sectors.

Agricultural production could improve its performance by specialising in high-quality and perishable products, as a consequence of the reduction in transport times to the consumers' markets. The most noticeable effect would concern products forwarded by rail, because the saving of time on the road would not be very considerable.

Industrial activity would increase especially for the direct and induced orders connected with the realisation of the project. Companies that would either be set up or be induced to expand their activity would find, in the improved connection with the Continent, an important factor in maintaining their competitiveness at a national level after the closure of the construction site. A reduced bankruptcy rate for companies is therefore predictable; on the other hand, the establishment or localisation of new businesses would generally benefit from improved accessibility, but only if this were accompanied by other factors such as the availability of energy, water, a qualified workforce, and the presence of an industrial infrastructure. A fixed link across the Strait of Messina is thus not a sufficient condition to promote this development, even though it can be a useful complement to well-timed stimulation and promotion policies.

With regard to the *service sector*, tourism would surely benefit from improved accessibility (even though the restraining effects of the existing crossing system seem moderate), but also from the attraction represented by such an exceptional infrastructure. The bridge and tunnel would have different types of impact on tourism, both for the reduced visibility of the latter (the impact would not be so impressive either on the eye or on the environment) and for the possible emotional opposition to the use of a submerged crossing.

The tourist attraction aspect of major engineering achievements has seldom been considered in appraisal studies of the social and economic impact of such infrastructures. As a result, some important benefits and some possible costs due to overcrowding have often been unestimated. The reason for this is that, on the one hand, the primary objective of these enterprises is not that of becoming a tourist attraction, and, on the other, it is extremely difficult to judge beforehand the extent to which tourists will be drawn to the structure.

The answer to these questions is the object of a new research project— by the same study group—which is yet to be completed and whose aim is to determine the most adequate analytical guidelines for the study of both tourist demand and supply. These guidelines would allow precise and timely forecasts of all indirect effects such as those mentioned, and give practical information on services which would enhance the attractiveness of large infrastructures.

The completion of a fixed link will also have an effect on the localisation of facilities in support of transit traffic, which at the moment are located near the embarkation and disembarkation points and which, in the presence of a direct link, would be eliminated or distributed around surrounding regions, close to the starting points or the final destinations of the journeys.

The changes in property prices in the Strait area could be considerable. New economic activities would probably settle close to the approaches to the fixed link with an attraction effect on residential buildings and with the consequence of an increase in the value of such areas. A decrease in the value of the land in noncontiguous areas can equally be expected. This situation may produce important redistribution effects (even though the final balance could be very moderate) but may also have considerable consequences on the Strait area and produce local effects of urban development or decay.

Finally, we can say that the most important effects of the improvement of accessibility are represented by a net change in the value of property. The increase in Sicilian exports induced by the reduction of the costs of transport will be at least partially balanced by a correlated increase of imports with the net effect depending on the respective elasticities and a national welfare effect depending on the increase of productivity of producers. As regards the stimulus to the creation of new economic activities—apart from the direct and secondary effects induced by the construction of the chosen infrastructure—the results will be quite moderate and in any case will not just arise from the construction of the fixed link; active development policies will also be necessary to generate positive results.

3.3 Impact on the environment

In this research we have paid particular attention to the environmental impact of a fixed link across the Strait. The paramount importance of the transport system for the link has already been exhaustively considered. Therefore, before identifying the impact that the infrastructure would have on the environment, we should briefly look into the relations between the economic system, the transport system, and the environment. Such relations are outlined in figure 1.

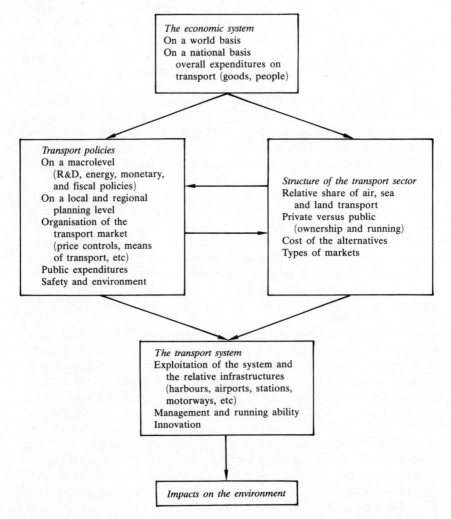

Figure 1. Outline of the relationships between the economy, the transport system and the environment.

In short, the transmission mechanism is the following: the more developed an area becomes, the greater its need for an advanced transport system which, in turn, depends on the structure and variety of the modes of transport available as well as on specific sector policies. The overall impact on the environment is basically a result of these two factors and of the aspects connected to the management and the use made of the transport system.

The types and, moreover, the magnitude of the impact essentially depend on the following five elements:
1. the technical characteristics of structures and infrastructures,
2. the management of infrastructures,
3. the intensity of utilisation,
4. the modes of transport,
5. the built-in technology.

Furthermore, the analysis of the potential impact on the environment should not simply be based on a single comparison between the initial and the final stages, but should also look in detail into all stages which shape the impact.

Some introductory tables (tables 5 and 6, see over) which sum up the characteristics and options of the various fixed-link alternatives have been laid out to allow an initial appraisal of the overall impact of the project on the Strait area. These tables have been set out as a basis for further and more detailed analysis which should be conducted with an interdisciplinary approach.

Because some of the fundamental specific information on the alternatives is not yet available, part of our research is of necessity approximate. However, an attempt has been made to bring out the more important types of impact on the environment, with particular attention being paid to the physical environment. Because it is, at present, impossible to produce exact quantitative values for the various types of impact on the environment, the qualitative aspects have been set out in tables which highlight the differences and the similarities between the alternatives more clearly.

4 Conclusions

In this chapter we have shown that the construction of a fixed link between Sicily and the Continent produces effects not only on the transport system, but also on economic activity, the environment, and the organisation of the regions. Summing up what has been said up to date about the various effects, it is possible to assert that greater importance should be attributed to effects on the transport system than to those on the economy. Furthermore, time savings and increases in demand predominantly affect local (30% of total) rather than long-distance traffic: this is because savings are relatively less important for long-distance travellers. These positive effects are, however, likely to be at least partly compensated by possible increases in travel costs and number of accidents.

Table 5. Possible impacts related to the different alternatives for the crossing of the Strait of Messina.

Impact	Null option	Improvement of ferry services
Description		Increase in the number of ferries and related enlargement of wharfs.
Impacts related to the type of terminals on land	Present situation.	New and improved docks needed to deal with the shipping of rail cars.
Transport capacity (people and goods)	Present traffic volume and bottlenecks.	Increase in transport capacity and in sea traffic in the Strait area.
Road infrastructures		New roads to the wharfs and bigger car parks near the dock area.
Construction activity		Increase in the ship-building activity; Possible delays on ferry crossing during the construction of the new docks.
Excavation rubble		Rubble from construction of new wharfs and new roads.
Consequences if project is abandoned		Difficult reutilisation of wharfs (see the Reggio Calabria airport wharf).
Safety and health	No changes.	Increased risks of collisions.

Table 5 (continued)

Bored tunnel	Submerged tube	Bridge
Tunnel bored at a depth varying between 120 m and 260 m below sea level.	Either one or three tubes at a depth varying between 40 – 50 m below sea level.	3330 m long single-span or multispan bridge at a height of approximately 80 m above sea level.
One new road and one new rail access ramp needed of a length of 5 – 10 km.	Two new rail access ramps needed of a length of 0.5 km.	Two particularly long access ramps needed for rail traffic.
Capacity would be greater than that of the ferry system, but no data available.	Capacity would be greater than that of the ferry system, but no data available.	Capacity would be greater than that of the ferry system, but no data available.
New access road to the terminals and between the terminals and the main urban centres nearby; Public transport services (road or rail) on these routes.	New access road to the terminals and between the terminals and the main urban centres nearby; Public transport services (road or rail) on these routes.	New access road to the terminals and between the terminals and the main urban centres nearby; Public transport services (road or rail) on these routes.
Increase of road traffic, noise, etc, during construction.	Increase of road traffic, noise, etc, during construction.	Increase of road traffic, noise, etc, during construction.
Considerable impact related to the disposal of estimated 16 million m^3 of rubble.	Impact related to the disposal of rubble would be considerable, but smaller than that produced by the bored tunnel alternative.	Problems related to disposal of rubble.
If construction works were interrupted, it would be impossible to find alternative uses for the tunnel or the parts of it already completed.	If construction works were interrupted, it would be impossible to find alternative uses for the tunnel or the parts of it already completed.	If construction works were interrupted before completion, the bridge piers would affect the landscape considerably.
Risk of giddiness-related accidents and possible aggravation of consequences through limited air circulation; Possible risk of becoming military objective.	Risk of giddiness-related accidents and possible aggravation of consequences through limited air circulation; Possible danger for shipping; Possible risk of becoming military objective.	Risk of accidents due to bad weather conditions (strong winds and gales); Risk of accidents for ships (multispan alternative); Possible risk of becoming military objective.

Table 6. Possible impacts on the environment related to the different alternatives for the crossing of the Strait of Messina.

Physical environment	Null option	Improvement of ferry services
Landscape	No change.	Impact on the landscape because of the construction of new wharfs, heavier ship traffic, and the construction of new or enlarged car parks, new roads, and infrastructures in general.
Animal and plant life on land	No change.	Land areas taken up by the various new sites; Increase in the noise level with negative effects on animal life.
Marine life	No change.	The increase in traffic may have negative consequences on marine animal and plant life because of both the actual increase in the number of ships crossing and the disappearance of the waterline caused by the contruction of the new wharfs.
Agriculture	No change.	No relevant change should occur to farmland.

Table 6 (continued)

Bored tunnel	Submerged tube	Bridge
No visible impact on the sea; Impact due to new road tunnel and terminal buildings on land and (possible) air-vents on the sea surface.	No visible impact on the sea; Impact due to new road tunnel and terminal buildings on land and (possible) air-vents on the sea surface.	Highly visible and damaging impact, especially of bridge piers on an area of great natural value; Impressive overall effect of the bridge structure.
Land areas taken up by the various new sites; Increase in the noise level with negative effects on animal life; Considerable problems related to the disposal of rubble; Air pollution in the case of air-vents on land.	Land areas taken up by the various new sites; Increase in the noise level with negative effects on animal life; Considerable problems related to the disposal of rubble; Air pollution in the case of air-vents on land.	Extensive impact of bridge piers and access ramps; Increase in the noise level with negative effects on animal life; Air pollution; Destruction of particular natural habitats.
No impact should result if the air vents are placed on land; However, if they are placed across the Strait, both the marine habitat and navigation would be affected.	Consequences on the marine habitat depend on the position of the tube (with respect to currents) and on submarine navigation; The problems for air-vents are the same as those related to the bored tunnel.	The bridge, especially if single span, should have little impact on marine life apart from effects connected to the disappearance of the waterline; Possible impact on marine animal life because of increased noise.
Possible reduction of farmland available; Possible air pollution may cause a reduction in land productivity.	Possible reduction of farmland available; Possible air pollution may cause a reduction in land productivity.	Possible reduction of farmland available; Possible air pollution may cause a reduction in land productivity.

Increases in property value caused by improved accessibility are particularly important economic effects. Their significance depends more on their redistribution consequences than on their actual value. Although economic activity is certain to increase during construction, as soon as this is completed, long-term effects on the economy would depend almost entirely on policies not specifically related to the link. In this sense, the link is but one of a number of necessary requirements for boosting the development of the area.

Needless to say, this entire study is based on theoretical hypotheses which require checking or adjustment following an in-depth analysis of the alternative chosen in 1988, as mentioned at the beginning of this paper.

References
• References not cited in the text, but used as a data source.
• AISCAT, 1986, "Piano decennale della viabilità di grande comunicazione: stato di attuazione" *AISCAT Informazioni* number 1-2, January-February, April-June, pp 33-45; Associazione Italiana Concessionarie Autostrade e Trafori (Italian Association of Representative Companies for Motorways and Tunnels), Via Sardegna 40, 00187 Roma
• CEREST, 1983, "Rapporto sui trasporti in Sicilia", Centro Regionale Studi Trasporti-Palermo (Regional Centre for Studies on Transportation), c/o Unioncamere Sicilia, Via Emerico Amari 11, 90100 Palermo
• CSST, 1983, "Traffico merci medio giornaliero autostradale su distanze superiori a 400 chilometri" *Bollettino d'informazione CSST* Supplement number 6, November-December, pp 20-21, 28-29; Centro Studi sui Sistemi di Trasporto (Study Centre on Transport Systems), Via Lucullo 8, 00100 Roma
• ISTAT, 1984 *Annuario Statitistico della Navigazione Marittima* Istituto Nazionale di Statistica (National Institute of Statistics), Via Cesare Balbo 16, 00100 Roma
• Ministero dei Trasporti, 1984 *Civilavia Statistica* Ministero dei Trasporti, Roma
Ministero dei Trasporti, 1988 *Conto Nazionale dei Trasporti 1988* Ministero dei Trasporti, Roma
Polese A, 1985, "Note sull'attraversamento stabile dello Stretto di Messina" *Vie e trasporti* number 528-529, July-August, pp 473-481
• Regione Sicilia, 1985 *Il Ruolo dei Trasporti nella Prospettiva di Sviluppo della Sicilia* Papers and Proceedings of the Second Regional Conference on Transport, Unione della Camere di Commercio della Regione siciliana, Palermo
Secchi C (Ed.), 1990 *Elementi per una Analisi Degli Effetti Economici di un Attraversamento Stabile dello Stretto di Messina* (Edizioni Scientifiche Italiane, Napoli)
• SOMEA, 1985, "Indagini di traffico sullo Stretto", in *Rapporto Finale per la Società Stretto di Messina* part 2, Società per la Matematica e l'Economia Applicata (Limited Company for Mathematics and Applied Economy), Piazza del Collegio Romano 2, 00186 Roma
Vickerman R W, 1987, "The Channel Tunnel and regional development: a critique of an infrastructure-led growth project" *Project Appraisal* **2** 31-40

Transport and the European Community:
The Opportunities of a Liverpool Landbridge

L Lesley
Liverpool Polytechnic

1 Introduction

Transatlantic trade between Europe and North America is the largest by volume and value worldwide (the second being transpacific). Britain's trade is now dominated by imports from and exports to other European countries, accounting for over 60% of UK trade. The trend in the last two decades has been for UK trade with Europe to grow while UK–world trade has declined and for imports from Europe to grow faster than exports.

This imbalance of trade is caused by the centralising of production resulting in economies of scale greater than the increased cost of transport resulting from fewer plants. The cause of this has been the historic decline in the cost of transport, principally the construction of motorways increasing road freight speeds, the increase in weight and size of heavy goods vehicles, and the trend to higher-value, lower-volume goods able to bear higher-transport costs.

These centralising trends have previously occurred for political (for example, England and Scotland), and transport reasons (for example, UK motorways). Indeed the Leitch Report (Leitch 1977) concluded that further improvements in transport links would not encourage regional growth, when in fact the opposite had occurred, with multiplants and multiproducts rationalising to single plants and single products.

The Channel Tunnel is likely to accelerate a trend which is already evident, namely the United Kingdom becoming a dependent economy, as a net importer from mainland Europe (Lesley 1989a). The bottom line is that economic activity in the United Kingdom will increasingly be in stockholding, distribution, and after-sales.

2 Future role for rail freight

Historically rail freight has declined in the United Kingdom, and is declining in mainland Europe, both as a result of the change of consumption to higher-value products and the relative improvement in road transport speed and cost compared with rail. This is shown in the increase in road average hauls and the declining market share of rail (table 1).

This historic decline can be further appreciated by examining individual commodities, where rail has almost no market share of high-value products, and even in low-value commodities (coal, metals) only a 40% market share (table 2).

For trade with the rest of Europe rail has an even smaller market share of under 5%, but if one considers the volumes involved (table 3) there could be considerable potential for rail. This is especially true as rail has a larger, though declining, market share in mainland Europe. As controls on road haulage are increased and hauls lengthen, then the balance of advantage could swing back to rail.

Table 1. UK freight haulage (source: DTp, 1988).

Year	Average length of haul (km)		Traffic by rail (%)	Year	Average length of haul (km)		Traffic by rail (%)
	road	rail			road	rail	
1952	36	128	42	1980	67	114	11
1955	38	125	38	1985	71	125	9
1960	40	119	30	1986	72	118	8
1965	43	108	21	1987	73	123	7
1970	53	120	18	1988	74	121	7
1975	61	119	15				

Table 2. UK commodity modal share, 1988 (source: DTp, 1988).

Commodity	Road (%)	Rail (%)	Commodity as % of traffic
Agriculture	93	2	6
Food	98	1	11
Solid fuel	34	40	5
Liquid fuel	7	3	31
Ores and waste	59	41	1
Metals	77	24	4
Building material	76	10	15
Fertilisers	85	10	1
Chemicals	92	5	5
Manufactures	85	8	20

Table 3. Commodity flows by road from the United Kingdom to Europe, 1988 (source: DTp, 1988).

Commodity	Exports		Imports	
	kt	Mt km	kt	Mt km
Agriculture	307	371	471	654
Food	592	641	677	661
Metals	197	248	144	155
Chemicals	748	839	454	456
Manufactures	1017	1208	1129	1247
Others	569	594	717	770
Total	3430	3901	3592	3943

The geographical distribution of these flows (table 4) shows concentrations in the larger members of the EC, also offering potential for rail freight.

Commodities which are most vulnerable to centralisation are: agricultural products, food and animals feeds, finished metals, building materials, fertilisers, chemicals, and manufactures, which together account for over 80% of UK – Europe trade. A small transfer of road freight to rail would increase rail traffic by over 1.0 billion t km^{-1} (or nearly 7% of current freight on British Rail).

These commodities are being increasingly transported in 'swap bodies' (that is, soft top containers) (Lesley, 1987), which make combined road – rail – road intermodal haulage practical and attractive.

Table 4. UK trade flows with other EC countries, 1988 (source: DTp, 1988).

EC Member	Exports		Imports	
	kt	Mt km	kt	Mt km
Belgium and Luxembourg	195	119	324	178
Denmark	7	9	8	9
France	718	807	744	593
West Germany	877	803	782	711
Greece	31	90	13	34
Italy	733	1198	800	1306
Holland	244	147	418	269
Spain	270	455	279	524
EC total	3263	3582	3438	3711
Non EC	132	169	127	162
Total	3395	3751	3565	3873

3 Europe – North American trade

Transatlantic trade flows are large, and the fastest growing modes are containerised and air freight (reflecting the rise in commodity values) (Lesley, 1989a). In 1988 nearly 200 Mt of freight were transported across the Atlantic in both directions. The value of this trade was nearly US $200 billion (table 5).

Over the last twenty years the proportion of traffic carried in International Standards Organisation containers has grown (PIEDA, 1989). Currently about 3 million containers are carried on dedicated container shipping lines, calling at East Coast American ports, Baltimore, New York and New Jersey, Boston, Halifax and St Johns, and in Europe at national ports in maritime EC countries, for example, Liverpool, Le Havre, Antwerp, Rotterdam, Bremerhaven, Felixstowe, Rotterdam and Hamburg. Two main types of service exist, slow at 13 knots and fast at 18 knots (being nearly three days shorter). One line (Maersk) is operating a

24-knot service. However, the speed across the Atlantic is negated by the time taken in multiport itineries, up to one week on each side.

Significant savings in shipping costs could be achieved following the example of transpacific trades by rationalising into single 'hub ports'. On the West coast of America four hub ports have replaced nearly twenty ports previously used. At the hub port, ships (un)load all containers which are then collected or distributed by land. A rationalisation of North Atlantic containerised traffic to one hub port on each side, would reduce shipping costs by at least 20%, and reduce average container transit times.

Increasing container throughput in ports has allowed for capital investment to replace labour and substantially reduce unit costs. A capital intensive port has a low marginal operating cost and reflects the scale economies possible, until the capacity of the port is reached when capital expansion becomes necessary which changes the unit costs. For Liverpool, with spare capacity, increasing throughput would reduce unit costs. For Rotterdam, already operating to capacity, new investments would initially increase unit costs, as would any reduction of throughput.

The replacement of part of a maritime transit by land, is called a landbridge operation and major examples are between East and West American coasts, and the Trans-Siberian railway between Europe and Japan. The carrying of containers on 'landbridge' rail services has developed rapidly, including the double stacking of containers on railcars in North America. An entire ship load can be carried on under twenty trains (Liverpool Polytechnic, 1989). Hub ports and landbridges reduce costs for shipping lines, and for shippers of high-value products because faster transits reduce interest charges on the capital tied up in goods in transit. Faster deliveries also mean faster payments, an important improvement of cash flow.

Table 5. North Atlantic trade ($billion), 1988 (source: UN International Trade Statistics, 1988).

From	To			
	EC	EFTA	USA	Canada
EC			84.3	10.2
EFTA			13.2	1.7
USA	59.4	6.7		
Canada	6.8	0.7		

Traffic:
Eastbound: $73.6 billion (48 Mt)
Westbound: $109.7 billion (140 Mt)

4 Liverpool as a European hub port?

Liverpool is the nearest major European port to North America, being conveniently on the shortest great circle route (Lesley, 1986). This was of course the main reason why Liverpool was such an important port in the 19th and early 20th century (Asteris, 1988). In sailing time alone this shorter route is about three days shorter than from mainland European ports on routes passing south of Ireland.

The Channel Tunnel and rail links mean that Liverpool will be less than 24 hours by rail transit from the majority of the EC (figure 1). Therefore other things [for example, port entry, berthing, (un)loading] being equal, traffic via Liverpool could be at least one day and up to five days (on multiport itineraries) faster. However, rail costs are higher than maritime

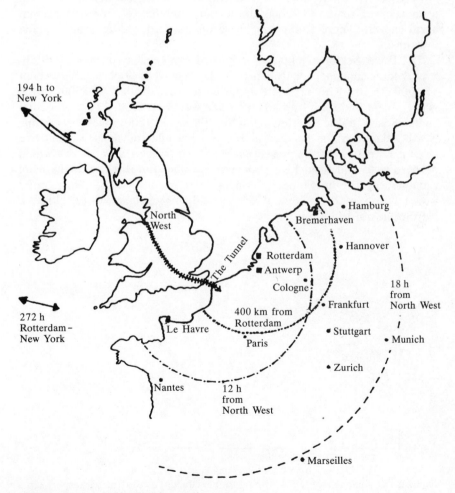

Figure 1. Liverpool landbridge service area.

and double-stacked rail cars are not possible in Europe because of loading gauge restrictions. The Port of Liverpool also had a poor reputation both among shipping lines and among shippers of freight.

An analysis of maritime and rail costs of transatlantic trade to and from mainland European centres via Liverpool or Rotterdam, shows (figure 2) that Rotterdam is cheaper for destinations near the North Sea Coast, and that Liverpool becomes competitive further inland (Fenyoe et al, 1987).

Since the abolition of the Dock Work Labour Scheme in 1989, the Port of Liverpool has been able to reduce operating costs, improve ship turnaround times, and establish a growing reputation for reliability and regularity. These have helped to increase port traffic and boost profits, so that for the first time in nearly two decades the port is on a virtuous growth curve, where increases in traffic will reduce unit costs from economies of scale. Provided traffic does not increase beyond present berth capacity, more traffic can be accommodated without major capital investment.

The Royal Seaforth container terminal has a capacity of about 500 000 twenty-foot container equivalents (TEU), and in 1989 handled about 150 000 TEUs. This gives an opportunity for a further 350 000 TEUs, which if captured from transatlantic trade would be about 12% of the total containerised traffic (Lesley, 1988b). These 350 000 plus the existing North Atlantic traffic handled at Liverpool would translate to about five ships per week (from the present two). About fifteen trains per day would be needed to and from Liverpool, which would run directly to the main economic centres in France, Germany, and Italy (figure 3). This traffic would represent over 20% of existing UK rail freight (on one line), a worthwhile traffic to capture.

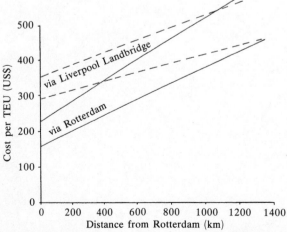

Figure 2. Comparison of TEU (twenty-foot container equivalents) transport costs from North America to Europe (1987 prices) (source: Lesley, 1988c).

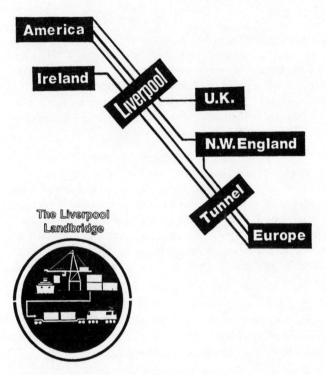

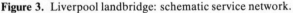

Figure 3. Liverpool landbridge: schematic service network.

5 Conditions to make Liverpool landbridge competitive

5.1 Shipping lines

One or more shipping lines will have to select Liverpool as a hub port. The operational savings possible could be partly realised in tariff reductions. Containers would have to be loaded at port of origin in the unloading sequence required at port of destination. As loading plans are already computerised, and this procedure is used for transpacific traffic, its use here would not be difficult.

5.2 Port of Liverpool

Royal Seaforth would have to be partly reorganised to facilitate the rapid (un)loading of containers between train and ship. Ideally, a train should leave hourly with containers unloaded in the previous hour (Lesley, 1988c). A computer-based container-tracking system is needed to allow shippers to locate their own containers and transport operators to ensure the smooth transit of traffic. Such a system could be located anywhere in America or Europe, but it would make operational sense to locate it in Liverpool.

5.3 British Rail
Dedicated container trains would have to operate between Royal Seaforth and the Channel Tunnel at an average speed of at least 80 km h^{-1} (Lesley, 1988a). A faster speed would be more advantageous. To achieve this speed and the reliability required, there should be no stops in Britain (for example, no change of engine). This means electrification from Edge Hill in Liverpool down to the Dock Terminal, at a cost of about £3 million, to allow electric haulage right through to France.

5.4 Channel Tunnel
At present the tariff proposed is speculation, but the worst-cost scenario would mean that the Channel transit itself would be more expensive than the rail cost, and greater than maritime savings. Given that the Liverpool landbridge trains would be a regular traffic and could be timetabled to avoid Tunnel peaks (for example, summer Saturdays and middays), then it would be reasonable for the landbridge to obtain a base tariff, which would be needed in any case if this traffic is going to be attracted via Liverpool.

5.5 Intercontainer
This is the European railways container-train-marketing cooperative. Already Intercontainer carries about one million containers per year. Liverpool landbridge would be a healthy additional traffic.

6 Regional impacts
The Liverpool landbridge would significantly change the transport geography of Britain. With up to fifteen unitised freight trains per day to major European centres, and a daily service to North America, the North West of England would enjoy levels of accessibility to Europe and North America greater than any other UK region. This would transform the North West from being a peripheral EC region (Lesley, 1989b; 1989c), to being a region between two major markets.

This level of accessibility can be judged by the fact that British Rail is planning only twenty-seven through freight trains per day from the whole of the United Kingdom through the Channel Tunnel. Liverpool and the North West would therefore have over one third of the UK–Europe freight train capacity, offering a range of destinations overnight, which no other region could support in the absence of public subsidies. On the deep-sea side, Liverpool is the most geographically central UK port, and a daily service to North America would reduce average transit times and costs for UK–American cargoes. This could raise the traffic through the port, and make it one of the top three (Lesley, 1990).

The Liverpool Freeport will be an attractive location for third parties wishing access to the mainland EC and North American markets. The Liverpool Freeport is already the most successful freeport in the United Kingdom and plans are currently in hand with the Merseyside

Development Corporation to expand the freeport area to accommodate growth already apparent. The North West has considerable spare and vacant industrial land. Unemployment is higher and wage levels lower than in much of the EC, and skill levels are high. This makes the North West a possible location for manufacturing expansion, especially for higher-value items which can bear the higher costs of transport. In particular, with the concentration and centralisation of industry within the EC, the North West might offer a location for companies seeking economies of scale in manufacture, and maximising market opportunities in North America and Europe.

7 Conclusion

The centripetal forces of the EC will tend to attract manufacturing and processing from the United Kingdom to automated 'megaplants' in mainland Europe. If rail was involved at an early stage, then there could be a significant role for rail in trunk haulage to UK storage and distribution facilities.

The dominance of road in UK – Europe trade means that rail has a significant potential for growth, provided that transit times and reliability are competitive with road. Here British Rail has a challenge to overcome.

Last, the Channel Tunnel would allow the Port of Liverpool and British Rail to try and attract up to 12% of transatlantic container traffic, onto a dedicated service offering price competition and faster transits compared with direct services to mainland European ports.

The opportunity and potential for Liverpool and British Rail are great. The opening of the Channel Tunnel will happen only once, and if this opportunity is missed, then the main European ports of Rotterdam and Antwerp will be very pleased to provide landbridge services into the United Kingdom, making UK ports redundant for deep-sea trades.

References

Asteris M, 1988, "British seaports: competition and trans-shipment" *National Westminster Bank Review* February, page 8

DTp, 1988 *Transport Statistics Great Britain 1977–1987* Department of Transport (HMSO, London)

Fenyoe R H, Sutcliffe P, Garratt M, 1987, "The European gateway" *Transmodal Industries Research* May, page 10

Leitch G, 1977, "Report of Advisory Committee on Trunk Road Assessment", Chairman Sir George Leitch, Department of Transport (HMSO, London)

Lesley L, 1986, "Channel Tunnel to aid Merseyside?" *TRIDENT, Merseyside Chamber of Commerce Journal* October, page 1

Lesley L, 1987, "Development of containerised freight transport in Britain and future directions", paper presented at the 5th Scientific Conference "Development of planning, organisation and management of transport and telecommunications", Transport and Telecommunications Technical College, Gyor, Hungary, May; copy available from the author

Lesley L, 1988a, "New market opportunities for rail: and a new role for Liverpool", paper presented at the North of England Regional Consortium Conference "The Channel Tunnel: making the most of the link in the north", Manchester, 5 February; copy available from the author

Lesley L, 1988b, "Potential traffic", paper presented at "The Liverpool Landbridge Symposium", Merseyside Maritime Museum, 15 September; copy available from the author

Lesley L, 1988c, "The Liverpool landbridge—a window of opportunity", paper presented at the Institute of Freight Forwarders Conference "The Competitive Edge", National Exhibition Centre, Birmingham, November; copy available from the author

Lesley L, 1989a, "The problem of peripherality", paper presented at the conference "Transportation and the Effects of 1992", Queen's University, Belfast, September; copy available from the author

Lesley L, 1989b, "1992: the effect of the single European Market on international air freight", paper presented at the Japan Air Lines Conference, Vienna, March; copy available from the author

Lesley L, 1989c, "The problem of peripherality", paper presented at the conference "Impacts of Channel Tunnel", University of London, June; copy available from the author

Lesley L, 1990, "The opportunities of a Liverpool landbridge", paper presented at the Regional Science Association Conference, University of Liverpool, September; copy available from the author

Liverpool Polytechnic, 1989 *The Liverpool Landbridge* Proceedings of a Symposium held 15 September 1988, Merseyside Maritime Museum

PIEDA, 1989, "The implications of the Single European Market and the Channel Tunnel for rail links to the North West Region", PIEDA, 10 Chester Street, Edinburgh EH3 7RA

The Channel Tunnel and the Impact on a Peripheral Region: A Study of the Northern Ireland Food Industry

K Greenan, M McHugh
University of Ulster

1 Introduction

The planned completion of the Single European Market in 1992, together with the opening of the Channel Tunnel scheduled for 1993, represents a major potential change in the competitive environment facing firms in a range of sectors in the regions of the United Kingdom. In particular, completion of the internal market will provide not only an opportunity to penetrate new markets but a threat to firms' existing domestic and export markets by, for example, opening up competition for public procurement contracts and reducing or eliminating many tariff and nontariff trade barriers (Commission of the European Communities, 1988; Emerson, 1988). Completion of the Channel Tunnel, by differentially altering the financial and nonfinancial costs of distance and accessibility, will affect the relative competitiveness of firms in different regions on both sides of the Channel (Keeble et al, 1982).

These changes are likely to be of particular significance to firms in Northern Ireland. Government and economic researchers have identified a lack of competitiveness as a major constraint on the Northern Ireland economy, and have targeted this as a major policy area (DED, 1987; Hitchens and Birnie, 1989; Teague, 1989). Despite the generally positive publicity campaign on the implications of the Single European Market, there is considerable concern that the competitive position of Northern Ireland may be further eroded after 1992, and that this may be reinforced by the effects of the opening of the Channel Tunnel, which have received almost no attention in the regional business community.

This reflects a more general concern that the nature of the existing transport infrastructure in the United Kingdom will reduce the potential benefits of 1992 and the Channel Tunnel to peripheral regions such as Scotland (Morris, 1987) and the North of England (Gunnell, 1988). More generally, it has been suggested that, at the aggregate level, the Channel Tunnel will have few differential regional effects (Vickerman, 1987), with the main impact observed in immediately adjacent regions such as Kent and Nord–Pas de Calais.

One consequence of the opening of the Channel Tunnel and the completion of the Single European Market will be that the relative accessibility of the South East of England, which contains 38% of the UK population, to the economic centre of the European Community will be increased. However, the economic distance between regions on the periphery and the economic centre will remain large. For example, after 1993 it is estimated that journey times between London and Paris or Brussels may fall from nine hours to around three hours; journey times from Belfast, however, will only fall from twenty-seven to twenty-one hours.

This differential change will place firms in peripheral areas such as Northern Ireland at a competitive disadvantage in a number of ways. First, given the importance of the ability to compete on delivery as an element in determining competitiveness (Fagerberg, 1988), the opening of the Channel Tunnel will give firms in the South East of England a relative competitive advantage over peripherally located firms in serving the European market. Second, reduced journey times after the completion of the Tunnel will improve the competitive position of Continental European firms presently or potentially serving markets in the South East of England, relative to those in the UK periphery. The combined impact of 1992 and the opening of the Channel Tunnel, therefore, will be to increase continental competition for Northern Ireland companies currently serving British markets. There is some evidence to suggest that Northern Ireland companies already rate improvements in speed and reliability and the introduction of more direct routes as the major required improvements to the transport infrastructure (Smyth and McNamee, 1982). After 1993, these will be increasingly important areas for improvement if the competitive position of Northern Ireland firms in the UK market is not to be further eroded. As Palmer (1989) has recently argued, poor transport infrastructure can be just as effective a barrier to trade as high tariffs. Third, and more generally, the increased accessibility of the UK market, and in particular the South East market, to Continental European producers may have an impact on the locational preferences of firms, and there are suggestions that some companies are considering locating investment in the Nord–Pas de Calais region, from which to service the UK market, rather than locating in the North West of Britain (Business Strategies Ltd, 1989).

In the light of this, the University of Ulster's Centre for Research in Management is currently investigating the likely competitive effects of the opening of the Channel Tunnel in 1993 on selected sectors of Northern Ireland industry. It could be argued that, although the implementation of the Single European Act (SEA) in 1992 will unite Europe legally, the opening of the Channel Tunnel will provide a physical link between Britain and Europe. It is a premise of this research that both of these events are strongly interlinked and that the likely effects of the opening of the Channel Tunnel can only be appraised with the assumption that the SEA will have been implemented.

2 The food industry
The food sector is a most important element in Northern Ireland's industrial base. The food, drink, and tobacco industrial group is the second largest manufacturing sector in Northern Ireland, and represented

around 20% of total manufacturing employment in 1986. The sector also accounted for around 20% of manufacturing gross domestic fixed capital formation between 1973 and 1981, and by 1981 capital spending per employee was 50% higher than in manufacturing as a whole (NIEC, 1985). However, 60% of this investment has been in the tobacco industry, where per-capita investment has been over three times the level in the food sector, and capital investment in the food sector has fallen by about 40% since 1973.

The food system is dominated by a large agricultural structure which, in 1988, produced output worth just over £820 million (Department of Agriculture for Northern Ireland, 1989, verbal communication). Black (1990) reports that argriculture in Northern Ireland is a more important economic activity than is the case for the industry in the United Kingdom or the European Community (EC). In 1985 agriculture accounted for 6% of gross domestic product (GDP) and 8.2% of civil employment in Northern Ireland (NIEC, 1985; NIAAS, 1987), compared with 2.1% of employment and 2% of GDP in the United Kingdom, and 7.6% of employment and 4% of GDP in the EC (CSO, 1986).

A very large percentage of agricultural output was processed by food manufacturers which added value of £225 million in 1988, (estimated by the Department of Agriculture for Northern Ireland), thus making the Northern Ireland food production and processing industry worth in excess of £1 billion (NIEC, 1985; Industrial Development Board, 1987, verbal communication). The importance of the food industry in the local economy is reflected in the turnover of the sector which is presented in table 1.

The local food processing industry is characterised by a large number of small processors. Individually these processors concentrate on specialist products, but collectively they produce a wide range of products. However, despite the large number of specialist producers, the bulk of food production is concentrated in a small number of companies. This is reflected in the employment statistics for the industry—in 1981, under 25% of food processing enterprises in the region employed fifty people or more.

Table 1. Turnover of subsectors of the Northern Ireland food processing industry 1985 (source: Industrial Development Board, 1986, verbal communication).

Sector	Estimated turnover (£million)	Estimated exports from Northern Ireland (£million)
Beef and lamb	383	308
Dairy produce	375	274
Pork	104	63
Poultry and eggs	107	63
Fish	13	12
Other	125	31
Total	1107	751

Although a wide range of products are manufactured by Northern Ireland food producers, livestock and dairy products are predominant. In 1985 it was estimated that 87.5% of turnover in the industry was attributable to sales of livestock and dairy goods (Industrial Development Board, 1985, verbal communication) (this value excludes animal feeds). Thus, although small specialist processors are important, the Northern Ireland food industry is dominated by large companies involved in the processing of livestock and milk.

2.1 Food production
Food production has fluctuated between 1978 and 1989 as can be seen from table 2. Throughout the 1980s food production in Northern Ireland has not risen at the same rate as in Britain. This discrepancy may be attributed to the product structure of the Northern Ireland food processing industry and to the structural contexts within which it operates; namely a high dependence upon livestock and milk in a period of changing market preferences and the terms of the EC Common Agriculture Policy.

Table 2. Index (1989 = 100) of food production for the Northern Ireland food industry 1978 – 89 (source: DED, verbal communication).

Year	Index	Year	Index	Year	Index
1978	103	1982	96	1986	100
1979	105	1983	100	1987	96
1980	103	1984	96	1988	97
1981	98	1985	100	1989	100

2.2 Employment in the food industry
Employment trends in the Northern Ireland food processing industry for 1971 – 1989 are outlined in table 3. Employment in the local food industry has declined steadily since 1971. Recent analysis by the Northern Ireland Economic Research Centre (NIERC) has indicated that many job losses within the food industry are attributable to plant closures and to contraction of other surviving enterprises.

Table 3. Employment change in the Northern Ireland food, drink, and tobacco industry 1971 – 89, SIC (1968) Order III (1980) 41/42 (source: DED, 1990, verbal communication).

Year	Employment	Year	Employment
1971	26870	1981	22340
1976	23980	1986	20780
		1989	19160

Change 1971 – 89 (%): −28.7

2.3 An investigation of the food industry

The food industry was selected as the focus of this investigation for a number of reasons. In addition to its absolute importance to the Northern Ireland economy, the food industry is also one which is most likely to be affected by the opening of the Channel Tunnel. As indicated by Vickerman (chapter 5), certain key sectors may be more affected than industry in general; such sectors include food where reduction in transport time could lead to significant gains. Companies located in mainland Britain or on the Continent may experience such beneficial effects. However, because of the location of Northern Ireland, it is unlikely that these anticipated gains will benefit local food companies. The development of a physical link between mainland Britain and Europe will have a significant impact upon the competitiveness of an industry currently located in a region which is regarded as being on the periphery.

The work of Porter (1980) lends support for this argument. Briefly, Porter asserts that the competitiveness of an industry is determined by the interplay of five competitive forces, these are: the power of buyers, the power of suppliers, the threat of substitutes, the threat of new entrants, and, the degree of internal rivalry. In order to gain competitive advantage it is necessary for an individual firm to position itself so that the negative effects of these forces are minimised. This is achieved through the pursuit of a generic strategy which emphasises either product differentiation or overall cost leadership, or alternatively, a focused strategy which emphasises product differentiation or overall cost leadership for a targeted market segment.

On the basis of the Porter model it can be suggested that following the enforcement of the SEA in 1992, the opening of the Channel Tunnel will lead to an intensification of three key competitive forces in the food industry. These are: the threat of new entrants, internal rivalry, and the power of buyers.

Of primary importance is the threat of new entrants. The SEA and the Tunnel are likely to make mainland Britain a more accessible and, consequently, a more attractive market for Continental food producers. It might also be suggested that some Continental markets may appear more attractive and accessible to British food producers. Thus Northern Ireland food companies currently selling a significant proportion of their output to customers in mainland Britain and Europe are likely to experience an increase in the number of competitors within the industry. This increased number of competitors will lead to an intensification in the degree of rivalry within the industry. The power of buyers, and particularly large multiples, has been highlighted recently by Martin (1990). Because of the greater choice of food suppliers these buyers are likely to become even more powerful after 1993.

Thus, it would seem inevitable that the Northern Ireland food industry will experience enhanced levels of competitive pressure after the opening of the Tunnel in 1993.

The vulnerability of the local food industry outlined above is exacerbated by the peripherality of Northern Ireland as a region and the consequent time and costs of transporting goods to customers in distant locations (relative to food companies in mainland Britain and in Continental Europe).

Vickerman (chapter 5) indicates that infrastructure developments such as the Channel Tunnel have a variety of direct and indirect effects on the economic performance of other regions possibly quite remote from it. The indirect effects of such developments concern the *relative* competitiveness of a region as a consequence of the infrastructure. Thus, the creation of a new link into a peripheral region may bestow competitive advantage to that region, relative to a similarly located region which does not have such a link. In the context of this paper, the Channel Tunnel may be viewed as a new link in one peripheral region.

After the opening of the Channel Tunnel, Northern Ireland and the Irish Republic will be the only regions which do not have a physical link with other countries of the EC. Thus, this major development in infrastructure is likely to have a significant impact in regions far removed from where the infrastructure is built.

In this research project we set out to investigate the likely impact of the Channel Tunnel on the competitiveness of the Northern Ireland food industry—an industry which is likely to be most affected by a major new infrastructure development. It is a premise of this study that local food companies, which have a relatively high dependence upon markets outside Northern Ireland, will be adversely affected by the Channel Tunnel. The adverse effects will be caused by an interplay between the following:

(1) the cost and time savings in transport experienced by competitors in mainland Britain and Europe,

(2) the increased attractiveness and accessibility of British markets to Continental competitors,

(3) the increased attractiveness and accessibility of Continental markets to British competitors.

The study aimed to assess: the market dependence of local food companies, the current basis for competition, for example, product price or 'quality', the current transport times and costs, and, the preparedness of the food industry for a major new infrastructure development in terms of strategy formulation and evolution.

3 Research method
The research was undertaken in two stages: stage 1 was a pilot study and stage 2 was a detailed study.

3.1 Stage 1: the pilot study
A pilot study was carried out in May 1989 to obtain a profile of the Northern Ireland food industry. The investigation focused upon four

major segments within the food industry, meat products, dairy products, fish products, and miscellaneous products, which constitute approximately 60% of employment in the industry. A representative sample was taken of companies in these segments which had ten or more employees.

A total of eighty-one companies participated in a telephone survey, based on a short structured questionnaire which sought information on age, size, growth, products, and market dependence.

The pilot study revealed some important features of the Northern Ireland food industry in terms of its dependence on nonlocal markets and its vulnerability to increased competition when the SEA is implemented and the Channel Tunnel is opened. Companies which are likely to be most affected are those which could be described as 'best-prospect companies', which are fast growing, large, and relatively young.

These companies had been most successful in developing their presence in nonlocal markets (see Greenan et al, 1989; Harrison, 1989). The opening of the Channel Tunnel may well cause this nonlocal market dependence to be a source of vulnerability. In stage 2 of the project we built upon stage 1 by selecting a sample of twenty-six best-prospect companies and carrying out a detailed analysis of the likely impact of the opening of the Tunnel upon them.

3.2 Stage 2: the detailed study

3.2.1 *Methodology.* This study was carried out in Autumn 1989 and took the form of personal interviews in the companies by means of a structured questionnaire. These interviews aimed to ascertain for the selected sample of best-prospect companies: their knowledge of the transport consequences of the opening of the Channel Tunnel, degree of market dependence, performance, strategies, competitive perceptions.

3.2.2 *Profile of respondents.* Eighteen companies comprising nine from meat, four from fish, four from dairy, and one from miscellaneous food products took part in the survey.

Respondents held senior managerial positions in the companies. Thus it is suggested that the data provided are authentic and are of high quality.

Although the sample is relatively small, it is representative of the food industry, and the economic importance of the participating firms can be seen from their total sales and total employment. In 1988 their total sales were approximately £25 million and their total employment was approximately 4400.

There was great variation in the sales of individual companies, from circa £1 million for a fish company to over £60 million for a meat company. Average sales growth for the sample for the period 1985 to 1988 ranged from 5.9% for dairy companies to 15.6% for fish producers.

The weighted average number of employees for each firm in the sample was 243. Once again, however, large variations were evident between the segments. The smallest employment figure was recorded for miscellaneous food producers (54 employees), whereas meat producers were the largest employers in the entire food industry (average 398 employees). The meat and dairy segments had, on average, a much higher number of employees than either fish or miscellaneous food producers.

Ten out of the eighteen companies were locally owned limited companies, three were UK-owned subsidiaries, three were cooperatives, one was a locally owned and managed company, and another was a subsidiary of a parent company in another country. This indicates that a relatively large proportion of Northern Ireland food companies are in some form of local ownership and that strategic decisionmaking should take place within Northern Ireland. Therefore it is imperative that strategies to cope with the consequences of the opening of the Tunnel are developed by local management.

Fifteen out of the eighteen participating companies were described as integrated manufacturers and engage in a variety of activities: manufacturing, distribution, sales, and marketing.

4 Regional dependence
A primary assertion of this research is that the Channel Tunnel will have the greatest impact upon those companies which currently depend most upon markets in the South of England, France, Germany, Belgium, and Holland. To measure the regional dependence of participating companies, respondents' sales were disaggregated into the following eleven regions: Northern Ireland, the Republic of Ireland, South of England, North of England, Scotland, Wales, France, Belgium, Germany, Holland, and 'other'. Regional dependence was assessed in three ways:

1. *Actual regional dependency of individual companies*: the actual sales value that each company had in each region.
2. *Percentage regional dependency of individual companies*: the proportion of sales that each company had in each region.
3. *Weighted average regional dependencies*, which captured the magnitude of regional dependence, calculated from actual segment sales to each region divided by total segment sales. For example, the total sales of the meat segment to Northern Ireland were £52.3 million and the overall total meat segment sales were £217.3 million. Thus the weighted average of the meat segment on the Northern Ireland market would be given by $100 \times 52.3/217.8 = 24.0\%$.

The results indicated that large amounts of locally produced foods are sold in markets outside Northern Ireland. More specifically, they revealed that the food industry is heavily reliant upon customers in England, Wales, France, Germany, Belgium, and Holland, which accounted for 67% of the sales of the sampled companies, with 40% to the English and Welsh markets alone.

The results indicate differences in the market dependence of the four segments. For example, 23% of meat, 58% of fish, but only 15% of dairy products were sold in South East England; whereas very little fish, but 24% of meat and 41% of dairy products were sold locally in Northern Ireland. France took as much as 18% of meat but only 5% of fish and negligible dairy products.

The average dependence of the sampled companies on the more local markets of Northern Ireland, the Republic of Ireland, and Scotland was found to be 33%. Companies which were most dependent upon these markets, that is which sold 33% or more of their products in these regions, experienced an average sales growth from 1985 to 1988 of 11.75%, compared with the average sales growth rate for those respondents which are more reliant upon nonlocal markets of 7.68%.

The average sales of companies which are most dependent upon local markets was calculated at £14.48 million. For those companies which sell relatively large percentages of their products in nonlocal markets, the average sales figure was slightly higher—£16.28 million.

Conversely, companies which are most dependent on local markets have a slightly higher average number of employees (270) than those which trade in nonlocal regions (245).

The youngest companies in the sample, that is, companies which have been established within the last ten years, are most dependent on markets outside Northern Ireland, the Irish Republic, and Scotland. Indeed, there would appear to be a direct relationship between company age and market dependence. Taken together these findings suggest that the longest established companies are: fastest growing in terms of sales growth and numbers of employees, and most dependent upon the local market.

This would seem to indicate that those companies which are highly dependent on markets likely to be affected by the opening of the Tunnel are younger companies which are currently experiencing higher levels of competitive pressure. This would seem to indicate that older companies follow different growth strategies to younger companies. Ansoff (1965) asserts that companies may grow through the pursuit of one of four strategies, these are outlined below in table 4.

On the basis of this analysis it might be suggested that older companies grow through market penetration and product development within Northern Ireland, whereas younger companies adopt a strategy of market development outside the province. Companies trading within the local

Table 4. Growth-vector components.

Mission	Product	
	Present	New
Present	market penetration	product development
New	market development	differentiation

market experience less intense competitive pressure than those which seek customers elsewhere. This may be partly explained by the fact that buyer power is less significant in Northern Ireland where the predominant customer group is small retailers.

5 Customer dependence

We investigated the types of customers which are served by Northern Ireland food producers in each region and then assessed the extent to which the food industry is dependent upon each customer group.

The sample has three main customer types: large multiples, wholesalers, and industrial buyers, whereas small retailers are the predominant customer group in the Northern Ireland market. Thus knowledge of the operations of large multiples, wholesalers, and industrial buyers may be important for companies considering extending their operations outside the Northern Ireland market.

Further analyses of the data revealed regional variations in customer types for the four segments. In particular it was found that a large percentage of sales from the meat industry, (which is heavily dependent on regions which are likely to be affected by the Channel Tunnel), are to large multiples (figure 1).

The majority of the survey participants cited 'quality' as being the basis for the success of their company in markets outside Northern Ireland. It is perhaps significant that 'quality' is the primary competitive weapon of respondents who trade in the South East of England and in Continental Europe; that is, markets which are most likely to be affected by the Channel Tunnel. Thus it would seem to be the case that as delivery speed is not a critical success factor, the anticipated shortened journey times which are likely to result from the Tunnel may have a much smaller impact upon local companies trading in Britain and the Continent than was originally expected. However, this is not meant to minimise the anticipated impact of the Tunnel, but rather to focus attention on the *nature* of its anticipated impact. Thus it is expected that in preparing for the opening of the Tunnel, local producers ought to pay particular attention to

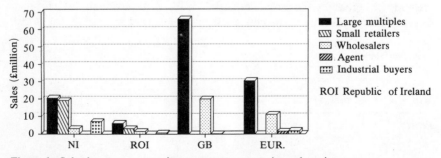

Figure 1. Sales by meat companies to customer types in each region.

the quality of their products relative to Continental competitors. 'Quality' is measured not just by physical features of the product, but includes other attributes such as reliability and security of delivery.

6 Knowledge and perceptions about the Channel Tunnel

The commercial success of food producers regardless of location is, to some extent, dependent on the service which they provide. As food products are perishable this would seem to suggest that components of this service should include speedy and reliable delivery. Faster delivery times permit companies to transport food products in very fresh condition and should therefore be a factor in gaining competitive advantage.

Reliable delivery refers to a company's ability to deliver goods according to the time schedule agreed with customers and is an important factor for companies located in regions such as Northern Ireland, where large percentages of outputs are exported to nonlocal markets.

It would seem likely that the opening of the Tunnel in 1993 will adversely affect Northern Ireland food companies which sell a significant proportion of their output to customers in nonlocal markets, particularly the South East of England and other European regions. These companies may find themselves facing intense competition from continental rivals who may avail themselves of any benefits provided by faster delivery times through the Tunnel.

Figure 2 indicates that, although journey times between Belfast to London will remain unchanged after 1993, there will be a significant reduction in freight journey time between London and Paris or London and Brussels.

For Northern Ireland food companies which sell a relatively large percentage of goods to markets in the South East of England and/or other European regions, the implications of these changes in freight journey times, combined with the implementation of the Single European Act, are potentially very serious. It seems likely that the legal and physical unification of Britain and Europe will encourage new continental competitors to enter into direct competition with Northern Ireland companies in their nonlocal markets, and that the South East of England appears to be particularly susceptible to this development. Thus, respondents' knowledge and perceptions of the Channel Tunnel were investigated.

Respondents were asked to indicate their knowledge of freight journey times between London and other major Continental European cities at present and after 1993. Around 50% or less of respondents were aware of the actual current or anticipated journey times. The largest number of correct responses were given for the journey time between London and Paris.

It is interesting to note that, although the meat segment was most aware of *current* journey times, the fish segment was most knowledgeable with regard to *anticipated* journey times. This is perhaps a reflection of the views put forward by the majority of respondents from meat companies that the opening of the Tunnel will have little impact on the way in which they transport products to customers.

Although the majority of meat and dairy producers in the sample regarded the Channel Tunnel as a potential threat to their company, this belief was not shared by the fish segment. This difference in perceptions may be a result of a combination of the following two factors:

(a) Meat and dairy respondents sell a much larger percentage of their output to Continental markets than sampled fish producers.

(b) Fish producers do not believe that any of their products will be adversely affected by the Tunnel. This is perhaps because of the unique nature of the local fish industry and the fact that its main product, breaded scampi, is not in demand outside the United Kingdom, consequently local fish producers are not engaged in direct competition with their foreign counterparts in other regions.

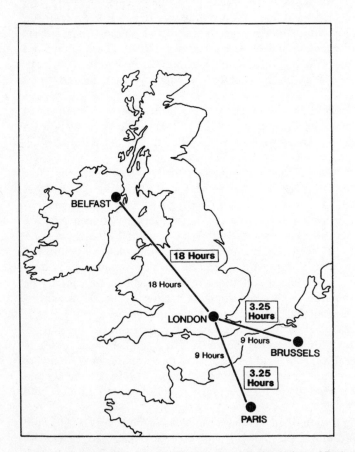

Figure 2. Journey times between Belfast, London, Brussels, and Paris 1989 and 1993.

A significant number of respondents believe that the opening of the Channel Tunnel is likely to affect their sales in English markets, especially to customers in the South East region. This would seem to suggest:
(1) An awareness by local food companies of the likelihood of increased competition from Continental rivals in English markets after the opening of the Channel Tunnel. The physical and legal links between Britain and the Continent are likely to make the English market appear more accessible to Continental competitors.
(2) The markets which respondents believe are most likely to be affected by the opening of the Channel Tunnel represent important outlets for the products of the Northern Ireland food industry.

6.1 Anticipated strategic changes
McNamee (1988) indicates that the fundamental reason for the development of new strategies is that the environment faced by all organisations is constantly changing. Consequently, organisations can only ensure their continued existence, (or success), by successfully tracking their environment and adapting their strategies in response to change. Respondents were thus asked if they anticipated any change in their current strategy as a consequence of the Channel Tunnel.

Most participants do not expect any change in their strategy after the opening of the Channel Tunnel; it is perhaps interesting that in the fish segment none of the respondents anticipated any change in strategic direction after 1993. This may be attributed to the unique nature of the fish industry and its products as discussed above.

These results are somewhat surprising when they are considered alongside those concerning threats presented by the Tunnel. Nine out of eighteen respondents viewed the Channel Tunnel as a threat to their company. Thus it would seem to be the case that, although the Tunnel is perceived by many as posing a threat to the food industry, few anticipate any change in current strategy to prepare for future competition.

6.2 Changes in the nature of competition
The meat and dairy segments anticipate a wide variety of changes in the nature of competition. Overall, 'faster delivery' is expected by the largest number of respondents, coupled with a greater variety of products. A minority anticipate the availability of higher quality products.

Fish companies do not expect any change in the nature of competition. However, this finding is not surprising when one considers the commonly held views within this segment regarding peculiarities in the demand for its products.

6.3 Opportunities presented by the Channel Tunnel
Relatively few respondents perceive the Tunnel to be a source of opportunity. Of those who did believe that their company would benefit from the Tunnel, the majority mentioned that such benefits would be residual

effects of the SEA. Many believed that the implementation of the SEA in 1992 would permit Northern Ireland companies to exploit new markets on the Continent and that it was possible that the Channel Tunnel could facilitate faster delivery of Northern Ireland goods.

Some respondents mentioned the fact that, although the Channel Tunnel may present new opportunities for their company, they also believed that the Tunnel may prompt Continental competitors to seek new trading links with customers in Great Britain and perhaps in Northern Ireland.

7 New competitors
Fifty percent of respondents believe they will experience an increase in the number of competitors after the opening of the Tunnel. The majority of these participants were from the meat and dairy segments.

Most new competitors are believed to be much larger in size than respondents' companies and are located in Great Britain. This is a signif-icant finding; thus it may be suggested that these larger competitors which are located on the British mainland, are in a prime position to avail of any potential opportunities presented by the Channel Tunnel. Consequently, the characteristics of these new competitors are such that they may be viewed as threatening to Northern Ireland food companies which are dependent upon markets in Great Britain and in other European countries.

Two new competitors from the dairy segment are believed to be located in France and Germany. Because of the physical and legal links effected by the Channel Tunnel and the SEA, these companies would appear to be ideally positioned to exploit new market opportunities in Britain and may also seek to develop new trading links in their own countries. Thus, as these new entrants will be competing directly with some of Northern Ireland's dairy companies they may be viewed as potentially threatening.

Respondents believe Continental markets are most likely to be threat-ened by new competitors. This finding was expected and provides some support for the views presented previously regarding potential opportu-nities for new English and Continental competitors.

8 Transport
Northern Ireland food products destined for mainland Britain and the Continent are generally transported by road to Larne Harbour which is located north of Belfast. From here they are shipped to Stranraer and are then transported by road once again to customers in Britain or to ports for further shipment to the Continent.

We investigated the various modes of transport used by respondents and the cost of each mode as a percentage of selling price. Figure 3 shows the modes of transport used by the sample.

The most frequently used mode of transport was 'mode 3' which is totally contracted. Many participants also reported that they used 'mode 1' which refers to the use of the firms' own vehicles for the transportation of products to customers. It was generally found that companies using their own vehicles for transportation, used this method to service customers in local markets, that is, Northern Ireland and the Republic of Ireland.

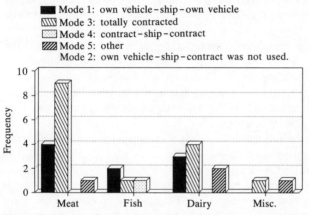

■ Mode 1: own vehicle – ship – own vehicle
▧ Mode 3: totally contracted
▨ Mode 4: contract – ship – contract
▨ Mode 5: other
Mode 2: own vehicle – ship – contract was not used.

Figure 3. Modes of transport used by respondents' companies.

8.1 Transport costs

Analyses of transport costs were carried out for a number of reasons:
1. to assess the current transport costs as a percentage of selling price,
2. to assess the likely impact of the Channel Tunnel on the transport of local food products to customers in Britain and on the Continent,
3. to permit some comment on the likely impact of the Channel Tunnel on the transportation of food products by British and Continental rivals who trade in similar markets to Northern Ireland food companies.

In order to investigate the actual cost of transport, further analysis was carried out to assess the average transport costs as a percentage of selling price. Figure 4 presents the findings for transport mode 3 (totally contracted). Transport costs ranged from 0.6% to 20% of selling price, both of these figures were recorded for the meat segment.

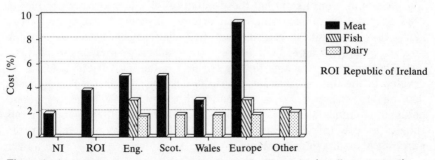

Figure 4. Average transport costs as a percentage of selling price (totally contracted).

When regional average transport costs are considered, not surprisingly the figure for Northern Ireland was lowest at 1.8%, with the highest average for the transportation of goods to Holland (12%).

In general, transport costs are most significant for the meat segment and least significant for the dairy segment. For meat companies average transport costs increase with distance, however this trend is not mirrored by the dairy and fish segments.

From these reults it might be inferred that, in terms of transport, the opening of the Channel Tunnel is likely to have the greatest impact on Northern Ireland meat companies. One of the anticipated effects of the Channel Tunnel is lower transport costs, thus it would seem to be the case that British and Continental rivals will be optimally placed to avail themselves of such potential benefits.

This may be a cause for concern in view of the overall value of meat segment sales and regional dependence referred to earlier. However, it is important to note that many respondents cited the quality of their products as being a major factor contributing to their success. Consequently, it might be suggested that, although the Channel Tunnel may provide cheaper transport for competitors in other regions, the 'quality' of food produced in Northern Ireland must be the competitive weapon used to promote sales of local companies in markets most likely to be affected by the Tunnel, that is, Britain and Continental Europe. Some support for this view is provided by the comments of respondents regarding their views on the criteria which they believe are of paramount importance in transport.

Reliability of delivery appeared to be the most significant factor in transport for the majority of participants, followed by speed of delivery and security of cargo.

These findings appear to indicate that the respondents in the Northern Ireland food industry believe that the primary level of competitiveness is not the cost or price but 'quality'. This view was endorsed by comments made by key personnel from major supermarket chains at a recent meat industry seminar organised by the University of Ulster. 'Quality', it would seem, is a concept which extends beyond the physical attributes of the product; instead it is primarily concerned with total customer satisfaction. Thus it would seem likely that the production of a high-quality product in itself does not guarantee commercial success. Instead, it would seem more likely that the highest returns will be achieved by companies which produce high-quality products of the type required by their major customers. The implication of this finding is that for the industry to continue to develop in the future, considerable resources must be devoted to ensuring that quality standards at least match those provided by existing and potential Continental rivals. This may become more difficult if such rivals choose to use the cost savings that the Tunnel may provide for the purposes of quality improvement.

The following hypothetical example demonstrates the possible significance of these cost savings.

Company A is located in Northern Ireland and Company B, which is highly similar, is located in Northern France. It is assumed that return on capital employed (ROCE) for both firms is currently 30%. This return is a combination of a net profit margin of 10% on sales and a turnover of capital employed of 3, that is, $30\% = 10\% \times 3$.

If transportation costs are currently 6% of sales, the potential savings of the Continental company, (Company B), because of the opening of the Channel Tunnel, and the consequent reduction in delivery time, may be as much as 4%, that is, a reduction of two thirds. For the Continental company such savings will increase the net profit margin to 14% of sales, thus raising the ROCE to 42%, that is $42\% = 14\% \times 3$. By comparison, the Northern Ireland company is significantly less competitive, with ROCE remaining at the original 30%.

Although transport costs account for a very small fraction of the total costs of most manufacturing firms, typically around 4%, this example serves to illustrate the relative importance of transport costs as a significant determinant of performance, a view supported by Tyler et al (1988).

9 Conclusions
9.1 Regional implications
This study has highlighted some important aspects of the Northern Ireland food industry and its markets. First, in terms of the regional economy the food industry is seen to be extremely important, through its contribution to GDP and employment. Second, the industry is highly dependent on sales outside the local region and is especially dependent on those regions which are most likely to be affected by the opening of the Channel Tunnel: England, Wales, France, Belgium, Germany, and Holland. Indeed, 67% of the sampled companies' 'exports' go to those markets. This would suggest that the opening of the Tunnel is an issue of major regional economic importance, and that it is essential for the food industry to be strategically prepared for this event.

The study casts major doubts over the 'preparedness' of the industry. Indeed, many of the companies appeared to be poorly informed about the opening of the Tunnel (only 50% knew the correct year) and the extent of its proposed operations (most respondents did not know which major cities which will be linked to the Tunnel railway network and an even greater number did not know the post-Tunnel rail journey times). Much more significant, however, is the fact that, although many respondents considered the Tunnel to be a 'threat' which would increase the degree of competition through the entry of new competitors offering faster delivery, lower price, higher quality, and greater product variety, there was a general view that no strategic changes in their companies' activities would be necessary after the opening of the Tunnel. This appeared to be a rather optimistic view. The case for suggesting that in the post-Tunnel era the degree of competition will be substantially higher is reinforced by the general view of respondents that its opening will provide few if any additional opportunities.

The environment within which the food industry operates seems destined to change with the opening of the Channel Tunnel. McNamee (1988) suggests that keen sensitivity to competitive forces plus the ability to react effectively to them is a vital element in determining strategic viability. Thus, companies which fail to react and adapt their strategies to a changing environment seem likely to experience intense competitive pressure and, ultimately, possible failure. This potential failure has serious implications for the Northern Ireland regional economy, where the food sector is a most important element in the industrial base.

9.2 Transport implications

Respondents generally seemed rather unconcerned about the transport implications of the opening of the Tunnel. A prevailing view was that the basis for the success of their products was quality and not price or speed of delivery. Furthermore, an important dimension of their perception of quality was *reliability of delivery* which included security and guaranteed delivery time. Indeed guaranteed delivery time was often cited as being more important than *actual delivery time*. Thus, most respondents were of the opinion that their customers placed a much greater premium upon say 'guaranteed delivery in 24 hours' than 'probable delivery in 12 hours'.

The significance of transport reliability has been noted in chapter 5. However, for Northern Ireland companies, guaranteed delivery depends upon the existence of good *road* and *sea* links. At present there would appear to be no proposed developments in infrastructure which will provide benefits for Northern Ireland manufacturers. The proposed development of the Dublin – Holyhead route with improved rail links as a means of serving Irish interests offers little to Northern Ireland industry. The reasons for this include the following:

(a) The port of Larne itself will suffer from this development because it is not only used by Northern Ireland industry but also generates a substantial income from traders in the Republic of Ireland.

(b) The rail network is not a suitable mode of transport for food haulage because of the necessity to deliver parts of a container load en route to the final destination.

(c) The frequent disruptions on the Belfast – Dublin rail link, because of the current volatile political situation, would mean that reliability of delivery could not be assured.

Therefore this proposed infrastructure development, by improving the competitive position of other regions, while providing no benefits for the Northern Ireland region, will make the competitive position of Northern Ireland companies relatively worse.

9.3 Competitive implications

This may have important implications for the development of the generic competitive strategies of firms in peripheral regions. Namely, it is important to recognise that it will always be impossible for firms in peripheral regions to compete, on the basis of speed of delivery and/or costs, in central markets with central based companies. Consequently, it is advocated that for peripheral regions the primary emphasis in the development of firms' strategies ought to be in the area of quality enhancement. Research evidence suggests that high relative quality is one of the major strategic influences on profitability and cash flow, (for example, Schoeffler, 1980). In other words, competitive redress for the opening of the Tunnel is most likely to be found in the area of product and delivery improvement rather than cost and time reduction.

However, improvements in quality are not without cost. The anticipated weakened competitive position, as a consequence of the Channel Tunnel, may make additional investment in 'quality' rather difficult. As highlighted previously in the example, the level of potential savings by continental firms will enhance *their* ability to invest in quality improvements.

The results of this research would thus suggest that the outlook for the Northern Ireland food industry is exceedingly bleak. The opening of the Channel Tunnel is likely to further increase the level of competitive pressure experienced by Northern Ireland food companies.

9.4 Future research directions

This research is not complete. Currently efforts are being made to match the firms in this sample with similar enterprises in other peripheral and central regions of Europe. The objective of this analysis is to generate comparative data, (particularly in the areas of product cycle times and the components of unit costs), so that a more accurate comparison between peripheral and central regions can be made.

Acknowledgements. This paper was prepared by the following staff in the University of Ulster: K Greenan, J Hanna, R Harrison, E McAleer, M McHugh, and P McNamee.

References

Ansoff H I, 1965 *Corporate Strategy: An Analytic Approach to Business Policy for Growth and Expansion* (McGraw-Hill, New York)

Black C W, 1990, "Corporate policy in a peripheral economy in a period of recession and recovery: the case of the food industry in Northern Ireland", unpublished manuscript, Department of Geography, Queen's University Belfast, Belfast

Business Strategies Ltd, 1989, "Chunnel or Transmanche: business location and regional opportunities", May, Business Strategies Ltd

Commission of the European Communities 1988 *The Economics of 1992* European Economy No. 35

CSO, 1986 *Regional Trends* number 21, Central Statistical Office (HMSO, London)

DED, 1987, "Building a stronger economy: the pathfinder process", Department of Economic Development, Northern Ireland, Belfast

Emerson N, 1988 *The Economics of 1992: The EC Commission's Assessment of the Effects of Completing the Internal Market* (Oxford University Press, Oxford)

Fagerberg J, 1988, "International competitiveness" *Economic Journal* **98** 355-374

Greenan K, Hanna J, Harrison R, McAleer E, McHugh M, McNamee P, 1989, "The opening of the Channel Tunnel: implications for the Northern Ireland food industry" *Business Outlook and Economic Review* TSB Northern Ireland plc **4**(3) 29-32

Gunnell J, 1988, "A minimum investment programme for the North" *Town and Country Planning* May, pp 153-155

Harrison R, 1989, "The Single European Market, the Channel Tunnel and regional competitiveness: the implications for industry in Northern Ireland", paper presented at the Regional Science Association European Congress, Cambridge, 29 August-1 September; copy available from the author, Faculty of Business and Management, University of Ulster, Jordanstown Campus

Hitchens D, Birnie E, 1989, "Manufacturing productivity in Northern Ireland: a comparison with Great Britain", Northern Ireland Economic Research Centre, Belfast

Keeble D, Owens P, Thompson C, 1982, "Economic potential and the Channel Tunnel" *Area* **14** 97-103

Martin P, 1990, "Trolley fodder" *The Sunday Times* 4 November

McNamee P B, 1988 *Management Accounting: Strategic Planning and Marketing* (Heinemann Professional Publishing, Oxford)

Morris E, 1987, "When the Tunnel is built—the Scottish viewpoint" *The Planner* January, page 19

NIAAS, 1987 *Northern Ireland Annual Abstract of Statistics* (HMSO, Belfast)

NIEC, 1985, "Economic strategy: food, drink and tobacco", report 51, Northern Ireland Economic Council, Belfast

Palmer D, 1989, "Improving Britain's transport links with Europe" *National Westminster Bank Quarterly Review* August, pp 29-38

Porter M E, 1980 *Competitive Strategy: Techniques for Analysing Industries and Competitors* (The Free Press, New York)

Schoeffler S, 1980, "The nine basic findings of business strategy" *Profit Impact on Market Strategy Letter* number 1, The Strategic Planning Institute, Cambridge, MA

Smyth M, McNamee P, 1982, "Survey of transport services in Northern Ireland", unpublished report, Polytechnic Innovation and Resource Centre, Newtownabbey, Northern Ireland

Teague P, 1989, "Economic development in NI: has Pathfinder lost its way?" *Regional Trends* **23** 63-69

Tyler P, Moore B, Rhodes J, 1988 *Geographical Variations in Costs and Productivity* (Department of Trade and Industry, HMSO, London)

Vickerman R W, 1987, "The Channel Tunnel: consequences for regional growth and development" *Regional Studies* **23** 187-197

The New East–West Corridor: An Analysis of Passenger Transport Flows inside and through Germany in 2010

U Blum
University of Bamberg

1 Introduction

The unification of Germany and the opening up of Eastern Europe are beginning to rearrange European transportation flows. Even though the transportation infrastructure in the five new German provinces does not match Western European standards by a long way, it is somewhat superior to that of the remaining former Eastern Bloc countries and is expected to be modernised over the next ten years.

Transportation volumes within Germany will increase tremendously over the next few years simply to return to the 'normal' pattern of interaction, as its formerly separated parts grow together (Blum et al, 1990). Consequently, regional development in the five new provinces of Germany will depend heavily on the availability of an adequate transportation infrastructure. Furthermore, the transportation infrastructure of Germany will serve as a funnel attracting a large share of East–West transit traffic. Given its economic, and especially industrial, strength, interaction between Germany and its neighbours in the East will generate considerable additional transportation flows.

In this paper, I will deal with forecasts of passenger transportation flows in Germany for the year 2010. The analysis is based on data stemming from the year 1985. I assume in my optimistic scenario for the old German provinces an average annual economic growth rate of 3% to 4% a year. For the new provinces, this value will be much higher. Within the next ten years an economic miracle is expected to result in an average growth rate of up to 7% which will gradually decrease. Consequently, by the year 2000, the five new provinces will have attained 80% of the average German per-capita income which by then may be considered as a normal interregional variation.

I will describe in this chapter, first of all, the database used and address the problems arising from lack of data for Eastern Europe and the former GDR. In later sections I describe the models used in the forecasting process, and present and discuss the results.

2 Data particulars

2.1 The regional subdivision

The area of the former West Germany is subdivided into seventy-eight transportation regions and a seventy-ninth for West Berlin; they are common in all official transportation analyses.

These regions are aggregated from counties and, consequently, sufficient socioeconomic data are available for the analysis. In order to include the former GDR, its districts, of which fifteen existed until unification plus one for East Berlin, were used; at least some credible socioeconomic data could be obtained for these regions.

The remaining parts of Europe were included on the basis of sixteen regions in the analysis, and on the basis of forty-one regions in the forecasting process; in the latter case, subdivisions of those countries located close to Germany and building transportation corridors with it were used to include important border crossings.

2.2 The forecasting data

A transportation demand model was used as defined in Blum et al (1988). Initially, estimates for the period 1968–83 were generated and later recalculated for the years 1968–87. The data include variables on prices, income, infrastructure, economic activity, weather conditions, and aggregation, which are used to explain the demand for gasoline, the demand variable in the time-series analysis, which serves as a proxy for total transportation demand.

2.3 The distribution data

2.3.1 *Passenger flows for* 1985

For the year 1985 data on passenger transportation flows within Germany and between Germany and its neighbours were extracted from the regional subdivisions of Germany (78 + 1 regions) and the sixteen foreign neighbouring regions. Three modes (road, rail, air) and six trip purposes (work, education, shopping, business, vacation, leisure; for air transport only the last three) were used for the estimation process of the distribution model.

2.3.2 *Socioeconomic variables*

In order to estimate the distribution model, socioeconomic data had to be obtained that were also available for the Eastern countries. This implied that data on value added could not be used because of differing accounting rules combined with a lack of an appropriate spatial subdivision. Furthermore, incompatibilities in the price systems led to a rejection of all monetary variables. To avoid a structural break, only data on population and employment could be retained which were also available for the regional subdivisions.

We chose for our distribution model population, general employment, and employment in services as the major variables of attraction.

2.3.2 *Impedance data*

Using a shortest path algorithm based on the infrastructure network of the regions, impedance matrices were obtained. They include data on travel distance, travel length (in minutes), and travel costs (total and direct 'out-of-pocket' costs).

3 The forecasting model
3.1 The structure of the model and the estimation procedure
3.1.1 *The structure of the model*
The estimation of the model was performed in two steps:
(1) Transportation demand was derived, based on time-series data.
(2) The interregional distribution was generated from the regional distribution model.

There are three major reasons why forecasting was not performed within the framework of a single model:
(1) Data availability restricted the possibility of creating and estimating a single model that simultaneously allowed the forecasting and distribution of transportation flows.
(2) Even if data for Eastern Europe had been available, their use as a basis in an economic model would not have made sense and would have produced a structural break, as they reflected the situation in centrally administered economies; our time horizon, however, assumes that market economies will prevail.
(3) Elasticities of demand with respect to prices tend to be three to ten times higher for regional cross-sections than for time series. The results obtained from cross-sections reflect long-term structural relationships where adjustment processes have occurred, whereas those obtained from monthly time series relate to medium-term adaptation processes with considerable captivities and rigidities in modes and in transportation alternatives.

3.1.2 *The estimation procedure*
The formulation of the model is:

$$Y_t^{(\lambda_y)} = a_0 + \sum_{j=1}^{m} a_j v_{jt}^{(\lambda_j)} + u_t , \tag{1}$$

where Y_t is the endogenous variable of transportation demand, a_j are the coefficients of the explanatory variables, v_{jt}, λ_y, and λ_j are the transformation variables, and u_t is the stochastic term. The transformation is defined as

$$v_j^{\lambda_j} = \begin{cases} (v_j^{\lambda_j} - 1)/\lambda_j , & \text{if } \lambda_j \neq 0 , \\ \ln v_j , & \text{if } \lambda_j = 0 . \end{cases} \tag{2}$$

The linear case is obtained by setting λ_y and all λ_j to 1. Assuming a value of 0 for both yields the log model.

Often the error variance is not constant, especially once flexible forms are used which modify this variance. Therefore, it can be efficient to obtain homoskedastic results by applying a general error-term specification for heteroskedasticity (Gaudry, 1984; Gaudry and Dagenais, 1979):

$$u_t = \exp\left(\delta_o + \sum_{m=1}^{M} \delta_m Z_{mt}^{(\lambda_{zm})} \right)^{1/2} v_t . \tag{3}$$

Here, Z_m is the set of variables assumed to explain the heteroskedastic process; they are subject to Box–Cox transformations, defined in equation (2). If all δ_m except one are assumed to be 0 and the remaining one is set equal to 2 and $\lambda_z = 0$, then the classical univariate heteroskedasticity term is obtained as a special nested case of a more general formulation.

Autocorrelation of multiple orders may result from information in the endogenous variable not explained by the deterministic part of the demand function. The proper structures may be identified by means of Box–Jenkins techniques as well as a number of distinct orders to obtain white noise residuals, w_t.

$$v_t = \sum_{q=1}^{Q} \rho_q v_{t-q} + w_t. \tag{4}$$

3.2 Aggregate transportation demand

3.2.1 *Infrastructure and regional development*

The availability of infrastructure is a necessary, but not a sufficient, precondition for regional economic development. Its importance can be evaluated by estimating regional production functions that yield elasticities for road infrastructure of 0.1 to 0.3 depending on the type of road included (Blum, 1982; 1985). These values clearly are highest if the respective infrastructure category tends to become a bottleneck for regional production, as may soon be the case in the five new provinces of Germany. From a strategic planning approach, a supply-oriented infrastructure policy that makes decisions on where to invest, dependent on regional production potentials stemming from certain factor availabilities and locational factors seems most appropriate. However, this model predicts traffic volumes that will restrict local, provincial, and federal governments to a bottleneck-oriented policy.

Because of these considerations, we used a 'full' demand model in which gasoline consumption is explained by factors that relate to the supply side (infrastructure, regulations, etc) as well as to the demand side.

3.2.2 *Description of variables and their impact*

The list of explanatory variables contains seven major groups; these are listed below together with their code names.

Prices

Two price variables are used: the real price of gasoline (RBNS)—we expect a negative sign; the real price of other transportation modes (RPATM), excluding air transportation—we expect a positive sign because of a substitutive relationship.

Motor vehicles

The number of vehicles and their efficiency with respect to fuel consumption are relevant. Given the level of economic activities (see below) and the fuel consumption rate of vehicles, the stock of cars using gasoline (PKWB) reflects changes in the modal split. Consequently, its elasticities should be positive. The consumption rate of the stock of cars (SEVPKWB, in litres km^{-1}) should have a positive impact on gasoline demand.

Infrastructure

Six variables are used to represent the infrastructure; three relate to the regulatory environment, two others define the quantity and quality of the road infrastructure, and the last reflects the competition with the public transit sector. Speed limits on state roads (but not on motorways) were introduced in 1972 and have been in effect since then. This variable (HHG), as well as further restrictions on state roads and motorways in 1973–1974 (NHG7374), and automobile-free Sundays in 1973 (SFV73), are expected to reduce the demand for gasoline. The length of streets (SL) is used as a quantitative indicator of the road infrastructure, whereas the share of motorways (*Autobahn*) to total street length (AASL) is a measure for road quality. The expected signs of both are ambiguous: a positive sign for SL could be attributed to high distances between activities, a negative to congestion effects; a positive sign for AASL would be a sign for an above average usage of motorways for travelling, whereas a negative sign would suggest a qualitative effect. The service intervals of the public transportation sector (BT) are an indicator of its quality; an increase of service intervals, and, consequently, a decrease in the quality of services provided, is expected to make private transportation more attractive.

Weather

Weather conditions influence fuel consumption. Good weather conditions should increase gasoline demand because of additional driving for leisure and recreational purposes; bad weather had no clear-cut impact on fuel demand, as it may be argued that people either drive less (because they reduce driving to a minimum) or drive more (because they do not want to get wet or cold). Three variables encompassing the weather conditions in Frankfurt ["too warm in Frankfurt" (ZWF), "too cold in Frankfurt" (ZKF), and a variable for the share of rainy days (RFPT)] were used as indicators for the nation as a whole.

Income

Real disposable income (RVEKP) is expected to have a positive impact on gasoline consumption.

Activities

Different variables were selected to describe intermediate and final economic activities which generate travelling and increase fuel consumption: the number of employees (E), which should have a positive effect on gasoline consumption; real retail sales (REUNB), which should increase gasoline demand; total overnight stays (UENG), an indicator for economic activity in services (exhibitions, congresses, etc), which should have a positive sign; long-distance transportation with trucks (in metric tonnes, FVLKW), an indicator of industrial activities, which should be positive. We added the weekly work-hours (TGA) to our initial model specification covering the period from 1968 to 1983 as we wanted to test the effect of time budgets on transportation demand. According to the time-budget argument, the impact of TGA should be negative, as a reduced work time should free additional time for other activities.

Other variables

The last category includes fuel tax changes and aggregation variables that account for the heterogeneity of months. The anticipation of real tax increases (RSEA) and the lagged anticipation of real tax increases (RSEAV) are indicators for rational consumer behaviour: tax increases in Germany are discussed in parliament and are therefore known beforehand. Thus the elasticity of the tax increase anticipation should be positive, and the elasticity of the lagged tax increase anticipation should be negative. The number of workdays (AT), Saturdays (ST), as well as Sundays and holidays (SF) are included as aggregation variables. Their multiple role as normalisation and implicit activity variables makes their expected coefficients ambiguous and without particular significance.

3.2.2 Results

The results displayed in column (5) of table A1 in the appendix and summarised in table 1 show that nearly all elasticity coefficients have the expected signs. The estimated price elasticity is -0.217 and the cross-elasticity with respect to the price of mass transit is 0.331: the first result is somewhat lower than that found in our previous analysis on Germany for 1968–83 that is listed in column 6 of table A1 as a matter of record.

The elasticity of the stock of cars (PKWB) is 0.075 and rather low, showing that for a given consumption rate and a given level of activities, a rise in the stock of cars has only a low impact on fuel demand because of specialisation effects. The elasticity of the cars' consumption rate (SEVPKWB) is 0.761. If fuel efficiency were improved by 1%, fuel consumption would decrease by less than 1%, as car users partly compensate for this effect through more driving.

As can be expected, road infrastructure—quantity and quality—plays an important role. Compared with our earlier analysis, we find a change in sign that we interpret as evidence for increased congestion: formerly the high elasticity of the length of streets, which also played a role as trend variable, was consistent both with the high elasticities found in trip-distribution models and the high interaction costs of increased distances among economic activities. Given the enormous increase in congestion in recent years, the addition of roads reduces fuel demand which explains the negative elasticity of -0.487 for SL and the increased importance of high-speed motorway links (elasticity of AASL is 0.550). Speed limits during or after the oil crisis (HHG), speed limits on motorways in 1973–74 (NHG7374), and Sundays without driving (SFV73) reduced gasoline consumption by 3.3%, 6.7%, and 2.5%. Longer service intervals of public transit (BT) have only a small negative influence on gasoline consumption (-0.112), which is difficult to explain and a different result than that found in our previous model.

Weather conditions show a small impact on gasoline consumption, which may be increased in times of good weather and reduced in times of bad weather.

Table 1. Demand for gasoline in Germany (January 1968–December 1987): elasticities of the final model (table A1, column 5).

Variable	Elasticity
Prices	
Real price of gasoline (RBPNS)	−0.217
Price of other transportation (RPATM)	0.331
Motor vehicle	
Total stock of cars using gasoline (PKWB)	0.075
Consumption rate of stock of cars (SEVPKWB)	0.761
Infrastructure	
Motorway length road share (AASL)	0.550
Public transit service intervals (BT)	−0.112
Lower speed limit 1972 and since 1974 (HHG)	−0.033
Lower speed limit 1973–74 (NHG7374)	−0.067
Sundays without driving (SFV73)	−0.025
Total road network length (SL)	−0.487
Weather	
Rainy days in Frankfurt per day (RFPT)	−0.015
Too cold in Frankfurt (ZFK)	−0.029
Too warm in Frankfurt (ZWF)	0.001
Income	
Real disposable income per capita (RVEKP)	−0.302
Activities	
Employees (E)	1.177
Long-distance truck transportation (FVLKW)	0.228
Real retail sales food and clothing (REUNB)	0.267
Total overnight stays (UENG)	0.044
Daily work hours per week (TGA)	−0.208
Other variables	
Workdays (AT)	0.347
Real tax anticipation increase (RSEA)	0.005
Real tax anticipation increase, lagged (RSEAV)	−0.021
Sundays and holidays (SF)	0.083
Saturdays (ST)	−0.057
Transformation	
$\lambda(Y)$	0.820
$\lambda(X)$	1.252
Autocorrelation	
ρ_1	0.203
ρ_{12}	0.456
R^2	0.966

A negative value of −0.302 for the income (RVEKP) elasticity is surprising, as it contrasts with our earlier results given in column 6; the latter, however, was already considerably lower than values given by other studies. We conclude that, in recent years, the relative constancy of the per-capita income in Germany related to an increased labour demand reflected in the employment variable is responsible. If we add the elasticities of the variables of economic activity to the elasticity of income, the total is 1.414 compared with 1.252 in our old study, which is about the value found by others in much smaller models. If the elasticity of employment is excluded, the sums fall to 0.237 and 0.766, respectively. We conclude that the influence of economic activities on travel demand has fallen considerably.

It is quite plausible to have a high elasticity of employment; the value above 1 which is double that found earlier (and double that given by the previous experiments in columns 1 to 4 of the appendix table that do not account for autocorrelation) seems to relate to special conditions pertaining to the period added to our sample. The values of 0.267 and 0.228 for retail sales (REUNB) and long-distance transportation with trucks (FVLKW) show the importance of intermediate activities for gasoline consumption, whereas the amount of overnight stays (UENG) is less important (0.044).

From the elasticities computed for the tax increase anticipation variables we must conclude that consumers are rational and buy less gasoline just after, and sometimes more gasoline just before a tax increase.

In order to forecast future changes in the demand for transportation we assumed the following changes in certain variables for 2010, compared with 1985 (variables not listed were assumed to remain constant):
gasoline price (RPBNS): +85%
price of other transport modes (RPATM): +30%,
activities (RVEKP + FVLKW + REUNB + UENG): +150%
weekly work hours (TGA): −10%.
These assumptions imply an increase in the level of gasoline prices above the level presently experienced, complemented by a rise in the price of public transit, which usually follows the rise in the price of gasoline in a deficit-reducing policy. Activities from which transportation demand is derived increase by 150% according to our optimistic scenario, but allow a decrease in work time of 10%.

We estimated a model that relates car expenditures to income and found an elasticity of 0.555 which allowed us to make a forecast on the development of the stock of cars, assuming that half of the expenditures relate to improvements in the quality of cars and half to the purchase of new cars: stock of cars (PKWB): +40%.

From these data, the demand for passenger road transportation in the area of West Germany over the next 25 years (1985–2010) is estimated to increase by 52%.

We derived the demand for passenger railroad transportation by assuming that the share of this mode would decrease from 7.4% to 6.5% in regard to flows and from 10% to 9% in regard to passenger kilometers (pkm); consequently, railroad transportation flows over distances covered would increase by 35% from 1985 to 2010.

By analogy, using a gravity model, the underlying total transport demand was expanded to East Germany: to obtain a consistent estimation, this approach seemed superior compared with others that base their transportation forecasts for East Germany on highly unreliable present data.

3.3 Spatial distribution

3.3.1 *The gravity model*

Because of the lack of data, we used the following simple gravity model for our analysis:

$$t_{ij}^{(\lambda_t)} = a_0 + a_1 L_i^{(\lambda_1)} + a_2 L_j^{(\lambda_2)} + a_3 s_{ij}^{(\lambda_3)} + u_{ij}, \tag{5}$$

where t_{ij} are the flows from i to j, L_i and L_j are the socioeconomic variables of attraction from the origin and the destination, and s_{ij} is the impedance. We specified impedance and socioeconomic variables according to the related trip purpose (table 2); the elasticities estimated later relate to the effect of a 1% change in trip costs or trip time on the number of trips per year. We did not include infrastructure variables in our flow distribution model so as not to prejudice future flows by having to give exact forecasts of future networks, these operate through time and cost variables. We did not estimate vacation trips, as most of the flows go to foreign countries.

We performed a careful analysis of the data set for leisure trips, using road or rail, where the matrix was full and contained above its diagonal 3003 observations ($78 \times 77/2$; we excluded West Berlin). As our TRIO algorithm only allowed a maximum of 1500 observations, we had to split the data set in half and drop the last three observations, which, however, did not produce a structural break.

We discovered that the elasticities of the socioeconomic variables approach the value 1, with that of the destination variable slightly higher than that of the origin. This asymmetry is supported by the transformation

Table 2. Trip purpose and related variables.

Trip purpose	Socioeconomic variables (L_i, L_j)	Impedance (s_{ij})
Work	employees	out-of-pocket costs
Education	population	out-of-pocket costs
Shopping	population	out-of-pocket costs
Business	employment in services	trip time
Leisure	population	out-of-pocket costs

variables which, if they are allowed to choose their optimal values, leave a small difference that is, however, statistically insignificant. Heteroskedasticity of the general form could be detected at the 10% level, which, however, turned to an exponential form in the two variables, L_i and L_j. Asymmetry is the consequence of using pooled travel data. For instance, trips that originate in A and end in B and return to A are pooled with those that originate in B and end in A and return to B. Of course we know that even within a class of trip purposes, the respective motivations may be very different.

Consequently, we reduced our model to the classic multiplicative gravitation approach, with unit elasticities for L_i and L_j. We found the following results, given in table 3. The results state that the elasticities increase with trip purposes of a shorter distance. It is interesting to note that this outcome contrasts with the intuitive understanding of the elasticity formula as, for a given partial derivative, higher distances and smaller flows should create higher elasticities. We do not find this result here if we compare short-distance and long-distance transportation flows within Germany as well as trips inside or outside Germany. We explain this with the variables of attractiveness through which the flows are divided (and thus normalised) and the fall of the partial derivatives over distance.

Table 3. Estimates of regional trip distribution in Germany, 1985.

Purpose	Road			Rail		
	elasticity	R	number of observations	elasticity	R	number of observations
Trips inside Germany						
Work	−2.9	0.60	616	−3.6	0.62	505
Education	−3.1	0.58	588	−3.4	0.63	506
Shopping	−3.7	0.64	611	−3.9	0.63	478
Business	−3.0	0.85	2987	−1.3	0.65	3001
Leisure	−2.2	0.79	3003	−1.2	0.67	3003
Maximum			3003			3003
Trips outside Germany						
Business	−2.3	0.60	864	−1.9	0.52	1082
Leisure	−2.6	0.58	894	−1.3	0.38	1091
Maximum			1248			1248

3.3.2 Correction for attractiveness
Because of the necessary simplicity of the gravity model employed here, we were not able to capture effects of special attractiveness beyond our variables L_i and L_j. However, we wanted to include those unexplained differences in our forecast. Consequently, we have used the estimation error found for the West German estimation to construct a correction

factor for attractiveness in the following way. Let

$$a_{ij} = \frac{t_{ij}}{\hat{t}_{ij}}, \qquad i = 1, ..., 78; \quad j = 1, ..., 78; \quad i \neq j. \tag{6}$$

If all rows and columns of a_{ij} for West Germany are summed, we obtain

$$\hat{a}_i = \sum_{j=1}^{78} \hat{a}_{ij}, \qquad i = 1, ..., 78,$$

$$\hat{a}_j = \sum_{i=1}^{78} \hat{a}_{ij}, \qquad j = 1, ..., 78, \tag{6a}$$

$$\hat{a}_i = \hat{a}_j,$$

$$\hat{a} = \sum_{i=1}^{78} a_i.$$

For each transportation region in the new provinces, we selected a comparable region in West Germany. A correction factor, c_i (or c_j), was established to correct for differences in population size (this factor represents the share of population of the Eastern region with respect to the reference region).

The estimates of the flows were corrected by

$$t_{ij}^{*2010} = \hat{t}_{ij}^{2010} \hat{a}_{ij}; \qquad i = 1, ..., 78; \quad j = 1, ..., 78; \quad i \neq j. \tag{7}$$

For the first seventy-eight provinces, the values of the weights are defined by formula 6; for all other provinces, we used the following formula to define the weights:

$$\hat{a}_{ij} = \frac{\hat{a}_i \hat{a}_j}{\hat{a}} c_i c_j, \qquad i = 1, ..., 94; \quad j = 79, ..., 94; \quad i \neq j. \tag{8}$$

In the case of $i = 1, ..., 78$, the c_i are 1.

4 Results

In *West* Germany long-distance railroad passenger flows will increase from 188 million trips or 30 billion pkm in 1985 (71% of total rail passenger transport in pkm) to 254 million trips ($+35\%$) or 38 billion pkm ($+31\%$) in 2010. Long-distance road passenger flows will increase from 2.3 billion trips or 242 billion pkm in 1985 (50% of total road passenger transport in pkm) to 3.5 billion trips ($+52\%$) or 336 billion pkm ($+39\%$). The values of the *united* Germany in 2010 are 433 million trips or 78 billion pkm for railroad and 5 billion trips or 651 billion pkm for roads.

Total long-distance traffic that originates in, ends in, or transits through Germany will amount to 483 million trips on railroads and 5.8 billion trips on roads.

It follows that the average travel distances in *West* Germany will fall (railroad: 158 km to 152 km; road: 104 km to 96 km); for the *united*

Germany, however, average travel distances will rise because of the increase size of the country and the redirection of transportation flows from intervening opportunities (railroad: 180 km; road: 130 km).

By dividing Germany into three macroregions, we were able to get an idea of the flow distribution; the following delimitations were used:

South Germany: Bavaria, Baden-Württemberg;

North Germany: Hesse, Rhineland-Palatinate, Saarland, Northrhine-Westphalia, Lower Saxony, Hamburg, Bremen, Schleswig-Holstein;

East Germany: Mecklenburg-Vorpommern, Brandenburg, Berlin, Saxony-Anhalt, Saxony, Thuringia.

Figure 1 shows the results, excluding data on transit, outgoing and incoming transportation flows. If they are included, the transportation flows in 2010 increase from 433 million trips to 471 million trips for the railroad and from 5 billion trips to 5.7 billion trips for the road.

We observe, for instance, that railroad passenger flows between the East and the West will increase from 6 million trips in 1985 to 43 million trips in 2010. The exchange with the North (28 million trips) is channelled

Figure 1. Distribution of transport flows in Germany, 2010 (million passenger trips per year).

through three railway corridors: Berlin – Frankfurt, Berlin – Hannover (–Köln) and Berlin – Hamburg. This estimated demand is sufficiently high to provide high-speed services on each of these routes. The same can be applied to the East – South exchange which basically favours the Berlin – München corridor with its two alternative paths: one is located more towards the East (via Regensburg) and the other more towards the Centre (via Nürnberg).

Concerning road traffic, a demand will arise for which—as in the case of railroads—infrastructure is not available, and, therefore, enormous additional investments will have to be made.

We were not able to include the complete matrices of flows in this paper; however, for a given subset of regions that are of special concern to us, we will provide more detailed information: Northern Bavaria is especially affected by the opening of the Iron Curtain and is expected to

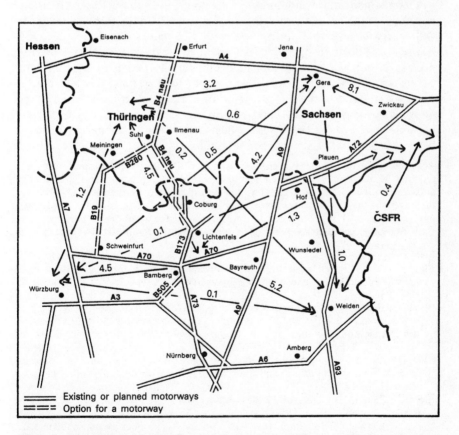

Figure 2. Distribution of long-distance road transport flows in Northern Bavaria, Southern Thuringia, and Southern Saxony. All data are in millions of passenger trips per year in 2010. The total flow in the corridor is 48 000 000 passenger trips.

establish strong economic relations with Southern Thuringia and Southern Saxony. The existing motorways that provide links to the North—the A9 in the East and the A7 in the West do not have sufficient capacity to handle the predicted flows and are too far apart to be able to take traffic from the more central regions, a developing axis from Nuremberg via Bamberg and Coburg to Erfurt. Consequently, we have proposed adding a motorway based on existing four-lane highways. The traffic flows in this corridor are shown in figure 2.

5 Conclusions
By using a two-level model, we were able to forecast and regionally distribute traffic flows, even though reliable economic and transportation data for the Eastern counties are not available. Our forecasts provide evidence for a tremendous growth in transportation flows, mainly caused by German unification and improved economic links to the East. The transportation volumes that cross the former Iron Curtain through Germany will increase sevenfold, compared with the values for the year 1985. Enormous efforts to provide an adequate infrastructure will become necessary, but will not be able to overcome short-term or medium-term bottlenecks. If new motorway links are not built in time, this will burden regions that suffer from congestion on their road network and hinder their future development. This may particularly affect regions on the former border between East and West, which instead of being peripheral have become central to the current economic changes.

Acknowledgements. The research in this paper was indirectly supported by the German Ministry of Transportation and the FCAR programme of Québec. The author is indebted to Marc Gaudry, Jan Kowalski, and Werner Rothengatter for their great help in discussing this project. The data set of the demand model was put together by Ulrike Schäfer, the respective estimations were performed by Catherine Laplante; their cooperation in this project is gratefully acknowledged.

References
Blum U, 1982, "Effects of transportation investments on regional growth: a theoretical and empirical investigation" *Papers of the Regional Science Association* **49** 169–184
Blum U, 1985, "The development and the effects of transportation investments in West Germany, 1960–1980", in *Transport Sector Investments 1960–1980: Analysis and Implications for the Future (Round Table 66)* (European Conference of Ministers of Transport, Paris) pp 37–66
Blum U, Foos G, Gaudry M J I, 1988 "Aggregate time series transport demand models: survey of literature and new evidence for West Germany" *Transportation Research A* **22A** 75–88
Blum U, Hautzinger H, Kessel P, Kowalski J, Kienzler H-P, Künzle K, Röhling W, Rothengatter W, Selz T, 1990, "Szenario zur Verkehrsentwicklung mit der DDR und dem Osten", Gutachten Nr. 98105/90 im Auftrag des Bundesministers für Verkehr, Institut für Wirtschaftspolitik und Wirtschaftsforschung/Kessel und Partner, Karlsruhe und Freiburg

Dagenais M G, Gaudry M J I, Liem T C, 1987, "Urban travel demand: the impact of Box–Cox-transformations with nonspherical residual errors" *Transportation Research B* **21B** 443–477

Gaudry M J I, 1984, "DRAG, un modèle de la demande routière, des accidents et de leur gravité appliqué au Québec de 1956 à 1982", Centre de Recherche sur les Transports, University of Montréal, Montréal, Québec

Gaudry M J I, Dagenais M G, 1979, "Heteroskedasticity and the use of Box–Cox transformations" *Economic Letters* **2** 225–229

Liem T C, Dagenais M M, Gaudry M J I, 1987, "L-1.2: A program for Box–Cox-transformations in regression models with heteroscedastic and autoregressive residuals", publication 510, Centre de Recherche sur les Transports, University of Montréal, Montréal, Québec

APPENDIX

Table A1 presents results for the final model. This table presents the elasticities of the expected value of the dependent variable, computed at the mean values of the positive observations of each independent variable. For a dummy variable, the percentage change of the estimated dependent variable caused by the presence of that dummy variable is defined as its elasticity (Dagenais et al, 1987). The full results give partial derivatives, and t-statistics in parentheses, which are conditional upon the optimal value of the Box–Cox parameters. The indications LAM under the t-statistics show the Box–Cox transformation that has been applied to this variable; the numbers, for example LAM 1, indicate the group of variables which were subject to a common transformation.

The optimal values for autocorrelation and functional forms, as well as R^2 and the values of the log-likelihood are given at the foot of the column.

The results and the tables were generated with the L-1.2 algorithms (Liem et al, 1987) used in the TRIO program package.

Columns (1) and (2) of the table show the reference models with a linear and a log–linear specification, respectively. In a third model (3), one Box–Cox was used for all variables of the model. With respect to the values of the log-likelihood function, this model is superior to those estimated in columns (1) and (2), as a change of one degree of freedom involves an increase in the log-likelihood function of more than 2 points. In a fourth model, one Box–Cox transformation was used on the dependent variable and another on the explanatory variables. Although the model given in column (4) did not dominate that of column (3), it was retained as the correction for autocorrelation in column (5) yielded a dominant model, essentially white noise residuals and a considerable spread of the transformation parameters: tests for heteroskedasticity did not yield a statistically significant gain in the log-likelihood function.

Table A1. Demand for gasoline in Germany (January 1968–December 1987).

	Variant and version					
	bvt1					bvs1
	1	2	3	4	5	6
	Elasticity Partial derivative (Conditional t-statistic)					
Prices						
RBPNS	−0.213	−0.222	−0.219	−0.217	−0.217	−0.278
	-0.32×10^6	-0.34×10^6	-0.33×10^6	-0.33×10^6	-0.33×10^6	-0.42×10^6
	(−5.07)	(−5.48)	(−5.09)	(−5.04)	(−6.00)	(−5.10)
	LAM 1	LAM 1	LAM 1	LAM 1	LAM 1	LAM 1
RPATM	0.202	0.129	0.169	0.154	0.331	0.407
	0.29×10^6	0.19×10^6	0.25×10^6	0.22×10^6	0.48×10^6	0.59×10^6
	(1.87)	(1.13)	(1.70)	(1.57)	(2.62)	(1.70)
	LAM 1	LAM 1	LAM 1	LAM 1	LAM 1	LAM 1
Motor vehicle						
PKWB	0.695	0.623	0.643	0.657	0.075	0.138
	0.64×10^{-1}	0.58×10^{-1}	0.59×10^{-1}	0.60×10^{-1}	0.69×10^{-2}	0.13×10^{-1}
	(2.06)	(2.20)	(2.10)	(2.10)	(0.22)	(0.38)
	LAM 1	LAM 1	LAM 1	LAM 1	LAM 1	LAM 1
SEVPKWB	0.486	0.383	0.439	0.452	0.761	0.668
	0.76×10^5	0.61×10^5	0.69×10^5	0.71×10^5	0.12×10^6	0.10×10^6
	(3.64)	(3.88)	(3.88)	(3.82)	(4.76)	(2.78)
	LAM 1	LAM 1	LAM 1	LAM 1	LAM 1	LAM 1
Infrastructure						
AASL	−0.008	0.248	0.118	0.102	0.550	−0.178
	-0.38×10^6	0.12×10^8	0.55×10^7	0.47×10^7	0.25×10^8	-0.81×10^7
	(−0.02)	(0.52)	(0.24)	(0.21)	(1.22)	(−0.32)
	LAM 1	LAM 1	LAM 1	LAM 1	LAM 1	LAM 1
BT	0.015	−0.014	0.004	0.028	−0.112	0.037
	0.36×10^3	-0.33×10^3	0.84×10^2	0.64×10^3	-0.26×10^4	0.86×10^3
	(0.24)	(−0.27)	(0.07)	(0.49)	(−1.50)	(0.50)
	LAM 1	LAM 1	LAM 1	LAM 1	LAM 1	LAM 1
HHG	−0.038	−0.048	−0.042	−0.041	−0.033	−0.021
	-0.64×10^5	-0.81×10^5	-0.71×10^5	-0.70×10^5	-0.55×10^5	-0.36×10^5
	(−2.13)	(−2.60)	(−2.40)	(−2.33)	(−1.45)	(−0.97)
NHG7374	−0.095	−0.122	−0.107	−0.109	−0.067	−0.059
	-0.16×10^6	-0.21×10^6	-0.18×10^6	-0.18×10^6	-0.11×10^6	-0.99×10^5
	(−3.51)	(−4.40)	(−4.18)	(−4.31)	(−2.30)	(−2.07)
SFV73	−0.011	−0.009	−0.009	−0.008	−0.025	−0.025
	-0.89×10^4	-0.73×10^4	-0.76×10^4	-0.66×10^4	-0.21×10^5	-0.21×10^5
	(−0.38)	(−0.32)	(−0.24)	(−0.21)	(−0.92)	(−0.97)
SL	1.000	0.500	0.802	1.033	−0.487	3.282
	1.00×10^1	0.50×10^1	0.80×10^1	0.10×10^2	-0.48×10^1	0.32×10^2
	(0.68)	(0.30)	(0.51)	(0.68)	(−0.30)	(1.86)
	LAM 1	LAM 1	LAM 1	LAM 1	LAM 1	LAM 1
Weather						
RFPT	−0.018	−0.013	−0.017	−0.019	−0.015	−0.013
	-0.10×10^6	-0.72×10^5	-0.96×10^5	-0.11×10^6	-0.87×10^5	-0.73×10^5
	(−3.19)	(−2.79)	(−3.05)	(−3.26)	(−3.49)	(−2.87)
	LAM 1	LAM 1	LAM 1	LAM 1	LAM 1	LAM 1
ZKF	−0.042	−0.033	−0.039	−0.042	−0.029	−0.043
	-0.78×10^4	-0.63×10^4	-0.73×10^4	-0.79×10^4	-0.54×10^4	-0.80×10^4
	(−4.22)	(−3.23)	(−3.64)	(−4.04)	(−2.76)	(−3.95)

Table A1 (continued)

	Variant and version					
	bvt1					bvs1
	1	2	3	4	5	6
Weather (continued)						
ZWF	0.002	0.003	0.002	0.002	0.001	0.002
	0.47×10^4	0.76×10^4	0.58×10^4	0.52×10^4	0.26×10^4	0.59×10^4
	(0.99)	(1.64)	(1.05)	(0.93)	(0.44)	(0.82)
Income						
RVEPK	−0.505	−0.710	−0.589	−0.568	−0.302	0.275
	-0.12×10^4	-0.17×10^4	-0.14×10^4	-0.14×10^4	-0.73×10^3	0.67×10^3
	(−2.34)	(−2.99)	(−2.45)	−(2.41)	(−1.54)	(1.01)
	LAM 1	LAM 1	LAM 1	LAM 1	LAM 1	LAM 1
Activities						
E	0.395	0.582	0.503	0.428	1.177	0.486
	0.26×10^{-1}	0.38×10^{-1}	0.33×10^{-1}	0.28×10^{-1}	0.76×10^{-1}	0.31×10^{-1}
	(0.71)	(1.19)	(0.94)	(0.79)	(2.01)	(0.82)
	LAM 1	LAM 1	LAM 1	LAM 1	LAM 1	LAM 1
FVLKW	0.267	0.264	0.267	0.262	0.228	0.243
	0.22×10^{-1}	0.22×10^{-1}	0.22×10^{-1}	0.22×10^{-1}	0.19×10^{-1}	0.20×10^{-1}
	(7.50)	(6.63)	(6.35)	(6.47)	(5.58)	(5.88)
	LAM 1	LAM 1	LAM 1	LAM 1	LAM 1	LAM 1
REUNB	0.240	0.292	0.260	0.254	0.267	0.231
	0.36×10^6	0.45×10^6	0.40×10^6	0.39×10^6	0.40×10^6	0.35×10^6
	(9.44)	(10.92)	(11.04)	(10.93)	(8.98)	(8.80)
	LAM 1	LAM 1	LAM 1	LAM 1	LAM 1	LAM 1
UENG	0.021	0.038	0.027	0.022	0.044	0.017
	0.19×10^{-2}	0.36×10^{-2}	0.25×10^{-2}	0.21×10^{-2}	0.41×10^{-2}	0.16×10^{-2}
	(1.45)	(2.46)	(1.63)	(1.41)	(2.38)	(1.26)
	LAM 1	LAM 1	LAM 1	LAM 1	LAM 1	LAM 1
TGA	−0.670	−0.770	−0.742	−0.774	−0.208	
	-0.28×10^5	-0.32×10^5	-0.31×10^5	-0.32×10^5	-0.86×10^4	
	(−1.29)	(−1.58)	(−1.60)	(−1.67)	(−0.47)	
	LAM 1	LAM 1	LAM 1	LAM 1	LAM 1	
Other variables						
AT	0.334	0.230	0.293	0.311	0.347	0.382
	0.27×10^5	0.19×10^5	0.24×10^5	0.25×10^5	0.28×10^5	0.31×10^5
	(4.43)	(3.08)	(3.64)	(3.90)	(3.58)	(4.34)
	LAM 1	LAM 1	LAM 1	LAM 1	LAM 1	LAM 1
RSEA	0.020	0.015	0.017	0.018	0.005	0.004
	0.76×10^6	0.57×10^6	0.65×10^6	0.67×10^6	0.20×10^6	0.15×10^6
	(0.97)	(0.74)	(0.66)	(0.65)	(0.17)	(0.10)
RSEAV	−0.023	−0.022	−0.022	−0.022	−0.021	−0.024
	-0.88×10^6	-0.83×10^6	-0.85×10^6	-0.85×10^6	-0.81×10^6	-0.91×10^6
	(−1.11)	(−1.07)	(−0.61)	(−0.61)	(−1.31)	(−1.14)
SF	0.096	0.070	0.087	0.091	0.083	0.087
	0.31×10^5	0.23×10^5	0.28×10^5	0.29×10^5	0.26×10^5	0.28×10^5
	(4.19)	(3.05)	(3.80)	(3.99)	(3.09)	(3.58)
	LAM 1	LAM 1	LAM 1	LAM 1	LAM 1	LAM 1
ST	−0.065	−0.084	−0.072	−0.069	−0.057	−0.065
	-0.25×10^5	-0.33×10^5	-0.28×10^5	-0.27×10^5	-0.22×10^5	-0.25×10^5
	(−2.72)	(−3.42)	(−2.89)	(−2.79)	(−2.28)	(−2.57)
	LAM 1	LAM 1	LAM 1	LAM 1	LAM 1	LAM 1

Table A1 (continued)

	Variant and version					
	bvt1					bvs1
	1	2	3	4	5	6
Regression constant						
	−1.251	−10.319	0.039	0.729	27.198	−53.882
	-0.21×10^7	-0.18×10^8	0.66×10^5	0.12×10^7	0.46×10^8	-0.90×10^8
	(−0.09)	(−0.55)	(0.01)	(0.09)	(1.19)	(−0.33)

Box – Cox transformations: (t-statistics $= 0$)/(t-statistics $= 1$)
      Parameter
      Conditional t-statistic (t-statistic $= 0$)
               (t-statistic $= 1$)

$\lambda(Y)$, BV	1.000	0.000	0.551	0.577	0.820	0.742
	fixed	fixed	(1.98)	(2.09)	(2.60)	(2.22)
			(−1.62)	(−1.53)	(−0.57)	(−0.77)
$\lambda(X)$	1.000	0.000	0.551	0.738	1.252	1.914
	fixed	fixed	(1.98)	(1.91)	(3.21)	(3.82)
			(−1.62)	(−0.68)	(0.65)	(1.82)

Autocorrelation
Order 1, ρ_1

					0.203	0.226
					(2.80)	(2.44)

Order 12, ρ_{12}

					0.456	0.364
					(6.23)	(3.99)

General statistics
Log-likelihood

	−2797.467	−2798.494	−2795.415	−2795.282	−2776.113	−2181.584

Pseudo-R^2: E adjusted for degrees of freedom

	0.960	0.959	0.960	0.959	0.966	0.965

Number of observations

	227	227	227	227	227	179

A New Airport for Firenze? A Demand and Supply Analysis

S Casini Benvenuti, G Maltinti
IRPET, Firenze

1 Introduction

In this chapter we examine the economic viability of a new airport in the central area of Tuscany (in particular the metropolitan area of Firenze) and its economic effects. The need for this infrastructure derives from the high mobility that arises in this part of the region, strongly affected as it is not only by tourist flows but also by business travel. The lack of airport capacity is, therefore, seen as acting as a constraint on regional economic development. At present there are two main airports in Tuscany, but only the airport of Pisa (S Giusto), 80 km away from Firenze, is of national and international importance. In 1989 this airport was used by about 1 million passengers whereas the most densely populated area of Tuscany—the central area—is served only by a small airport (Peretola) close to Firenze (6 km away from the inner city) that does not have the capacity to cope with air travel demand in this area.

There are three different solutions to the problem of an airport for this central area of Tuscany:
(1) the expansion of the airport of Pisa in conjunction with the improvement of the rail link with Firenze;
(2) the expansion of the present airport of Firenze;
(3) the construction of a new airport close to Firenze.

No single one of these solutions seems a priori to be the best. Perhaps the first one is the cheapest, but then Pisa airport is too far from Firenze. The second one is not completely satisfactory because geographical and environmental reasons would permit only a limited expansion of the present site. The third one would be more appropriate as far as solving the environmental and geographical problems is concerned, but would perhaps be the most expensive.

The evaluation of the three possible solutions has been carried out by means of the construction of a model for air travel demand, and by the application of a multicriteria analysis and a traditional cost–benefit analysis. In this analysis the level of air travel demand can be taken as indicative of the level of economic activity. The role which the capacity of infrastructure plays is assessed by comparing potential demand with that demand satisfied under each of the alternative investment scenarios.

2 Transport and regional development in Tuscany

The industrial structure of Tuscany is the result, on the one hand, of its historical roots in regional handicrafts, and on the other, of political choices made after the Second World War. Most postwar reconstruction investment (particularly in transport infrastructure) was, in fact, concentrated in Northwestern Italy, where there was heavy industry.

Tuscany, on the other hand, had to rely on the handicraft industry. Rapid export-demand growth, met by low-wage labour moving from the rural areas, led to rapid industrial expansion in the footwear, leather goods, clothing, and furniture sectors. Tuscany was able to take advantage of increasing international demand, to the extent of providing between 8% and 9% of total Italian exports.

The network of small plants has a high ratio of labour to capital and the productive process is fragmented. The development of light industry, which still forms the core of industrialisation in Tuscany, continued in this manner until the early 1980s.

During the last decade most of the advantages of the industrial district, based on small flexible firms in traditional industries, have been diminishing; big industries have regained flexibility by means of technological innovations and, at the same time, the traditional linkages to the market have become more and more inadequate. In particular, the weakness of those stages of production before and after the physical production of the goods seemed to be the crucial problem in this area. Research, planning, and design, on the one hand, and market and financial strategies, on the other, have not evolved enough to cope with the needs of light industries.

These functions are usually located in urban areas, but Firenze, even though it is the most important service centre of Tuscany, has always had a very limited role in this field of activities, as can be seen in comparison with other Italian metropolitan areas, increasing its dependence on other cities and hence its need for transport to support the local economy. Nevertheless, Firenze, with its surrounding area, is at the same time the main industrial pole of Tuscany and the commercial and cultural core of the region, even if, in this case, the Florentine economy has some evident weakness. In addition, Firenze is also one of the greatest tourist attractions in Italy.

Thus Firenze is a city with a very high standard of living: in terms of per-capita income Firenze is in the top ten towns of Italy and, as a consequence, the Florentines themselves spend a lot of time and money on tourism.

Transport demand is high because of high mobility for business, both departing from and arriving in Firenze, and tourism, mainly entering Firenze but also departing from Firenze (the latter is increasing rapidly), as table 1 demonstrates by comparison with other Italian towns.

Faced with this high and increasing transport demand, largely concentrated in the inner city of Firenze, the existing infrastructure is inadequate. The need to solve this problem is evident and requires a lot of different initiatives, some of which have already been planned: for example the creation of a new service centre on the outskirts of Firenze and substantial investment in different transport projects (highways, railways, the light metro, the airport).

In this context the problem of a new airport is crucial for the role that Firenze has, and could have, as a service pole for the Tuscan economic system. The present Firenze airport is in fact very small, and is completely inadequate for air travel demand in central Tuscany. But even if we take into account all the airports in Tuscany, the shortfall in supply for

Table 1. Mobility in the main Italian provinces: departures per 1000 inhabitants, 1985 (source: IRPET, 1989).

Province	Tourism	Business	Total
Torino	2330	200	2550
Milano	2650	260	2910
Venezia	1880	140	2020
Genova	1930	130	2060
Bologna	2410	240	2650
Firenze	2300	240	2540
Roma	2090	180	2270
Napoli	1300	80	1380
Bari	1350	90	1440
Palermo	1150	60	1210

Table 2. Number of passengers (regional percentages) in the main Italian airports, 1987 (source: Civilavia).

Italian regions	Total	Excluding Rome and Milan
Piemonte	2.6	6.2
Lombardia	26.0	9.3
Trentino Alto Aldige	–	–
Fruili Venezia Giulia	0.8	2.0
Veneto	4.8	11.5
Liguria	1.7	4.2
Emilia Romagna	3.3	7.9
Toscana	2.4	5.7
Umbria	–	–
Marche	0.3	0.7
Lazio	37.3	2.7
Abruzzo e Molise	–	–
Campania	4.0	9.6
Puglia	1.8	4.4
Basilicata	–	–
Calabria	1.2	3.0
Sicilia	7.3	17.5
Sardegna	6.3	15.1
Total	100.0	100.0

air travel is evident (table 2); this shortfall is a serious one even if the two international airports of Roma and Milano, with their national catchment area, are left out of the consideration.

This evident weakness in air travel supply is most problematic for the urban area of Firenze: in fact, if we can assume that the closeness of an airport is less important for tourism, Pisa (80 km from Firenze) could continue to cater for this demand; for business the distance is more problematic.

In the remainder of this chapter we estimate future demands for travel in the region and use this to evaluate alternative strategies for investment.

3 The demand for air travel
3.1 Introduction
It is well known that travel demand has two main features. The first is that travel demand, unlike the demand for other commodities, is a 'derived' one: normally a journey is only a means of reaching other goals (consumption, production, or leisure). The second feature is that travel decisions are related to many variables, such as location, infrastructure, and car ownership, that are fixed in the short term, whereas in the long term they could change, because of many factors including the evolution of transport systems.

It is evident, from the first feature, that travel creates not pleasure, but only costs (costs in the sense both of monetary costs and of time loss), and so the objective function for a traveller is to minimise the 'generalised travel cost' G:

$$\text{minimise } G = C + WT, \tag{1}$$

where
C is monetary cost,
T is time loss for the trip,
W is the value of the traveller's time.
The value of time is the crux of the problem and the economic literature on this point is fairly abundant. But the argument that only W is subjective is misleading: the monetary cost and the time loss both depend on the subjective perception of the traveller. Does the traveller have a correct perception of the petrol used during a car trip? Does he or she include fixed costs such as insurance or wear and tear? How long does the trip seem to be? Each of these questions has a reply that will differ not only for different travellers, but also for different trips by the same traveller.

Once the above problems have been solved we can assume that travel demand will depend on generalised travel cost, given certain structural features of the origin and the destination of the trip. Even if, in the long run, these features too could change, the assumption that in the short run they are unchangeable is acceptable.

In this study our task is to estimate the demand for air travel only as far as a new airport for Firenze is concerned; furthermore, because no direct survey had been made, the only data that can be used are cross-sectional data about air travellers between each pair of Italian airports and between each airport and the main European countries (we have selected only the fourteen largest Italian airports: Torino, Milano, Venezia, Genova, Bologna, Firenze, Pisa, Roma, Napoli, Bari, Palermo, Catania, Olbia, and Cagliari; and eight European countries: Austria, France, Germany, Greece, Yugoslavia, United Kingdom, Spain, and Switzerland).

The structure of the implemented model strictly depends on this data availability. First, a traditional gravity model has been constructed aimed at estimating the total travel demand in Italy, and to and from the other countries; then the number of trips generated by the gravity model has been split into air and nonair trips by means of a modal choice model. In other words, the whole model is composed of two sequential submodels (a gravity model and a modal split model): the results of the first model form the inputs of the second one. From a theoretical point of view this could appear a weakness of the model: trip generation and modal split are in fact simultaneous. However, even if some models of this kind exist (Quandt and Baumol, 1970), these models are often very difficult to estimate.

So, if the only data about the number of passengers for a certain number of air routes are cross-sectional, the procedure we have used to estimate the demand for air travel can be summarised as follows:
(1) estimate total travel demands arising from the places that gravitate around the selected airports (general mobility);
(2) estimate how much of the travel demand is relevant to air travel (a kind of potential demand for air travel);
(3) compare that potential demand with the present known demand, and estimate the influence of specific variables such as prices, income levels, quality of service, competitiveness, etc.

3.2 The gravity model
As it is probable that most Italian cities gravitate around the Italian airports here selected, the gravity model has been applied to the whole Italian population, located in the ninety-five administrative Italian districts (provinces), and to the passengers coming from ten foreign 'countries', that are represented by the above eight European countries, the 'rest of Europe', and the 'rest of the World'.

The model has been applied separately to business and tourist trips and could be summarised as follows:
(1) The estimate of the total number of origins (N_i) has been made according to the social structure of each origin $(i = 1, ..., 95)$ and the travel propensity, V_s, of each social group, s (the social groups considered are: farmers, self-employed in industry, white-collar workers in industry,

blue-collar workers in industry, entrepreneurs in industry, professionals, the self-employed in services, white-collar workers in services, blue-collar workers in services, and the nonworking population) ($s = 1, ..., 10$):

$$N_i = \sum_s P_{is} V_s ,$$

where
P_{is} is the number of persons making up social group s in origin i;
V_s is the travel propensity of social group s;
under the constraint that

$$\sum_{i \in r} N_i = N_r , \qquad r = 1, ..., 20 ,$$

where N_r is known, and r represents Italian region.
(2) The total number of destinations (N_j) is derived from the official data for all the foreigners ($j = 96, ..., 105$) who come to the Italian provinces.
(3) The estimate of Italian destinations for business travel is computed according to the following function:

$$N_r = f(B, Y) , \qquad r = 1, ..., 20$$

where
B is the number of per-capita business trips in Italy,
Y is the per-capita income of destination r.
The estimated function has been extrapolated to the ninety-five Italian provinces.
(4) The estimate of Italian tourist destinations is derived from official data.
(5) The estimate of the flows between i and j is made according to a traditional gravity model, where the impedance function is different for tourist and business trips.
     The results of the model are two different origin–destination (OD) matrices: the first for business trips and the second for tourist trips.

3.3 The modal split model
3.3.1 The choice of the most convenient transport mode
The first stage of the modal split model is aimed at estimating the potential demand for air travel on the existing routes and to extrapolate it to the new ones. The method results in an estimate of the number of trips for which air travel is more convenient.
     Instead of immediately measuring the generalised travel cost, the model assumes that air travel between the origin i and the destination j is more convenient than the most convenient among the other transport modes (generally the railway is the most convenient transport mode other than air travel) if

$$G_{ij}^1 < G_{ij}^2 , \tag{2}$$

where G_{ij}^m is the generalised travel cost between origin i and destination j when an aircraft is used for a certain stage of the whole journey ($m = 1$) or never used ($m = 2$).

According to the definition (1) of G, equation (2) is true if

$$C_{ij}^1 + T_{ij}^1 W < C_{ij}^2 + T_{ij}^2 W, \tag{3}$$

or

$$W > W^* = \frac{C_{ij}^1 - C_{ij}^2}{T_{ij}^2 - T_{ij}^1}. \tag{4}$$

In other words, air travel is more convenient if the value of time is (for the passenger) more than the marginal cost of one unit of the time saving using the plane. This value could be considered as a kind of 'threshold price' in the sense that flying is only in the interests of those travellers who give their time a value greater than W^*.

Normally $W^* \geqslant 0$ because air travel is more expensive but also faster; there are only two exceptions to this rule: when destinations i and j are very close (in such a case air travel could be both the most expensive and the slowest) or very distant (in such a case air travel could be both the cheapest and the fastest).

For a complete understanding of the method adopted it is necessary to clarify how times and costs between origin i and destination j are computed:

$$C_{ij} = C_{ik} + C_{kh} + C_{hr} + C_{rj}, \tag{5}$$

$$T_{ij} = T_{ik} + T_k + T_{kl} + T_l + T_{lm} + T_m + T_{mj}, \tag{6}$$

where
i is the origin of the trip,
k is the first airport,
l is the second airport (only in the case of transshipment),
m is the third airport,
j is the destination of the trip,
T_k, T_l, and T_m are the waiting times at different points in the trip.

There are obviously many different routes and modes between each pair of places: the method used allows us to compare the best of those ways which, at some stage of the whole trip, require the use of air travel, with the best one that does not. According to this procedure, for each pair of cities the model gives: (a) all the stages of the journey, as a combination of different points; (b) the value of the threshold price when at least two of these points are airports (table 3).

As far as the threshold price is concerned the price of L108000 between Firenze and Torino means, for example, that only those passengers who place on their time a value greater than L108000 have any interest in using the plane. In many cases the value is so low that, in practice, it is in the interest of *all* passengers to go by plane (for example when travelling to island cities such as Palermo, Catania, Olbia, and Cagliari).

Table 3. Value of threshold prices (thousand lire per hour, 1987) on the different routes (source: IRPET, 1989).

	Firenze	Pisa		Firenze	Pisa
Torino	108	57	Austria	–	58
Milano	84	65	France	24	22
Roma	–	57	Germany	25	18
Napoli	68	26	Greece	9	8
Bari·	28	15	Yugoslavia	–	–
Palermo	–	7	United Kingdom	9	15
Catania	–	8	Spain	17	14
Olbia	–	6	Switzerland	106	48
Cagliari	–	6			

3.3.2 Income distribution and potential demand
The number of trips made by passengers whose time value is greater than the threshold price can be determined according to the income distribution for each origin. The income distribution has been estimated by assigning to the social groups of each origin the per-capita incomes of their respective regions or countries.

For business journeys all passengers whose hourly income is greater than the 'threshold price' are potentially interested in flying; because the value of leisure time is lower than that of working time, the value of the threshold price for tourist trips has been multiplied by a factor that changes according to the length of the holiday (the shorter the holiday the lower the factor).

The demand generated by the model is not the actual demand because it exists only if a *route* exists, but it is not constrained by the capacity of the route and so it can differ greatly from real demand. In other words, demand is obtained by giving to the traveller a probability of 1 of using the plane on a certain route, if the air route exists and the value of the time for the passenger is greater than the threshold price, and is equal to 0 in all the other cases: in this sense it is a kind of potential demand.

In practice, however, the choice of the traveller does not depend solely on the fact that $W \geqslant W^*$ but it is also affected by other variables. The next stage of the procedure consists of the estimation of a demand function to include the effect of these other variables.

3.3.3 The estimation of the demand function
Once the potential demand, P, has been estimated we can assume that the actual demand, D, between i and j depends on P, but also on other factors

such as:

(1) the presence of day trippers (neglected in the gravity model) which should be linked to the number of flights whose turnaround times allow day trips;

(2) competitiveness with the railway (already considered in terms of costs) in terms of different frequencies of the service;

(3) subjective preference for the plane, probably linked to the income of the traveller (and so to the value of W^*);

(4) competitiveness with the two main Italian airports, in terms of distance from them;

(5) competitiveness of the nearest airport in terms of relative frequencies of the flight;

(6) capacity of the aircraft;

(7) size of the airports of origin;

(8) length of the air trip;

(9) cost of the flight;

(10) the share, for each route, of total tourist trips.

The function selected is the following:

$$D = \Omega P \exp\left(\alpha + \frac{\beta}{X} \right), \tag{7}$$

where Ω is a scale parameter that expresses a kind of share of the potential demand that is really satisfied (Ω could be also >1 because of the weight of day trippers, that are computed in D but not in P), $\exp(\alpha + \beta/X)$ expressed a kind of probability that the potential demand can be satisfied. In applying this function to the above ten variables the variables (4), (5), (8), and (10) have been excluded because they do not have an acceptable t-statistic.

The results of regression analysis (table 4) can be considered satisfactory not only because of the values of t and R^2, but also because the signs of the parameters confirm the expectations (a negative sign indicates

Table 4. Parameters of the demand function.

Variable [a]	Parameter	t-statistic
Ω	0.9548	8.328
α	7.1333	49.084
(1)	−2.5236	−6.268
(2)	−0.0178	−5.220
(3)	−3662.4	−5.053
(6)	−8.8501	−5.572
(7)	−0.0014	−3.821
(9)	68 198	2.901

$R^2 = 0.9187$

[a] See text for definition of variables.

a positive relationship between the independent and the dependent variables). Thus the model provides estimates of the demand for air journeys (in terms of number of trips between each pair of airports), according to our hypotheses of the independent variables that are linked to: (a) the characteristics of the supply of air journeys (prices, frequencies, size of the airport, distance from other airports, etc) and (b) the characteristics of other transport modes (mainly the railway).

Any change in the independent variables affect the number of air journeys.

3.3.4 The results of the model

The model has been applied first to the present state of travel flows and transport infrastructure. In this way, the potential demand has been computed from the OD matrices obtained by the gravity model and the threshold prices already described in table 1.

The results confirm the existence of a great gap between supply and demand for the two airports in Tuscany in 1987: the ratio between air trips from Firenze and those from Pisa is $1:11$, whereas the ratio between them in terms of potential demand, P, is estimated by the model as $1:2.7$. This means that a great part of the demand for air travel from Firenze cannot be satisfied by its airport and consequently it is diverted not only towards other airports (mainly Pisa) but also to the railway. The results obtained confirm the appropriateness of the model in that the estimated values of D are fairly similar to the real ones.

Next, the model has been applied to different future scenarios (for the year 2000), mainly to estimate the effects of the different hypotheses about the airport of Firenze.

(1) *Hypothesis about the supply of air travel.* For non-Tuscan airports, an increase of 20% both in the number of the flights and in the capacity of the aircraft has been assumed, so that the total supply increased by 44%. For the two airports of Tuscany, the supply (in the sense of the product of the capacity of the aircraft and the number of flights) has been increased as follows:

Firenze Airport
Hypothesis A: 200 000 passengers per year (ppy)—the present figure
Hypothesis B: 300 000 ppy
Hypothesis C: 450 000 ppy
Hypothesis D: 550 000 ppy
Pisa Airport
Hypothesis A: 1 200 000 ppy
Hypothesis B: 2 000 000 ppy

(2) *Hypothesis about the railways.* An increase in speed of 10 km h^{-1} over the whole network has been assumed, combined with the functioning of a high-speed line between Napoli and Milano (already planned and partially constructed) with an average speed of 140 km h^{-1}.

(3) *Hypothesis about the relative prices.* It has been consumed that relative prices between air and rail travel are unchanged.

(4) *Hypothesis about the evolution of demand for travel.* The increase in general mobility has been computed according to a relationship between the number of trips and per-capita income estimated on the basis of data covering the period 1970–89. By extrapolating the function as far as the year 2000 two new OD matrices (for business and tourism) have been obtained (the total number of trips increases by 35%).

The above hypotheses permit the definition of the values of all the exogenous variables of the model and thus the estimation of both the potential and the actual demand for air travel. In terms of potential demand the above scenarios point to a general increase in the demand for air travel of about 80% for Italian airports as a whole, whereas the increase is more than 120% for the airports of Tuscany (because of the greater increase in supply).

The results for the Tuscan airports turn out to be fairly similar over all the different combinations of the above hypotheses about supply in the two airports: the potential demand for the airport of Firenze is about 1.2 million passengers (greater than the supply in all the four hypotheses assumed), whereas the demand for the airport of Pisa is about 1.4 million passengers (that is greater than the supply in hypothesis A, but lower than the supply in hypothesis B.

There is a further argument in favour of a more appropriate location for the airport of Firenze in order to satisfy the demand for air travel in Tuscany as a whole. By introducing constraints on the supply side (mainly concerning the size of the new airport of Firenze) into all the hypotheses, the traffic diverted to the airport of Pisa (out of every 100 passengers who cannot be satisfied by the airport of Firenze, 62 choose the railway and 34 Pisa Airport) provides enough demand to ulitise its full capacity.

The actual demand to be satisfied by the two airports of Tuscany, if one takes account of the constraints on the supply side as well as computing

Table 5. The demand (number of passengers in the year 2000) for air travel in Tuscany (source: IRPET, 1989).

Hypothesis		Demand	
Firenze	Pisa	Firenze	Pisa
A	A	212 000	1 260 000
B	A	290 000	1 260 000
C	A	407 000	1 240 000
D	A	540 000	1 223 000
B	B	290 000	1 940 000
C	B	407 000	1 890 000
D	B	540 000	1 850 000

the diverted traffic, is described in table 5. The results obtained largely depend on the hypothesis about improvements in the railway network.

The model has also been applied to the hypothesis that the railway service will be unchanged: the results of this simulation show the effects of the high-speed railway between Napoli and Milano (table 6), with a general decrease in the demand for air travel of 20%, a decrease that is greater in the airports located near the new railway. Firenze, located at the midpoint of the high-speed line, has in fact the greatest decrease in the demand for air travel. Full utilisation of the capacity of both airports is forecast in all the assumed hypotheses about air travel supply and demand, even in the case of maximum supply (hypothesis D + hypothesis B) and with the competitiveness effects of the high-speed railway.

Table 6. The effects of the high-speed railway: decrease in the number of air travellers (source: IRPET, 1989).

	Percentage		Percentage
Torino	−23	Napoli	−20
Milano	−16	Bari	−22
Venezia	−15	Palermo	−7
Genova	−10	Catania	−15
Bologna	−28	Olbia	−2
Firenze	−42	Cagliari	−2
Pisa	−21		
Roma	−18	Italy	−20

4 The evaluation of the alternatives
4.1 A new airport for Firenze—but on which site?
The demand analysis shows the large proportion of air travel demand which is not yet being satisfied. Before the possible solutions and the feasibility of the different alternatives are studied, the actual availability of places where a new airport could be built should be verified.

A preliminary study has been devoted to examining the geography of the wide plain between Pistoia and Firenze in order to make sure that there actually is enough space to build an airport in. With this in mind, we have assumed a 'grade 3' airport, planned for domestic and European flights and for business passengers, able to accommodate 70-seat planes and up to 500 000 passengers per year, the length of the single runway is assumed to be limited to 2 km.

The strong demographic and economic development of the area, as well as the infrastructure network, place severe constraints on the location, above all because of both the intense land demand of an airport system and the pollution limits. Only five sites seem to have all the physical characteristics, two of them located close to Pistoia and Firenze (numbers 1 and 5, respectively, in figure 1) and the others on the outskirts of Prato (numbers 2, 3, and 4). Site 5 is very close to the existing airport of Firenze and the new runway would be placed in a more or less orthogonal position to the one that is currently in use. In order to evaluate the geographical suitability of these locations in more detail, two different planning areas were examined: the more restricted (200 ha) project area of the airport system (including the runways, terminal buildings, and parking areas) and the structural area (665 ha), in other words, the area which would be affected by the environmental and economic effects of the airport's operations.

The most relevant constraints of the different locations are shown in tables 7 (project area) and 8 (structural area). Locations 1 and 2 are affected by an important concentration of horticultural nurseries and, in addition, the air traffic in the first could be greatly handicapped by the topography of the surrounding area. These elements would seem to be decisive factors in giving up these sites. The number of houses which would be demolished does not vary so much as to tilt the preference towards one solution or another, but the risk of having floodwater on the runway is very high for locations 2 and 3 (table 8).

As far as location 5 is concerned, all the factors which have been examined are positive, with the exception of both the need for a great volume of earth to be moved and the trade-off with the planned land use (an extensive park for the metropolitan area).

If we take into account the existing constraints and the future land use, location 4 seems to be less problematic than the others, bearing in mind

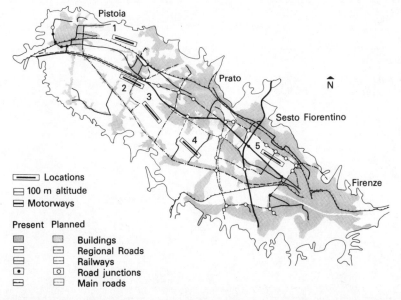

Figure 1. Possible locations and environmental constraints for a new airport.

Table 7. Project area (200 ha): land-use and environmental constraints (source: direct survey).

	Site				
	1	2	3	4	5
Constraints					
Number of buildings to be demolished	55	64	81	63	14
Present land use (%)	3.2	6.2	1.4	–	–
Residential areas	–	4.7	–	–	–
Industrial areas	–	1.5	–	–	–
Public services	3.2	–	1.4	–	–
Schools	–	–	–	–	–
Parks	–	–	–	–	–
Sports fields	–	–	–	–	–
Planned land use (%)	–	1.1	–	0.8	90.5
Residential areas	–	–	–	–	–
Industrial areas	–	–	–	–	–
Public services	–	1.1	–	0.8	–
Schools	–	–	–	–	–
Parks	–	–	–	–	90.5
Sports fields	–	–	–	–	–
Total	3.2	7.3	1.4	0.8	90.5
Constraints	9.9	–	5.1	1.7	93.8
Areas of archaeological interest	–	–	–	–	78.1
Marsh wildlife habitat	9.9	–	5.1	1.7	15.7
Plant-growing areas (%)	80.5	93.4	–	–	–
100	15.8	–	–	–	–
50	64.8	–	–	–	–
10	–	93.4	–	–	–

Table 8. Structural area (665 ha): land use (source: direct survey).

	Site				
	1	2	3	4	5
Constraints					
Present land use (%)	21.6	6.4	7.0	12.3	20.7
Residential areas	4.4	3.2	5.7	9.1	2.1
Industrial areas	17.2	2.9	0.3	2.8	15.5
Public services	–	0.1	0.8	–	3.1
Schools	–	0.2	0.2	0.3	–
Parks	–	–	–	–	–
Sports fields	–	–	0.1	0.1	–
Planned land use (%)	17.7	3.7	18.2	17.8	33.2
Residential areas	9.6	–	0.6	0.5	–
Industrial areas	2.0	2.0	1.0	0.3	1.9
Public services	4.1	1.7	0.2	0.6	–
Schools	–	–	0.3	–	3.2
Parks	2.0	–	16.0	16.4	28.2
Sports fields	4.3	–	–	–	–
Total	39.4	10.0	25.2	30.1	53.9

that, in any case, in a highly urbanised area any solution is always far from the ideal. On this basis a preliminary project related to location 4 (henceforth named Prato 1) was ˙commissioned in order to be able to compare the feasible alternatives from an economic point of view.

4.2 An economic analysis of the alternatives

The air of increasing the supply of air travel capacity in Tuscany could be attained by investing in a number of different schemes, each of which would raise the number of passengers to a total of between 100 000 and 1 200 000 passengers per year, according to the various scenarios. The maximum level of expansion is limited by two circumstances. (1) The closeness of the airport of Pisa to the city does not allow further increases in air traffic, and the airport of Firenze probably has the same limit. (2) A new airport could be of international status only if it were located outside the central part of Tuscany, but in this hypothesis the benefits to users would be very low.

The different combinations of airports with the maximum total passengers are shown in table 9. As far as Pisa airport is concerned, a project of investment in terminal buildings (Pisa 1) could increase the capacity to 2 million passengers without substantial modifications to the landing area. Firenze 1 includes the extension of the runway, the building of a taxiway, and the widening of the terminal buildings, whereas Firenze 2 is aimed at overcoming certain present operating difficulties by means of a new runway in orthogonal position to the existing one as well as a completely new terminal building. The Prato 1 project (involving a completely new airport) might be less costly in terms of investment than Firenze 2 owing to the better ground situation (that is, the amount of earth to be moved) but because of bureaucratic red tape (expropriations, planning permission, etc) it would take at least six years before the work could begin (table 10).

Table 9. Proposed airport systems in Tuscany.

Airport	Ppy[a]	Scenario								
		0	1	2	3	4	5	6	7	8
Pisa 0	1 200 000	•	•	•	•					
Pisa 1	2 000 000					•	•	•	•	•
Firenze 0	200 000	•					•			
Firenze 1	300 000		•					•		
Firenze 2	450 000			•					•	
Prato 1	550 000				•					•
Max. no. of passengers[b]		1400	1500	1650	1750	2000	2200	2300	2450	2550

[a] Ppy passengers per year.

[b] Maximum number of passengers expressed in thousands.

The need for an economic analysis of the projects derives from the 'public goods' nature of the airports. In fact, as in many other transport infrastructures, the costs and the benefits of the investments are both financial and social. Particular attention has been paid to the externalities, among which pollution effects are the most relevant. The number and range of the relevant effects are such that a selection among them becomes unavoidable: the main criteria for selection have been measurability and relative importance. On this basis some elements (such as atmospheric pollution, the effects on landscape, the risk of air crashes) and certain pecuniary effects (changes in property values, for instance) have been excluded from the evaluation because of their counterbalancing nature.

Even if this part of the study has had the traditional structure of a cost–benefit analysis, an attempt to evaluate the different 'points of view' of different social groups was also made by applying a multicriteria technique (for a multiobjective analysis of an airport facilities problem, see Keeney, 1973). A summary of the measured effects, related either to the construction phase or to the operational state of the airports, is shown in table 11.

A few details of the evaluation method are in most cases enough; however, in some circumstances a more detailed description of both the assumptions and the methodology is appropriate.

The ground displacements (their costs are already included in the total cost of construction) form part of the first category. They have been considered here as a 'proxy' for the nuisance to the inhabitants during the construction period (in terms of noise, increased traffic, dust, etc).

The operating costs and revenues have been evaluated with reference both to the direct financial flows affecting the airport agencies and the indirect ones concerning the government, who provide the public services generally required by air traffic, such as fire protection, police, and customs. The smallest airports suffer from negative turns to scale which makes the international structures relatively more efficient (in terms of overheads) owing to the greater utilisation of services and equipment.

The costs for the reduced working of the airport during adverse meteorological conditions have been estimated on the basis of the statistical frequency of these phenomena, such as fog and crosswinds, as well as

Table 10. Investment costs (billion lire in 1989 prices).

Projects	1991	1992	1993	1994	1995	1996	1997	1998	1999	Total
Pisa 1	11.2	15.4								26.6
Firenze 1		7.5	7.5							15.0
Firenze 2 [a]		7.5	7.5		5.5	19.2	25.6	25.7		91.0
Prato 1						10.0	15.0	15.0	23.0	63.0

[a] Firenze 2 project includes Firenze 1 because the new runway should not involve the decommissioning of the first one.

on the costs for the passengers and for airlines. Firenze is in the worst situation, for almost 20% of the flights could be cancelled for these reasons, whereas the best location from this point of view is Pisa, where a better climate and the availability of an instrumental landing system (which is impossible to set up in Firenze) reduce this percentage to the minimum.

The crucial points of the evaluation, however, are the estimates of time savings and noise pollution. In fact, time savings are usually the most important benefit in a transport project and different shadow prices would greatly affect the results of a cost–benefit analysis, whereas noise pollution is the biggest obstacle to the building of new airports.

Time savings should be evaluated both for the actual users of the means of transport (aircraft and their substitutes) and for the potential users (who give up travelling owing to the difficulty of reaching the airport). A good evaluation of this second group of users would require a direct survey (which is not available) and, in consequence, what has been stressed is the *time* saved both by those who choose to divert from the train to the plane and by the present airport users. The modal split model described above allows us to overcome most of the difficulties related to the estimate of the unitary value of time, which is here the threshold price. This value has been applied to the total travel hours saved in the different scenarios (expressed as a difference between 'zero hypothesis' and the situation after the fulfillment of each of the projects in table 10).

Table 11. Evaluated effects (year 2000).

	Project			
	Firenze 1	Firenze 2	Prato 1	Pisa 1
Growth in number of passengers	100 000	250 000	350 000	800 000
Construction phase				
Investment costs (10^9 lire)	15.0	91.0	63.0	26.6
Noise pollution costs (10^9 lire)	3.0	1.0	1.3	44.9
Ground displacements (10^3 m^3)[a]	300	1650	1100	
Buildings to be demolished (number)[a]		17	60	
Operational phase				
Increase in operational costs (10^9 lire)	2.1	5.4	7.5	16.7
Increase in working revenues (10^9 lire)	1.8	4.6	6.4	18.5
Time savings (10^9 lire)[b]	8.0	19.4	21.9	11.7
Costs of cancelled flights (10^9 lire)	1.2	0.8	0.3	1.1
Traffic increase (10^3 cars per day)	0.8	1.1	1.5	1.7
Total area (ha)	125	270	200	360

[a] These effects have already been included in the total construction costs and have been restated only as a 'proxy' for the troubles affecting the inhabitants.

[b] Domestic users only.

In figure 2 the curve AA represents the values of time corresponding to the total time employed in the different scenarios (and thus by the same number of travellers) [see equation (4)]. Because the only difference between the two scenarios is represented by the different capacity of the airports, this is the sole cause of the time savings.

The total time in the 'zero hypothesis' is equivalent to T_0, and the first investment will reduce this value to T_1. The new air travellers are those whose time value is between W_0 and W_1, and the total value of the time savings (that is $T_0 T_1$) is the area $CBT_0 T_1$. A good proxy of this area is obtained by applying to the time savings $T_0 T_1$ the average of the threshold prices before and after the investment. Thus the value of the total time savings due to the nth investment will be:

$$R_n = \tfrac{1}{2}(T_{n-1} - T_n)(W_{n-1} - W_n),$$

corresponding to the shaded area in figure 2.

Noise too, is very difficult to evaluate, because

"the impact of aircraft noise on a community is dependent upon several factors, including the magnitude and frequency distribution of the sound, the duration of noise, the flight paths during take-off and landing, the number and types of operations, the operating procedures, the aircraft mix, the runway system utilization, the time of day and season, and meteorological conditions. The response of communities to exposure to aircraft noise is a function of the land and building use, the type of building construction, the distance from the airport, the ambient noise level, sound attenuation due to physical or meteorological conditions, and sociological considerations" (Horonjeff and McKelvey, 1983, page 575).

A good indicator of noise pollution, which takes into account most of the previous factors, is the WECPNL index (weighted equivalent continuous perceived noise level) which has been used to trace the isophonic curves referring to the different projects. Pollution under 75 WECPNL

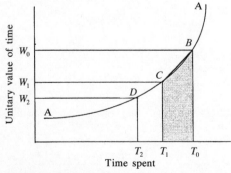

Figure 2. Time savings.

has not been quantified; noise in the range of 75–77 WECPNL was measured but not evaluated in terms of costs, but the potential cost of eliminating noise when it exceeded the level of 77 WECPNL was estimated. With this aim the basis of the evaluation was the total number of newly polluted houses, as well as a unitary cost (10% or 20% of the average value, respectively, if the noise is lower than or greater than 82 WECPNL). As can be seen from table 11, the Pisa 1 project could be strongly affected by this problem, because of both the extreme closeness of the runway to the city (2 km) and the customary flight procedures, whereas the cost of the other solutions is very low.

4.3 A summary of the selection criteria
The synthesis of all the evaluated elements is the trickiest phase of every method aimed at the selection of projects. Each element usually has different units of measurement and a different degree of importance; therefore whatever technique is used to summarise them will inevitably be arbitrary. The first method to be used was a traditional cost–benefit analysis, even though we were aware that the basic assumptions and the main procedures of this method have often been criticised. Of this criticism the most significant is whether or not the method can give a monetary measure to every effect and actualise it by using a social discount rate.

We applied this method to the data summarised in table 11, using a discount rate of 4% for a 25-year period. The results show that the Prato 1 project prevails from the points of view of the net present value, whereas Firenze 1 has the best internal return rate because, although it shows fewer benefits, it has lower costs. Firenze 1, on the other hand, is penalised in all comparisons by its high costs and relatively low benefits; the only factor in its favour seems (like Pisa 1) to be the easier feasibility of an expansion of an existing airport rather than the building of a new one. A possible answer to the above criticism could be looked for in the use of multicriteria analysis to choose the best strategy for Firenze (see Fedelino and Mealli, 1990).

The evaluated strategies, produced according to different investment timescales, are:

Strategy 1 Firenze 1
Strategy 2 Firenze 2
Strategy 3 Firenze 1 + Firenze 2 (after 6 years)
Strategy 4 Firenze 1 + Firenze 2 (after 9 years)
Strategy 5 Firenze 1 + Prato 1 (after 6 years)
Strategy 6 Firenze 1 + Prato 1 (after 9 years)
Strategy 7 Firenze 0 + Prato 1 (after 7 years)

Table 12 contains the information relating to the seven strategies previously defined with reference to seven criteria; note that one of these (the first) is measured in a qualitative way.

Table 12. Evaluation of the strategies according to each criterion.

Criterion	Min or max[a]	Strategy 1	2	3
Hydrogeological risk	min	0	0	0
Construction costs	min	15	91	91
Ground displacement	min	562	2 062	2 062
Noise pollution	min	142 293	132 892	133 593
Maintenance costs	max	−12 046	−9 086	−9 235
Time savings	max	240	536	513
Cancelled flights	min	1 980	1 818	1 830

[a] The criterion should be minimised (min) or maximised (max).

The techniques we have applied are the Promethee methods (see Brans and Vincke, 1985; D'Avignon and Mareshal, 1989), belonging to the family of the outranking methods, that is, methods in which a set of potential actions are considered and it is concluded that action A outranks action B, if the arguments in favour of the choide of A over B are significant, whereas those in favour of the contrary preference are not so relevant.

The results of these techniques are strongly affected by: the specification of the preference structure, that is, the width and outline of the indifference area between two strategies referring to a defined criterion; the specification of weights, that is, the measure of the relative importance of each criterion. In order to take into account the points of view of some of the groups involved in the decision (the policymakers, local residents, and the airport users), three systems of weights have been chosen to represent the different objectives, as in table 13.

The results are shown in figure 3; both the partial preorder (where incomparability between two strategies is possible), and the complete one for each subject, are shown. The stability intervals of the policymaker

Table 13. Absolute and relative weights from different points of view.

Subjects' criterion	Local residents		Airport users		Policy-makers		Stability intervals
	abs.	rel.	abs.	rel.	abs.	rel.	
Hydrogeological risk	5	0.143	8	0.203	7	0.126	0–0.39
Construction costs	2	0.057	5	0.127	7.5	0.135	0.127–0.567
Ground displacement	1	0.029	10	0.253	6.5	0.118	0–0.622
Noise pollution	3	0.086	10	0.253	10	0.180	0–1
Maintenance costs	4	0.114	2.5	0.063	7	0.126	0–0.715
Time Savings	10	0.288	1	0.025	10	0.180	0–0.92
Cancelled flights	10	0.288	3	0.076	7.5	0.135	0–1

Table 12 (continued)

Strategy			
4	5	6	7
0	1	1	1
91	88	88	63
2062	1842	1842	1280
134637	48893	60101	43799
−9470	−8118	−7516	−8156
479	549	531	547
1848	1580	1760	1460

weights (the degree of influence on the rankings of the deviation in the values of weights) give strategy 7 a high probability of being in first position, even if the system of weights were really fixed by the policymaker and not predicted by the analyst.

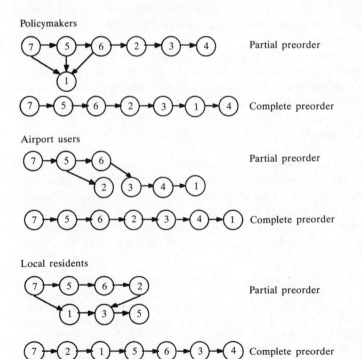

Figure 3. Multicriteria analysis: a comparison among the hypotheses according to different points of view.

5 Final remarks
The analysis of demand for air travel in Tuscany has revealed some striking results. First of all, at present there is a great gap between potential and actual demand in the two main airports of Tuscany (Firenze and Pisa): the airport of Firenze can satisfy only a small part of demand as far as the central area of Tuscany is concerned, and, therefore, part of the demand is diverted to the airport of Pisa, which is the largest airport in Tuscany.

This gap implies a constraint on future economic development of the region and justifies not only the provision of a new airport in the central area of Tuscany, but also the planned enlargement of the airport of Pisa, if the demand for air travel grows as expected in the near future. The different solutions concerning the airport of Firenze (the extension of the present runway, the construction of a second runway, and the construction of a new airport) and the enlargement of the airport of Pisa have been analysed both by means of cost–benefit and by means of multicriteria analyses.

The cost–benefit analysis takes into account, not only the monetary effects, but also the costs and the benefits mainly deriving from (a) time savings and (b) environmental effects; the method has been applied separately to the three scenarios for Firenze and to the enlargement of the present airport of Pisa.

The construction of a new airport for Firenze has the greatest net present value, mainly because it facilitates the greatest amount of time savings, whereas the extension of the present runway has the greatest internal rate of discount mainly because it gives the lowest construction cost.

Multicriteria analysis has been applied to the different hypotheses for the airport of Firenze (assuming also different timetables for construction) and taking into account three different points of view (policymakers, airport users, and local residents). The results obtained confirm that the best solution is the construction of a new airport for Firenze, and the decommissioning of the old one; this result seems to be independent of the views of any particular interest group. This is only the first stage of the analysis, however, because it does not allow for any induced effects on the structure of the local economy consequent on the provision of extra capacity.

Acknowledgements. In this paper the main results of the research: "Il Trasporto Aereo in Toscana: Individuazione di una soluzione aeroportuale adeguata alle esigenze dell'area Firenze–Prato–Pistoia", by IRPET, are presented. The research group, coordinated by M Badii was composed of P Baglioni, M Cartoni, S Casini Benvenuti, A Cavalieri, A Fedelino, A Floridia, M Grassi, P Lattarulo, G Maltinti, R Masci, F Mealli, M C Meini, G Pozzana, F Sforzi.

References
Brans J P, Vincke P, 1985, "A preference ranking organization method: the PROMETHEE method for multiple criteria decision-making" *Management Science* **31** 647–656
D'Avignon G, Mareshal B, 1989, "Specialization of hospital services in Quebec: an application of the PROMETHEE and GAIA methods" *Mathematical and Computer Modelling* **12** 1393–1400
Fedelino A, Mealli F, 1990, "Analisi delle decisioni a criteri multipli: un'applicazione al sistema aeroportuale toscano", mimeo, IRPET, Firenze
Horonjeff R, McKelvey F X, 1983 *Planning and Design of Airports* 3rd edition (McGraw-Hill, New York)
IRPET, 1989, "Il trasporto aereo in Toscana", final report, Regional Institute for Economic Planning of Tuscany, 50137 Firenze
Keeney R L, 1973, "A decision analysis with multiple objectives: the Mexico City Airport" *Bell Journal of Economic and Management Science* **4** 101–117
Quandt R E, Baumol W J, 1970, "The demand for abstract transport modes: theory and measurement", in *The Demand for Transport Modes: Theory of Measurement* Ed. R E Quandt (Lexington Books, Lexington, MA) pp 83–101

Infrastructure for Regional Development: Advice and Support to New Small Businesses

P M Townroe
Sheffield City Polytechnic
K Mallalieu
University of East Anglia

"... those running small businesses still need to have (or have access to) the knowledge and skills necessary to identify accurately what the problems and opportunities are, and the full range of options available to them in tackling ... problems"

(*Labour Market Quarterly Report*, November 1990, page 6)

1 Introduction

The act of founding a new small business may be likened to launching a small craft onto the waters of an estuary opening onto the sea, where the sea is the national economy. There will be dangers not only to successful passage but also to survival, especially if the craft is badly designed or poorly skippered. Whereas some craft are pushed into the water in the relative safety of a sheltered creek, finding a market niche, others are more bravely launched into the broader expanses, looking to the open sea perhaps, hoping to catch a favourable tide. However, there is turbulence on the water in this economy as well as hidden shoals beneath and there are sandbanks to avoid. And for the unwary, a turn of the tide or the passage of much larger craft, looming perhaps out of the darkness or the fog, may present danger, setback, or even loss.

Over the centuries, a considerable infrastructure has been built up around sea coasts to assist the captains of small craft. Lighthouses, buoys, fuel berths, radio links, radar surveillance: all may be regarded as infrastructure, designed to complement the equipment maintained upon the small boat itself, such as the compass, the two-way radio, the radar reflector, the wind gauge, etc. The cautious navigator has need of very little of this hardware, either that on the boat or that provided around the estuary. And the more experienced and skilled navigator may spurn such aids, content to use a compass alone, with the feel of the wind and the tide, and a good set of charts when he or she is in unknown waters. But when the weather turns foul, both seamen will be glad of the infrastructure that is provided.

If the lighthouses and the buoys and the communication links in this metaphor represent 'hard' infrastructure investment, which will assist all craft, small and large, the successful navigation of a small craft may be assisted also by the support of 'soft' infrastructure. The soft infrastructure is like the hard infrastructure: it is available to all, but some elements of it will be particularly important to small craft. Charts are needed by all, as is a broad knowledge of tide and weather. However, the small boat may suffer in rougher seas by virtue of its initial construction, and be guided into danger or set into pathways of slow progress or of grounding by the inexperience and lack of knowledge of the skipper.

Similarly, the new small business may be launched successfully and continue to make progress as it develops, or it may develop to a certain point and go no further, or it may founder on obstacles and adverse conditions. The state of the national economy with reference to the particular sector of activity of the new firm, major institutions and competitors: all may affect the progress and performance of the new small business. The owner of the new small business needs not only to understand these infrastructural frameworks but also to be able to use them to good effect. This competence may be enhanced with instruction as well as built up by experience.

Such competence lies in the recognition and appreciation by the individual of the ever-changing environment of the market and in linking this appreciation to the needs of his own company. The owner of a new small business has to 'read' his or her product market, as well as the labour market, the availability of finance, the offer of new equipment embodying new technology, etc, in order to negotiate the economic environment. This negotiation includes monitoring the business (cash flow, fund use, efficiency of workforce, etc), adjusting its performance and investing in new equipment. There is a range of competencies involved here which, together with the way in which soft infrastructure may assist in their acquisition and execution, are the subject of this chapter.

In the next section there is a brief discussion of the concept of entrepreneurial roles and entrepreneurial competencies involved in the running of a small business. This is associated with relevant soft infrastructural support elements, both from the public and from the private sectors. In section 3, the discussion is illustrated by the findings of an extensive survey of new small business in two rural counties of England, Devon and Northumberland. This survey enquired into the educational and experience background of those starting up small firms, and then asked about sources of advice and support. The respondents were also asked about their perceptions of their competencies: their strengths and weaknesses as fledgling businessmen and women. In the final section we point towards some lessons for regional economic development, especially in regions where the tradition of entrepreneurial activity may be low and the birth rate of new small businesses is well below comparative regions elsewhere in the nation (or elsewhere in the European Community).

2 Entrepreneurial abilities

In the literature on regional economic development, infrastructure has been seen as a necessary but not sufficient condition for progress. This is only partially true. As Hirshman (1958) has stressed, creative entrepreneurs will work around deficiencies in infrastructure. And, at a local level, each small firm will tend to find that its competitors are as hampered by inadequate infrastructural support as it is itself. However, a regional economy clearly benefits from the support of relevant infrastructural services. These services come from hard infrastructure investments: in the utilities, in transport, in telecommunications, and from what has been termed 'community infrastructure' (Diamond and Spence, 1989) in the form of schools, colleges and universities, health care facilities, leisure and environmental amenities, and public safety, as well as housing and the provision of land suitable for development. All of these forms of infrastructure provide services which not only influence the location, and hence the locational efficiency, of companies, but also which can have a direct bearing on productivity, competitiveness, and growth.

One specific example of local 'community' or 'soft' infrastructure which has only recently been identified in research terms is a pool of providers of informal risk capital. There are individuals outside of the immediate family circle (that is, they are 'Business Angels' rather than 'Aunt Agathas') who are prepared to invest in loans and equity in start-ups and growing small firms. The available limited evidence (Mason et al, 1991) suggests that, understandably, these investors prefer to invest locally, particularly because a majority wish to have an active participation to accompany their investment. The availability of this source of capital may be regarded as an infrastructure support in a region.

For new small firms there is a further kind of local or regional infrastructure to those listed above, a further form of 'soft infrastructure' which has a clear geographical variation. This is the support that is available to the entrepreneur in the form of relevant training and advice which enhances and sharpens what may be termed 'entrepreneurial competencies'. This support comes both from the private sector (banks, accountants, lawyers, consultants of various kinds) and from the public sector (training agencies, colleges, local government, regional development corporations, etc). Some of the advice comes at a price; other assistance comes at a zero financial cost, although at what may be a significant opportunity cost in terms of time and access costs for the recipient. And some training and advice comes with finance for investment, either commercially from the private sector or with some element of subsidy from the public sector. It follows that there is a supply side and a demand side to transactions in entrepreneurial competence. The demand side may be manifest or latent, but overall, from the point of view of local and regional economic development, it is possible to see a marketplace in these competencies (Townroe and Mallalieu, 1990).

The entrepreneurial competencies required to launch a small business successfully follow from the various roles the entrepreneur is called upon to perform. These roles have been much discussed in the literature on entrepreneurship and on small firms (for example, Casson, 1982).

Nine may be identified, each having related necessary skills and abilities:

(1) *Risk taking* This conception of the entrepreneur has a long history. Cantillon (1755) is often cited as the originator of this view in the literature of economics. He saw entrepreneurs as those who are involved in exchanges in the marketplace at their own risk in order to yield a personal profit. The origin of entrepreneurship thus lies in the lack of perfect foresight. The skills required involve 'judgment', decisiveness, self-confidence and self-knowledge, and persistence in the face of adverse outcomes.

(2) *Innovation* This is the conception of the entrepreneur that comes from the Austrian School of Economics, seen in the writings of Schumpeter (1934). The entrepreneur needs skills of imagination and creativity in order to carry through into the marketplace new products and new processes, or to find new markets, new sources of supply, or new forms of organisation and structure.

(3) *Arbitrage* Here the entrepreneur is a calculator of uncertainty, analysing trends and linking his or her analysis to skills of purchasing and selling. The entrepreneur is responding to market disequilibria. This view has been associated with the Chicago School of Writing (for example, Knight, 1921; and, more recently, Schultz, 1975).

(4) *Marketing* In the role of marketeer, the entrepreneur must seek to establish 'the unique selling proposition', having an understanding of consumer tastes and the role of advertising and other avenues of investment in sales.

(5) *Application of technology* There is an entrepreneurial task in being aware of the latest developments in technology relevant to the activities of the business and in being able to acquire and then apply this technology both creatively and profitably.

(6) *Quality control* Here the entrepreneur needs to know the market and to use market feedback to relate quality of the product and of the service to the offer price. There is judgment to be exercised here, to ensure profitability.

(7) *Production supervision* A more technical role, involving technical and practical knowledge, but a knowledge that is related to the commercial realities of the chosen marketplace and to the cost structures of inputs when related to the productivity yield in the process of adding value.

(8) *Financial management* In this role the entrepreneur is starting to look more like an executive manager, with a premium on monitoring and controlling the net cash flow position of the new firm. However, in many small firms there are clear aspects of this role involving innovation and skills of creativity.

(9) *Team building* Once the entrepreneur moves beyond being a one-man band, there are skills required of organisation and communication, and eventually of delegation. This last attribute is often one of the hardest consequences of successful growth for the owner of a small business to accept.

Each role requires certain skills and abilities for successful execution. Overall it is possible to agree with Casson (1982) that the entrepreneur, in setting up a new small business, has to possess certain qualities in his or her personality. Some of these qualities are difficult to enhance through advice or education and training. These include drive and determination, self-knowledge, imagination, and skills in communication. But other qualities are capable of enhancement and can be seen as being elements in the transactions which take place in the marketplace for entrepreneurial competencies. These qualities include technological knowledge, financial knowledge, market knowledge, analytical capabilities, skills of search and assessment, skills in delegation and organisation, and judgment in the face of uncertainty.

The preliminary results of a survey of the founders of small businesses in the rural counties of Devon and Northumberland provide a picture of the demand-side link in the market for entrepreneurial competence between the characteristics of entrepreneurs and their own opinion of their competencies, and the possible supply of support through advice and training. These findings need to be set into the context of a rising number of new small businesses in Great Britain through the 1980s.

It should be noted that the sample of small businesses in this study is weighted towards very small businesses. In such firms, the owner/manager will tend to find it easier to screen for his or her own level of competence in specific roles or tasks than if he or she is running a larger concern with a measure of delegation. This proposition, if correct, will mean that it is methodologically more accurate to analyse means and methods of adopting new skills in very small firms when the research involves contact with only a single individual in each firm.

3 Small businesses in rural Britain
In 1989 the number of businesses registered for value added tax in Great Britain (the best available source of information on business births and deaths) rose by 86 000, to approximately 1.611 million. This was from an accelerating trend in the 1980s, although the high interest rates of 1990 have been slowing registrations and speeding deregistrations. The trend links in with the growth of self-employment in the 1980s, to 3.4 million in June 1990 in Great Britain, or 17% of men in the workforce and 7% of women. Nearly one third of these (32% of self-employed men and 29% of self-employed women) employ others.

The failure rate of small businesses, as shown up in the deregistration statistics for VAT, is highest in the second and third years of life after registration, with considerable variation by sector and by region. Common problems include the effect of rising interest rates, access to finance, monitoring cash flow, coping with government regulations and paperwork, and a lack of skilled and trained employees. And yet the available survey evidence suggests that the number of employees nationwide seriously considering becoming self-employed within a year is equal to around one quarter of those already in self-employment. And over 80% of these prospective entrepreneurs had sought or intended to seek advice, particularly on taxation issues, obtaining capital, and on getting business and making sales.[1] A need for soft infrastructure is recognised.

Small businesses in rural areas face particular problems in obtaining advice and training, in spite of the policies of the district councils and the county councils, Enterprise Agencies, and the Rural Development Commission. Also, the new Training and Enterprise Councils cover rural as well as urban areas in England and Wales. Evidence from the survey in Devon and Northumberland suggests that these bodies will face some resistance from new small businesses as they offer their services, there being a degree of disillusionment with the advice many entrepreneurs in the survey had already received. (The most common complaint was that those who give advice have "never had experience of business themselves"). The mere availability of this form of soft infrastructure is not enough. Supply alone does not generate demand from more than a limited proportion of the prospective 'customers'.

Listings of the names and addresses of small businesses provided by the local offices of the Rural Development Commission and the county council industrial directories were used to send some six hundred questionnaires to entrepreneurs randomly selected in Devon and Northumberland. Each county received three hundred of an A questionnaire and three hundred of a B questionnaire. These questionnaires had a common core, but the A questions focused on the entrepreneur as an individual, considering his or her background, education, and training, as well as on the importance of the rural setting of the business; whereas the B questions focused on the process of starting up the new small business and the subsequent constraints on growth. In this way the benefits of a longer fuller survey instrument were obtained without facing respondents with more than six A4 pages of questions.

The small businesses were all located in fully rural environments or in villages or small towns with a maximum population of 15 000. The range of sectoral activity of the respondents was wide, including manufacturing activities ranging from craft products such as pottery to more capital-intensive engineering concerns, as well as many service sector businesses. Of those originally approached 5 to 7% had stopped trading, had moved away, or were too large. The survey was conducted in August and September 1990.

The response rate to the postal survey was 80 (or 27.3%) out of 300 for questionnaire A in Northumberland, and 59 (or 19.6%) for questionnaire B.

---

[1] Survey evidence reported in the *Labour Market Quarterly Report* of the Department of Employment in August and December 1990.

In Devon, the response rate was 88 (or 29.3%) for questionnaire A and 72 (or 23.6%) for questionnaire B. These levels of response are in line with what might be expected from a well-run postal survey. They reflect a considerable interest in the themes of the questioning by the respondents, an interest which overcame any reluctance to answer fairly personal questions. One possible source of bias in the pattern of respondents is towards the better educated. This is acknowledged and the results presented need to be seen in that light. This possible bias does not weaken the force of the lessons from the survey, however, because we know that those entrepreneurs with higher levels of achievement in education and with more years of experience in managerial tasks as an employee are more likely to set up businesses which grow and expand in terms of output and employment.

The postal survey is being extended to two further counties, Derbyshire and Norfolk, (the pilot survey was in Norfolk) with a similar initial target of six hundred small businesses in each area, split between the two questionnaires. The postal survey results will be supplemented early in 1991 with an interview survey, with visits to approximately 80 of the postal survey respondents split between Derbyshire and Norfolk. The interviews will pick up the theme of competency and the entrepreneur in greater depth and will include an experimental question to assess the degree of risk averseness of the entrepreneur. This question arises from the work on the regret theory of choice by Loombes and Sugden (1982).

The general characteristics of the respondents from Devon and Northumberland, in addition to their rural location, reflected a pattern of new (over 60% less than five years old) and very small business (90% with 10 or fewer employees, and half this number with 2 or fewer). Half operate as sole traders, with the remainder split almost equally in status as partnerships or limited companies; so that under one quarter, or 38 of 168, have incorporated. Three quarters of the responding entrepreneurs were male; with 70 of the 168 being in their thirties, 37 in their twenties, and the remaining 61 aged forty or more. Half had owned or had previous experience of running a business, the vast majority as owners. In fact, 18 respondents said that they were in the process of rebuilding an earlier business.

Although the demand for soft infrastructure support in starting up a new small business may be manifest, it may also be latent, as noted earlier. The starting point in judging this potential is an assessment of the level or degree of competency of the entrepreneur in the performance of the various facets of his or her role. And this assessment may usefully start with a self-assessment. In the rural small business survey the respondents were asked: "Which of the skills and tasks listed below do you feel you are competently endowed with and which do you feel you could improve upon?" The results are set out in table 1.

Several features stand out from this table (and the patterns of response were very similar in the two counties): first, the large minority of respondents who recognise that their skills and abilities could be improved upon across a very wide range of business activities; second, the (understandable) prominence given to financial management as an area for improvement; and, third, the relatively high level of confidence shown in the skills of risk taking, perhaps reflecting essentially conservative approaches to uncertainty. It is also interesting that the often quoted weakness of new small businesses in the area of marketing comes out as one of the least quoted tasks as being satisfactory on the basis of personal experience alone. The proportion of the 168 respondents not answering all or part of this question is also noteworthy and revealing.

The fact that a relatively high proportion of respondents had had prior experience of running a business as an owner (81 of 168 respondents to questionnaire A) perhaps explains why a relatively low proportion turned externally for advice and training as they established the current business. Those who sought (or were given) advice did so from a variety of sources (where more than one source could be quoted):

Enterprise agency	19%
Bank manager	29%
Solicitor	14%
Accountant	43%
Friends and relatives	17%
Similar tradesmen	23%
Local government	7%
Central government	11%
Consultants	5%
None	33%

Table 1. Competence in business skills and tasks: 168 respondents in Devon and Northumberland (source: postal survey, 1990).

Task	Satisfactory, gained by personal experience (%)	Satisfactory, gained by education and training (%)	Could be improved upon (%)	Number of respondents
Risk taking	70	5	25	148
Innovation	67	3	30	135
Arbitrage	64	3	33	132
Marketing	53	10	37	133
Application of technology	54	6	40	134
Quality control	63	6	31	141
Production supervision	58	8	34	140
Financial management	49	8	43	154
Team building	53	8	39	131

The importance of bank managers and accountants stands out in the figures above, but this is advice for which, directly or indirectly, a fee is normally chargeable. Overall, of 97 respondents to whom the question was relevant, 39 (or 40%) said that they had had to pay for the advice given; meaning that well over half of those entrepreneurs acknowledging that they had received advice did so for a zero cash price. However, following the earlier discussion, receipt of advice could have involved a considerable cost in terms of time and in indirect expenditure (travel, etc). This indirect cash cost can influence the demand pattern for advice on entrepreneurial skills, just as it can also influence the take-up of opportunities of the infrastructure represented by training courses.

Twenty eight (or 21%) of the entrepreneurs responding felt that the advice which they received was either confusing or different from one source as compared with another. The difficulty of speaking the same language as accountants and bank managers was commented upon in a number of the returns. This difficulty in communication in a one-to-one situation certainly points to a need for training courses for bank managers and accountants in communication skills. But it also points to a benefit which can arise from attendance by the new entrepreneur on training courses which steer the newcomer into asking the right questions of the relevant experts as well as gaining an appreciation of the resulting answers.

Across the two questionnaires, 80 out of 299 respondents attended some kind of training course related to the establishment of their business. The courses ranged from afternoon or evening courses to longer periods of intermittent study. 'Management' and 'marketing' were the leading themes cited; with the courses being organised in approximately equal proportions between the private sector (especially accountancy companies) and the public sector (the Rural Development Commission, the Enterprise Agencies, local government, and central government through the Small Firms Service, the Ministry of Agriculture, etc). We came across few examples of a budding entrepreneur attending a college or university course. The linking of financial aid to start up businesses with a mandatory requirement to attend such a course is now widely advocated.

Of those attending a course of some kind, 14 (of the 70) in retrospect saw the course as 'essential'; 33 saw it as very useful; 24 as of 'some use'; and 6 as 'no use'; with 3 not answering this question. There is a well-recognised issue here of the marketing of such courses.

The problem of the founders of new small businesses not recognising their own limitations and not recognising that the soft infrastructure of training and advice in their local area or region can help them to growth and to profit, is reflected in the pattern of replies to two further questions in the Devon and Northumberland surveys. Respondents were asked "... to identify the main problems associated with the growth of [your] business", by agreeing or disagreeing with a list of factors which might be said to have held back growth in the past or which might be expected to constrain growth in the future.

The list presented to the entrepreneurs emphasised factors external to the business, as may be seen in table 2. Factors relating to finance (access to finance, interest rates, terms of bank loan) stand out as the constraints on growth in the past and as factors identified as likely to hold back growth in the future. And with these factors, and indeed in 17 of the 23 factors listed in table 2, there is a degree of pessimism shown between the view of the past and the view of the future, as the percentage of respondents listing them as constraints rises. This perhaps reflects the difficult trading conditions in the summer of 1990 following a sharp rise in interest rates, as the UK economy suffered high inflation and a slide towards recession. The recession shows up particularly strongly in the local authority rates (the local property tax) factor, in the market demand factor, and in the skilled labour factor.

Table 2. Constraints upon growth in 131 rural small businesses in Northumberland and Devon in 1990.

Constraint	Percentage citing as 'very important', 'important' or 'sometimes important'	
	in the past	in the future
Insurance liabilities	22	25
Access to finance	50	51
High interest rates	56	69
Available supply of key inputs	25	24
Market demand for product	44	49
Obtaining skilled labour	46	57
Availability of training for workforce	29	34
Technical problems in		
product development	17	21
production process	24	23
Paperwork, secretarial	41	38
Problems of manageability	31	31
Local authority rates	34	43
VAT	35	40
Employment legislation	26	28
Health and safety legislation	23	29
Company law requirements	14	18
Land-use planning restrictions	28	27
Availability of premises	34	37
Price of premises	33	39
Trade credit		
providing	24	22
obtaining	16	17
Terms of mortgage	14	15
Terms of bank loan or overdraft	51	52

The factor 'problems of manageability' was cited by only 31% of respondents, and there is little hint in the other replies that the entrepreneurs saw their own acknowledged limitations holding back the development of their business. And yet, the various entrepreneurial competencies listed earlier provide the skills, when linked to determination, to remove or steer around the obstacles to growth implied and listed in table 2. Financial pressures, for example, are often more pressing for those small businesses not on top of their cash-flow situation; and legislation and tax burdens do not normally differentially hit competitiveness. It is noteworthy that problems related to secretarial and 'paperwork' issues decline somewhat into the future.

Finally, in this selective extraction of evidence from the rural small business survey, it is interesting to note that 50 of 128, a very high proportion of respondents, said "no" to the question: "Is the continuing expansion of your business (in outputs, employment, or turnover) a necessary precondition to the personal satisfaction you have in running your business?" For these entrepreneurs the satisfaction came in the quality of the product or the service or in the status achieved; or, for 17, there was simply no wish to expand. When asked about their criteria for business success in the A questionnaire, 88 of 165 respondents across both Northumberland and Devon placed "quality of product or service" as "very important". As a general criterion of satisfaction, this was cited by nearly three times as many respondents as the criteria of profitability, growth in sales, or providing employment.

4 Conclusion
A regional economy may be developed by bringing in resources of capital and labour from elsewhere. These resources may be applied directly to the export base or to import substitution in the region, or they may be used to support the infrastructure of utilities and communications and social facilities on which economic growth depends. Alternatively or concurrently a regional economy may be developed by enhancing the productivity of the resources of capital and labour already in the region when combined with locally generated investment. A progressive investment in infrastructures is a necessary handmaiden of this rising stock of productive capital and of increases in the productivity of capital and labour achieved by new technology and improved organisation.

Small businesses need the support of these 'hard' infrastructure services in the regional economy as much as the large companies. But the efficiency, productivity, and growth of small businesses will be enhanced by the additional support of 'soft' infrastructure; and in particular where this soft infrastructure serves to raise the skills and competencies of the entrepreneurs. The economic application of the creativity of the entrepreneurs founding and running the smaller businesses in a region not only provides a spawning ground for the future emergence of large companies, but it also (and really more importantly) provides a flexible, responsive, and inventive underpinning for the regional economy. A vibrant small firm sector not only serves regional consumers but also buoys up the larger enterprises operating in the region: as efficient suppliers of components and services. Raising the productivity of the small business contributes to a rising productivity in the larger company.

The survey findings referred to in this chapter are taken from responses made by entrepreneurs running very small businesses. But even at this level there is an awareness by a large minority that their skills and competencies could be improved upon. This is in spite of mixed experiences in receiving advice and attending training courses. The challenge to regional economic development organisations implied by these survey findings is to improve the mechanisms of delivery both of advice and of training for the founders of new small businesses; and to convince them that training should not cease once the business is initially on its feet. It is human nature for the small businessman or woman to see external circumstances as holding back his or her efforts to grow and expand, rather than to examine his or her ways of doing things and becoming aware that there is room for improvement. And, of course, there is a large minority of owners of small businesses who have no desire to grow and expand. But part of the delivery of the soft infrastructure of advice and training is to ensure that those running a small business can see that choices exist and that competency can be enhanced with external assistance.

Acknowledgements. This chapter has been prepared under the research project "The Characteristics of the Founders of Rural Small Businesses", part of the ESRC Small Business Initiative. Acknowledgement is made to Barclays Bank, the Rural Development Commission, the European Economic Community, and the Department of Employment, as well as to the Economic and Social Research Council, for financial support to the Initiative. Any views expressed do not necessarily reflect those of the sponsoring organisations.

References
Cantillon R, 1755 *Essai sur la Nature du Commerce en Général* reprinted 1931, Ed. H Higgs (Macmillan, London)
Casson M, 1982 *The Entrepreneur: An Economic Theory* (Basil Blackwell, Oxford)
Diamond D R, Spence N, 1989 *Infrastructure and Industrial Costs in British Industry* Department of Trade and Industry (HMSO, London)
Hirshman A O, 1958 *The Strategy of Economic Development* (Yale University Press, New Haven, CT)
Knight F H, 1921 *Risk, Uncertainty and Profit* reprinted 1971, Ed. G J Stigler (University of Chicago, Chicago, IL)
Loombes G, Sugden R, 1982, "Regret theory: an alternative theory of rational choice under uncertainty" *Economic Journal* **92** 805–824
Mason C, Harrison R, Chaloner J, 1991, "Informal risk capital in the UK: a study of investor characteristics, investment preferences and investment decision-making", mimeo, Urban Policy Research Unit, University of Southampton, Southampton, Hants

Schultz T W, 1975, "The value of the ability to deal with disequilibria" *Journal of Economic Literature* **13** 827–846

Schumpeter J A, 1934 *The Theory of Economic Development* (Harvard University Press, Cambridge, MA)

Townroe P M, Mallalieu K, 1990, "Entrepreneurial roles and entrepreneurial competence in regional development", mimeo, Economics Research Centre, University of East Anglia, Norwich

Infrastructure and Metropolitan Development in an International Perspective: Survey and Methodological Exploration

F Bruinsma, P Nijkamp, P Rietveld
Free University, Amsterdam

1 Infrastructure and transport at the crossroads

Infrastructure and transport have become focal points of vivid policy debates in recent years. The increased interest in these issues is mainly addressed to two constituents of infrastructure and transport, namely international (or long-distance) fast links (for example, the Channel Tunnel, the French TGV, the German ICE), and urban infrastructure (for example, the new plans for Paris). Especially in the recent past, urban transport policy has become an important item on the urban policy agenda. Some cities (for example, Oslo, Stockholm) have in the meantime decided to reduce private transport (or at least to charge the user of urban roads) by means of a system of urban road pricing or urban toll roads.

The idea of focusing transport policy instruments (for example, user-charge principles) on the city first makes sense. The large majority of our current world population lives in urban areas (at present at least 70%), and there are no signs of a reversal of this trend. Therefore one may plausibly take for granted that the future of Europe will be an urban future. This is also recognised in various major international initiatives to promote the role of large agglomerations in the emerging new European Community, witness the Euro-city association, the CITIES programme, etc.

The critical position of cities in European economic development is not only a current phenomenon. Cities have always played a crucial role as nodes in a logistic network in the history of Europe. For instance, Andersson and Strömquist (1988) have distinguished four major phases in the history of European economies: the Hanseatic period, the Golden Age, the Industrial Revolution, and the Informatics Era. In all these phases cities appeared to be the engines of action.

Transport and communications are the major features of a logistic network, and hence it is evident that the position and development of cities are to a large extent determined by the functioning of their intra-urban and interurban infrastructure (compare Vaughan, 1987). Transport and communications generate urban nodes, and urban nodes evoke transport and communications.

The high density of transport needs and of infrastructure supply in urban areas is evident, as large agglomerations are the areas par excellence where economies of scale and scope are generated. But at the same time, such agglomerations are also glaring examples of where the social costs of transport (for example, environmental pollution, lack of traffic safety, congestion) are the highest.

The above conflict is not easy to resolve. It has been demonstrated on the one hand that productive investments and social overhead investments (notably infrastructure investments) need each other in order to arrive at a balanced economic development (for instance, see Hirschman, 1958). In general, the spin-off effects of new infrastructure investments—provided they are tailor-made for spatial eonomic needs—are significant. For example, in a recent study, Bruinsma et al (1990) point to high employment effects of integrated infrastructure investments.

On the other hand, the social costs of transportation may be very high. In a recent OECD report (1989) various costs of traffic have been assessed:

Noise annoyance, both damage costs (for example, productivity losses, health care costs, decline in property values, and loss of psychological well-being) and abatement costs (for example, adjusted vehicle technology, antinoise screens, double glazing, etc). Studies in various countries show a relatively high level of social costs of traffic noise:

Country:	USA	Netherlands	Norway	France
Percentage of GDP:	0.06–0.12	0.10	0.06	0.08

Air pollution both damage costs (for example, damage to health, buildings, or forests) and environmental protection costs (for example, air pollution control, new vehicle technology, catalytic converters, etc). Numerical estimates of air pollution costs caused by transport show some variation, but all point in the same direction: social costs of transport are high:

Country:	Germany	Netherlands	USA	France
Percentage of GDP:	0.4	0.2	0.35	0.21

Lack of safety, mainly resulting in accidents, leading to damage costs and recovery costs (including damage to vehicles, medical treatment, productivity losses, police and emergency service expenditures etc). Various cost estimates have been made which show high financial burdens:

Country:	Germany	Netherlands	United Kingdom	Luxembourg
Percentage of GDP:	2.54	1.67	1.5	1.85

Country:	France	Belgium	USA
Percentage of GDP:	2.6	2.5	2.4

The estimated figures lead to the conclusion that on average the social cost of road transport in developed countries falls in the range of 2.5–3.0% of GDP even without the inclusion of congestion costs.

This relatively high figure has serious implications for transport and infrastructure policy. In order to make transport part of an ecologically sustainable economy, intensified efforts have to be developed to make the demand for transport compatible with the needs of European economies. A decline in the social costs of transport requires a more efficient operation of current networks and a better, that is more coherent, design of new infrastructures. Cities may provide the basis for a new infrastructure policy.

There is apparently a clear tension between transportation needs and social costs of transportation. This tension has led to an increased policy interest in controlling the growth of mobility. Any policy effort to influence the transport sector should focus attention on both the user side and the supplier side. The user side refers to both the consumptive and productive value of transport systems as needed by households and firms. The supplier side refers to the necessary infrastructure equipment, in terms of design, construction, maintenance, management, control, and policymaking.

Both the user side and the supplier side have experienced economic dynamics recently and will no doubt experience further drastic changes in the foreseeable future. Such changes are, to a large extent, related to broader global and European developments (economic, political, technological), but are reflected at all spatial levels (local, regional, national, international). Bottlenecks in the matching between supply and demand will hence also be found at all spatial scales.

Despite the increasing popularity of just-in-time (JIT) systems and related concepts, the actual practice of both commodity and passenger transport is still disappointing and often frustrating. Severe traffic congestion at the urban or metropolitan level (for example, Athens, Rome, Paris); unacceptable delays in medium-distance and long-distance transport during peak hours; unsatisfactory service levels of European railway systems (and public transport in general); unreliable airline connections because of limited airport capacity; and slow technical and institutional renewal of air traffic control in Europe: all these phenomena illustrate the difficult position of the European transport sector, and there is no clear perspective for a drastic improvement of this situation. On the contrary, it is increasingly claimed that a free European market (beyond the year 1992) and further deregulation of the European transport sector may lead to unacceptable levels of accessibility in major regions in Europe (European Round Table of Industrialists, 1990).

As mentioned above, another important complicating factor will be environmental policy. In contrast to the deregulation of pure transport-market phenomena, environmental policy is critically dependent on a great deal of regulation and intervention on both the supply and demand side. In particular, technical restrictions are likely to be imposed, for example, limited emission levels for motorcars or even a prohibition of the use of certain transport modes. Recently, a plea for a car-less city has even been made. Other cities (for example, Paris) are trying to build subterranean road infrastructure.

Consequently, transport policymakers in most European countries find themselves in extremely complicated situations. A large number of interest groups, ranging from multinational companies to local environmentalists, urge them to take action, but often in quite different directions. On the one hand, it becomes obvious that the environment imposes limits on the volume, character, and pace of extension of transport infrastructure, whereas on the other hand the competitive position of firms is hampered by an inadequate infrastructure.

In the light of the previous discussion on infrastructure and transport—with a particular view on urban areas—it is no surprise that there is a growing interest in the functioning and impact of urban infrastructures. The question is whether such infrastructures are detrimental to—or just supportive of—what has been termed urban sustainability (compare Nijkamp, 1990).

So far we have pointed out that the city needs infrastructure as a vital tool for its survival and growth, while at the same time this tool may be costly from a social perspective. This holds for all types of infrastructure, but in particular for infrastructure to be used for transport and communication.

Two main economic effects of infrastructure can be distinguished. First, infrastructure exerts positive external effects both on firms and on households, leading to a higher productivity or utility level than would occur without that infrastructure. Second, the provision of infrastructure leads to relocation of mobile production factors such as labour and private capital, giving rise to differential growth rates in a multicity network.

Surprisingly, the social costs of transport and infrastructure mentioned above do not frequently occur in analyses of infrastructure and urban development.

2 Impact models for urban infrastructure analysis
Various methods and models have been developed to study infrastructure impacts on urban or regional economies. In this section three classes will be distinguished.

2.1 Factor-productivity approach
In the factor-productivity approach it is taken for granted that the positive external effects of infrastructure projects lead to an improvement of the productivity of other production factors, compared with the situation without such projects. As long as infrastructure had a point character (airports, industrial estates, educational institutions, etc), their influence on urban productivity can be analysed by means of traditional production functions.

A general formulation of a production function for sector i in city r, with various types of infrastructure is:

$$Q_{ir} = f_{ir}(L_{ir}, K_{ir}; I_r^A, ..., I_r^N), \tag{1}$$

where

Q_{ir} is value added in sector i, city r,
L_{ir} is employment in sector i, city r,
K_{ir} is private capital in sector i, city r,
I_r^A, ..., I_r^N are infrastructure of various types in city r.

This formulation may still be generalised by taking into account spatial spillover effects: the impact of infrastructure may transcend the boundary of an urban agglomeration. For example, a certain city may not have its own university or airport but still benefit from a university or airport nearby. This may be solved by using the concept of *accessibility* of certain types of infrastructure in the production function.[1]

A summary of models using the production-function approach is given in table 1. It appears that in most of the models a simplified version of equation (1) is used. The most complete ones are those developed by Mera (1973) and Fukuchi (1978) for Japan, and Snickars and Granholm (1981) for Sweden.

Sectoral detail is important in these studies. This is shown by Fukuchi (1978) and Blum (1982), who found that the productivity increase due to infrastructure may be quite different in different economic sectors.

Table 1. Examples of the production-function approach to infrastructure modelling.

Author	Country	Number of sectors	Number of types of infra-structure	Presence of		Form of production function
				labour	private capital	
Biehl (1986)	EC	1	1	yes	no	C–D
Blum (1982)	FRG	3	8	no	no	C–D
Andersson and Strömquist (1988)	SWE	1	7	yes	yes	C–D[a]
Snickars and Granholm (1981)	SWE	21	5	yes	yes	Leontief
Nijkamp (1990)	HOL	1	3	yes	no	C–D
Fukuchi (1978)	JPN	3	3	yes	yes	C–D
Kawashima (1978)	JPN	8	1	yes	no	linear
Mera (1973)	JPN	3	4	yes	yes	C–D

Key to abbreviations: C–D Cobb–Douglas; EC European Community; FRG Federal Republic of Germany; HOL The Netherlands; JPN Japan; SWE Sweden.
[a] Modified Cobb–Douglas production function.

---

[1] There is also a statistical advantage to using the concept of accessibility in this context. Certain types of infrastructure may simply be absent in a region. This causes statistical difficulties when using a Cobb–Douglas production function, the form usually chosen in this type of analysis. It is questionable practice to replace the 0 by an arbitrary small number. Introducing an accessibility measure removes this difficulty.

2.2 Factor-mobility approach

Infrastructure improvements or expansions may also lead to a relocation of labour and capital between urban regions. Most empirical studies in this field focus on the influence of interurban network infrastructure.

Improvement of transportation infrastructure leads to a reduction of travel time or cost and hence to an improvement in accessibility of markets or inputs. This may in turn lead to a relocation of labour and capital. Accessibility, A, of a certain variable Z in urban regions can be defined as

$$A_r(Z) = \sum_{r'} Z_{r'} f(c_{r'r}), \tag{2}$$

where $c_{r'r}$ is an index of travel costs between regions r' and r, and $f(c_{r'r})$ is a distance decay function. The variable Z may refer to employment, production, inputs, etc.

Botham (1983) used the following relationship between regional employment and accessibility:

$$\Delta E_r = a_1 D_r + a_2 w_2 + a_3 L_r + A_r(Z), \tag{3}$$

where D, w, and L denote employment density, wage rate, and an index of labour availability. For Z, several variables mentioned above have been tried. Last, ΔE is the differential shift in employment, as defined by shift-share analysis.

Another approach to accessibility is followed by Mills and Carlino (1989). They measure accessibility by means of the density of the interstate highway network and find that it has a clearly positive impact on employment growth in US states.

In most studies in this section, a positive relationship is found between accessibility and total employment. One must be aware that such a result is not guaranteed by theory, however. Improved accessibility leads to an intensification of competition, so that it is not impossible that some cities will be negatively affected by an improvement in accessibility.

Improving urban infrastructure has both *distributive* and *generative* effects. Distributive effects relate to a redistribution of economic activity among cities, the overall figure remaining constant. On the other hand, generative effects occur when the overall total changes.

2.3 Interregional trade approach

This subsection will mainly be concerned with *inter*regional or *inter*urban models. In order to be applicable for our purpose, these models should at least contain the following linkages: (1) between transport infrastructure and transport costs, (2) between transport costs and trade flows, (3) between trade flows and regional development. These linkages can easily be discerned in figure 1, which presents an example of such an interregional model. Here we will pay particular attention to the second linkage, the relationship between transportation costs and trade flows.

Amano and Fujita (1970) put forth the following formulation for a Japanese interregional model:

$$t_{irs} = K_{ir} \exp[-\beta_i(p_{ir} + v_{irs})] \left/ \sum_q K_{iq} \exp[-\beta_i(p_{iq} + v_{iqs})] \right. , \tag{4}$$

where the subscripts q, r, and s refer to regions, and i refers to sectors. K_{ir} and p_{ir} denote capacity and price level in sector i of region r. Furthermore, v_{irs} is transportation cost per unit of i between r and s, and t_{irs} is the share of region r in the deliveries to region s for goods produced in sector i.

Liew and Liew (1985) propose another modelling procedure. Their model of departure is a Cobb–Douglas production function with capital, labour, and intermediate purchases for each sector and each region.

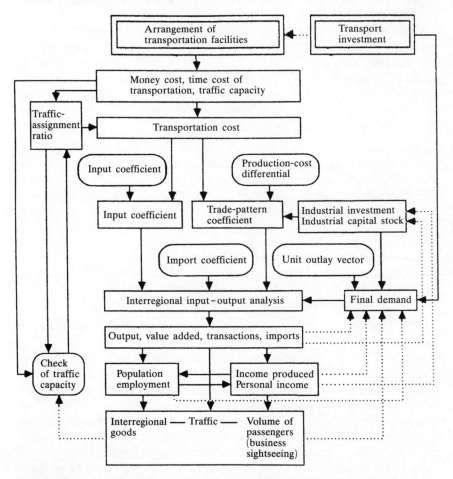

Figure 1. System chart of the Amano and Fujita (1970) interregional model. Dashed lines denote a time lag of one year.

They assume that consumers fully absorb the advantage of a decrease in transportation costs: the equilibrium purchase price in region s is the sum of the equilibrium price of the good in region r plus the cost of shipping it from region r to region s.

Another assumption is that, in equilibrium, transportation costs are a constant fraction of the equilibrium price. Using a profit-maximising approach, Liew and Liew derive a linear logarithmic system of price frontiers. Changes in transportation costs give rise to changes in equilibrium prices in the various regions. These in turn give rise to substitution effects in the production process. Thus, it is not only interregional trade shares which change as a consequence of changes in transportation costs, but all input–output coefficients may change as a result of it. In this respect, Liew and Liew's model is more general than Amano and Fujita's, where input–output coefficients are assumed to be constant.

Sasaki et al (1987) constructed an eight-region model of Japan, which is more general again than Liew and Liew's. A main difference is that Sasaki et al do not take into account only the influence of transport costs on prices of inputs and outputs (and hence on input–output coefficients), but also on final demand. Road construction does not only lead to a decrease in transportation costs and a change in trade patterns, but also to an increase in final demand in the region concerned.

2.4 Retrospect
Various attractiveness factors may be distinguished that play an important role in the contribution of infrastructure to the development of an urban agglomeration. Unfortunately, diseconomies from urban infrastructure are hardly considered in any of these studies. Also the dynamic generative impact of urban infrastructure is usually not very adequately considered.

3 Cross-urban comparative studies on infrastructure
The previous sample of infrastructure impact studies showed that comparative studies on the impact of urban infrastructure are rare. In this section we will deal with three of those comparative studies.

3.1 The attractiveness of European cities from the viewpoint of multinational firms: the NEI study
NEI (1987) carried out an exploratory study for seven West European urban agglomerations: Randstad, London, Paris, Hamburg, Frankfurt, München, and Brussels–Antwerp. The study focused on the attractiveness of the locational profiles of these agglomerations from the viewpoint of internationally oriented firms. Five groups of activities were distinguished: corporate headquarters, research and development establishments, high-tech production, distribution establishments, and producer services.

The data problems, which inevitably arise in such international comparisons have been solved by using qualitative (ordinal) data, based partly on secondary data and partly on expert judgment. Ordinal data are also used

Table 2. Locational profiles of urban agglomerations from the viewpoint of the distribution sector (source: NEI, 1987).

Location factor and ranking	Randstad	London	Paris	Hamburg	Frankfurt	München	Brussels – Antwerp
Demand-side factors							
1 Size of national market	6	5	4	1–3	1–3	1–3	7
1 Distance to point of gravity of European market	3/4	7	2	5/6	1	5/6	3/4
Institutional factors							
2 Fiscal laws	2	1	7	4–6	4–6	4–6	3
3 Facilities for custom-free entrepot	1	2–7	2–7	2–7	2–7	2–7	2–7
2 Speed of customs procedures	1	2–7	2–7	2–7	2–7	2–7	2–7
2 Computerised processing of administrative data by customs	4/5	1–3	1–3	4/5	6/7	6/7	1–3
3 Government acquisition policies	2	1	4–7	4–7	4–7	4–7	3
3 Investment premiums	3	2	7	4–6	4–6	4–6	1
3 Political stability	4	6	5	1–3	1–3	1–3	7
3 Stability in labour relationships	1	7	5	2–4	2–4	2–4	6
3 Attitude of population	1	7	6	2–4	2–4	2–4	5
Infrastructure							
2 Proximity to international airport	3	7	2	4–6	4–6	4–6	1
3 Costs of handling goods at airport	1	4	5	3	6/7	6/7	2
2 Proximity of seaport	2	4/5	4/5	3	na	na	1
2 Costs of handling goods in seaport							
2 Connection with international road network							
2 Location near waterway	1	4	3	5	na	na	2
2 Connection with international railway network							
2 Accessibility by lorry							
2 Availability of new telecommunication facilities		1/2	1/2	4–7	4–7	4–7	4–7
3 Quality of telecommunication	7	1	2	5–7	5–7	5–7	4
3 Tariffs of telecommunication	3						
3 Presence of transport firms	1	2–7	2–7	2–7	2–7	2–7	2–7
3 Price level of transport services	1	2–7	2–7	2–7	2–7	2–7	2–7
Quality of accommodation							
2 Availability of appropriate sites							
4 Price of land	7	1	5/6	2–4	2–4	2–4	5/6
3 Availability of appropriate premises							
4 Price of premises	2	3	7	4/6	4/6	4/6	1

in the weighting process of these factors. The various locational factors received a rank ranging from 1 (most important) to 6 (least important). The concept of urban area used here is rather loose: the use of qualitative data allows for some indeterminacy in this respect.

An example of the locational profile for distribution establishments is given in table 2. Infrastructure components obviously play a prominent role here. Network aspects of infrastructure are especially emphasised. Also tariffs for the use of infrastructure play a role here.

Multicriteria analysis has been used to generate a final ranking of urban agglomerations on the basis of table 2.

Table 3 gives the ranking of the urban agglomerations for the other types of economic activities. For each activity a specific list of location factors and the corresponding weights has been used.

The most striking aspect of the table is the very favourable result for London: it is unambiguously ranked first for three of the five activities. Relatively favourable results are also found for the Randstad, Frankfurt and Paris. The profiles of Hamburg, München, and Brussels–Antwerp are least favourable.

Among the weak aspects of this study are the soft character of the data used and the lack of an empirical basis for the weights. No efforts have been made to reinforce the analysis by linking these data to actual behaviour of internationally oriented firms. Thus, it is impossible to say whether firms will indeed evaluate urban agglomerations according to the rankings presented in table 3. Attractive aspects of this study are the sectoral detail used, and the network properties of infrastructure taken into account.

It is also surprising that no push effects (for example, high social costs, low environmental quality, congestion) are taken into consideration (see section 1 of this chapter), so that some reservations in interpreting the

Table 3. Attractiveness of urban agglomeration as a location for international economic activity (1 = most attractive) (source: NEI, 1987).

Urban agglomeration	Activity				
	corporate headquarters	research and development	high-tech production	distribution	producer services
Randstad	3/4	6/7	1/2	1	2 – 5
London	1	1	5 – 7	2 – 6	1
Paris	2	2 – 5	5 – 7	2 – 6	2 – 5
Hamburg	7	2 – 5	3/4	2 – 6	7
Frankfurt	5/6	2 – 5	1/2	2 – 6	2 – 5
München	5/6	2 – 5	3/4	7	6
Brussels– Antwerp	3/4	6/7	5 – 7	2 – 6	2 – 5

results are necessary. Nevertheless, the need for such comparative research is evident; in the following sections a new approach to an analysis of infrastructure in different European cities will be outlined.

3.2 Measuring and explaining the performance of the EC's urban regions: the Cheshire et al study

Urban problems are multidimensional and the construction of an aggregate index to measure the intensity of urban problems is accordingly a difficult task. One possibility is to apply a priori weights to individual problem indicators in order to arrive at an aggregate problem index. But it is not easy to find a sound basis for such weights. Another approach is followed by Cheshire et al (1986). They estimate the weights of individual problem indicators on the basis of expert opinions about which EC cities are healthy and which are unhealthy.

The statistical tool used by Cheshire et al is discriminant analysis (see Hand, 1981), which enables one to estimate coefficients (weights) which minimise the variance within groups of cities and maximise the variance between the groups.

The analysis was carried out for 103 cities in the EC in 1984. Data have been used at the level of the functional urban region (FUR). Experts agreed on a set of thirteen cities to be classified as 'unhealthy' and sixteen as 'healthy'. The variables taken into account are:

X GDP per capita,
U rate of unemployment,
M net migration rate,
T travel demand index (measured as a weighted sum of hotel beds per capita).

This leads to the following discriminant function:

$$\text{score} = -5.02 + 0.089U - 0.32M - 0.56T,$$
$$\quad\quad\quad\quad\quad (5.20)\quad\quad (-2.30)\quad (-4.39)$$

where figures in parentheses refer to t-values. GDP per capita was excluded because it was not significant. The signs of the coefficients are consistent with a priori ideas, although, as Cheshire et al admit, the use of the travel demand index may seem somewhat frivolous. Once the coefficients have been estimated, they can be used to generate the values of the problem index of all cities, including those which had not been classified before by the experts. Thus, one arrives at a ranking of European cities according to the degree of health, ranging from Frankfurt in first place to Liverpool with rank 103 as the most unhealthy city. Cheshire et al investigated the relationship between the problem score and the rate of population growth of cities. They find that a large majority of FURs with urban problems have a declining population, although some notable exceptions exist.

In a more recent study, Cheshire (1990) gives an update for 1988 in which cities from Spain and Portugal are also included. The main pattern observed is fairly stable. An important element is that an explanatory analysis is given of the *change* in the problem index between 1971 and 1988. The results are shown in table 4.

The negative sign of the population variable indicates that, ceteris paribus, the problems of large cities have been mitigated compared with smaller cities during the period considered. Another explanatory variable is the change in economic potential, measured by means of the gravity model. Major reasons for changes in economic potential are changes in the composition in the EC. This result means that cities in the Northern and Western periphery of the EC have been facing increasingly severe urban problems.

Most of the other variables relate to economic structure. Cities in regions with a strong orientation towards industry, agriculture, and coal mining experienced increasing urban problems. A similar result holds true for cities with a large natural change in population. There is only one *infrastructure* variable among the independent variables and it has an increasing influence on urban problems: the dependence of the local economy on ports (measured on a scale from 0 to 4 to indicate the volume of seaborne trade). This reflects the negative influence of containerisation on employment in ports during the period considered. The loss of employment may relate both to the substitution of labour by capital and to indirect effects on processing industries because containerisation means

Table 4. The changing incidence of urban problems, 1971–88 (*t*-values are given in parentheses) (source: Cheshire, 1990).

Independent variable	Result	
Constant	17.2	
Log total population (1981)	−0.96	(−2.95)
Change in economic potential	−4.82	(−5.31)
Percentage of labour force in wider region, 1975		
in industry	0.067	(2.16)
in agriculture	0.169	(1.86)
in agriculture (value squared)	−0.0056	(−2.44)
Dependence of local economy		
on port	0.63	(3.85)
on coal	1.21	(3.42)
Natural rate for population change	0.174	(2.75)
Country dummies		
Spain	4.54	(3.55)
Italy	−3.74	(−4.50)
France	−3.50	(−5.12)
United Kingdom	−3.75	(−4.62)
Adjusted R^2	0.80	

that ports lose their initial locational advantage compared with other cities (Cheshire, 1990).

The overall pattern emerging from table 4 is that skill-based cities have fared better than cities with a basis in natural resources. Except for the port variable, infrastructure does not play an explicit role in the explanation, but Cheshire indicates that it may play a role in the unexplained variance. He suggests, for example, that favourable developments in cities such as Paris and (more recently) Rotterdam are the result of coherent strategic plans for development and modernisation of their (intraurban) transport infrastructure. In addition, it plays an implicit role in the economic potential variable, because this variable depends on transport costs which in its turn depends on the (interurban) infrastructure network (see section 2.2).

In table 5 some numerical results are presented for a set of larger cities, mainly in the Northwestern part of the EC. Most of these cities have a problem index below the EC median in 1981, that is, they are relatively healthy. Also, from the viewpoint of change most of the cities perform well compared with the EC average. The worst development observed occurs with London and some cities in Northern and Central Germany.

Cheshire's idea of using discriminant analysis to construct an index of urban problems is quite interesting, although some of the variables used

Table 5. Incidence of urban problems in European cities (source: Cheshire, 1990).

City	Urban problem index (1981)	Change in urban problem index (1971–88)
Copenhagen	−2.14	not available
London	−4.35	3.92
Amsterdam	−8.16	−0.22
Rotterdam	3.19	0.69
The Hague	−0.05	0.19
Antwerp	−2.11	−0.89
Brussels	−10.59	−5.09
Paris	−1.71	−0.98
Lyon	−2.71	−0.39
Milan	−4.94	1.66
Hamburg	−5.02	4.70
Essen	−0.43	4.51
Düsseldorf	−8.25	4.06
Köln	−3.10	2.74
Frankfurt	−18.24	−3.56
München	−10.67	3.29
EC average	−0.17	3.29

may be questioned. The use of the transportation index (hotel beds) as an inverse indicator of urban problems is not entirely convincing (why is it not used as an explanatory variable?). In addition, we note that the scope of the urban problem indicators is rather limited. Problems related to the urban environment, housing, or transport are not taken into account.

The explanatory analysis of changes in the problem index yields plausible results, but it is a pity that infrastructure did not receive more systematic attention as a policy variable. Although data on public investments may be difficult to obtain, one might use other infrastructure data, such as the presence or accessibility of airports.

3.3 The performance of European cities; the DATAR report

In 1989, a French study (DATAR) was published on the socioeconomic performance of 165 European cities with a population of more than 200 000 inhabitants. Data relate to functional urban regions. The performance of the cities is measured by means of sixteen indicators which can be classified as follows:

1, 2   population (size, growth),
3 – 5   infrastructure (airports, ports, telecommunication),
6 – 9   skills (high-tech industry, R&D, skills of labour force, universities),
10 – 12 knowledge exchange (congresses, exhibitions, press)
13, 14   international relations (headquarters of multinational firms, financial institutions),
15, 16   cultural (museums, festivals, etc).

The cities have been rated on a scale from 1 (least attractive) to 6 (most attractive). An index of the aggregate socioeconomic performance of cities is constructed by unweighted summation. Thus, infrastructure variables contribute 3/16 of the aggregate index. The results for a subset of cities are presented in table 6. According to this table London and Paris have by far the highest scores, followed by Milan.

Table 6. Aggregate performance of European cities (source: DATAR, 1989).

City	Aggregate index	City	Aggregate index
Copenhagen	56	Milan	70
London	83	Hamburg	57
Amsterdam	63	Essen	35
Rotterdam	55	Düsseldorf	44
The Hague	44	Köln	51
		Frankfurt	65
Antwerp	44	München	65
Brussels	64		
Paris	81	EC (average)	28
Lyon	53		

Although the DATAR report brings together interesting information, it can be criticised for various reasons. First, it is not clear what the aggregate index actually stands for. Second, for several of the underlying variables quantitative data are readily available so that an unnecessary loss of information occurs by using a scale such as (1, 2, 3, 4, 5, 6). Third, no basis is given for the assumption of equal weights, although the DATAR report mentions that sensitivity analysis reveals that other assumptions lead to approximately the same results.

Fourth, the definition of the variables is not always mutually consistent. Most of the variables relate to absolute figures. Thus, Paris and London score 5 or 6 for most variables simply because of their size: these cities host most people, they have the biggest airports, most students, etc. Thus, it is no surprise to see that the figures in table 6 are closely related to population size. Such an approach is defendable, but it is not easy to understand why in some cases a standardisation is used. For example, the university variable is based on the absolute number of students but the labour-force skill variable is based on the *share* of people in the labour force having certain skills.

3.4 Retrospect

Given the growing importance of the international dimension in urban infrastructure policies we surveyed three recent studies on the role of infrastructure in the development of EC cities: NEI (1987), DATAR (1989), and Cheshire (1990). NEI and Cheshire follow the location-factor approach. The approach followed by DATAR is difficult to classify. Also the type of data used are quite different in the three studies. Concerning the role of infrastructure, Cheshire finds that the main influence of infrastructure runs via the potential variable. But one must be aware that changes in the potential variable may be both the result of changes in transport costs and of changes in the composition of the EC. It is therefore not possible to say precisely what the contribution of infrastructure is to the amelioration of urban problems. In the NEI study, infrastructure is assigned a very important role as a location factor, but no statistical testing is carried out. The role of infrastructure in the DATAR study is more limited, but statistical tests are not used here either.

The three studies considered give rankings of European cities in order of attractiveness. These rankings express different things, and it is therefore no surprise to see that they may be so different. For example the largest metropolitan areas, London and Paris, have very high scores in the NEI and DATAR studies, but in the Cheshire study their rank is much more mediocre.

4 Concluding remarks

In this exploratory chapter we focused attention on theoretical and modelling work on the (positive and negative) role of (mainly) transport infrastructure, followed by some examples of recent fieldwork.

The most important lesson that could be learned from this exploration is that there appears to be a gap between the various modelling approach and the empirical studies carried out in the EC countries.

To close this gap and to stimulate cross-national comparative research it will not be sufficient simply to carry out more empirical studies. It is of utmost importance that the databases of various urban economies are harmonised in terms of both quantity and quality. This does not only mean that an extended set of data should become available, but also that the various databases on urban economies should become more standardised so that data on urban economies become compatible.

In light of the completion of the Single European Market in 1992 it is not only interesting for scientists to work on inter-European urban relations and development, but it is also important both for national governments and for the business community to have better information about the possibilities this new European market has to offer. In the introduction it was stated that the large majority of our population is already living in urban areas. As a consequence the position of an urban area within the total European network and its relations within this network will represent the possibilities for that urban economy within Europe. It may be expected that the synergetic effect would be considerable if urban economies could use an exact notion of their relative position within the European network to their advantage.

Working on such a comparative study it has become clear that the lack of reliable, compatible data severely hampers fruitful research. Therefore we end with a plea for a freer exchange of data sets at least between universities.

References
Amano K, Fujita M, 1970, "A long run economic effect analysis of alternative transportation facility plans—regional and national" *Journal of Regional Science* **10** 297–323
Andersson A, Strömquist U, 1988, "The emerging L-society" *Transportation in the Future* Eds D F Batten, R Thord (Springer, Berlin) pp 33–48
Biehl D (Ed.), 1986 *The Contribution of Infrastructure to Regional Development* Final Report of the Infrastructure Study Group, Commission of the European Communities, Luxembourg
Blum U, 1982, "Effects of transportation investments on regional growth" *Papers of the Regional Science Association* **49** 151–168
Botham R, 1983, "The road programme and regional development: the problem of the counterfactual", in *Transport, Location and Spatial Policy* Eds K J Button, D Gillingwater (Gower, Aldershot, Hants) pp 23–56
Bruinsma F R, Nijkamp P, Rietveld P, 1990, "Employment impacts of infrastructure investments: a case study for the Netherlands", in *Infrastructure and the Space-economy* Ed. K Peschel (Springer, Berlin) pp 209–226

Cheshire P, 1990, "Explaining the recent performance of the European Community major urban regions" *Urban Studies* **27** 311–333

Cheshire P, Carbonaro G, Hay D, 1986, "Problems of urban decline and growth in EEC countries: on measuring degree of elephantness" *Urban Studies* **23** 131–149

DATAR, 1989 *Les Villes 'Européennes'* (Maison de la Géographie, Montpellier)

European Round Table of Industrialists, 1990, *Missing Networks in Europe* (NECTAR Report), Brussels

Fukuchi T, 1978, "Analyse économie-politique d'un développement régional harmonisé" *Collectional INSEE* **61** 227–253

Hand D J, 1981 *Discrimination and Classification* (John Wiley, New York)

Hirschman A O, 1958 *The Strategy of Economic Development* (Yale University Press, New Haven, CT)

Kawashima T, 1978, "Regional impact simulation model BALAMO", in *Models for Regional Planning and Policy Making* Eds H Straszak, B Wagle, International Institute for Applied Systems Analysis, Laxenburg, Austria, pp 143–158

Liew C K, Liew C J, 1985, "Measuring the development impact of a transportation system: a simplified approach" *Journal of Regional Science* **25** 241–257

Mera K, 1973, "Regional production functions and social overhead capital" *Regional Urban Economics* **3** 157–186

Mills E S, Carlino G, 1989, "Dynamics of country growth", in *Advances in Spatial Theory and Dynamics* Eds A E Andersson, D Batten, B Johansson, P Nijkamp (North-Holland, Amsterdam) pp 195–205

NEI, 1987, "Plaats en functie van de Randstad in de Nederlandse economie" Nederlands Economisch Instituut, Rotterdam

Nijkamp P, 1990 *Sustainability of Urban Systems* (Gower, Aldershot, Hants)

OECD, 1987, "The social cost of land transport" Environment Committee, Environment Division, OECD, Paris

Sasaki K, Shinmei M, Kunikisa S, 1987, "Multiregional model with endogenous price system for evaluating road construction projects" *Environment and Planning A* **19** 1093–1114

Snickars F, Granholm A, 1981, "A multiregional planning and forecasting model with special regard to the public sector" *Regional Science and Urban Economics* **11** 377–404

Vaughan R J, 1987 *Urban Spatial Traffic Patterns* (Pion, London)

Index